GOING TO MAINE

ALL THE WAYS TO FALL ON THE APPALACHIAN TRAIL

SALLY CHAFFIN BROOKS

RUNNING WILD

Going to Maine:
All the Ways to Fall on the Appalachian Trail

text copyright © 2024 Reserved by Sally Chaffin Brooks
Edited by Rebecca Dimyan
All rights reserved.
Published in North America and Europe by Running Wild Press. Visit Running
Wild Press at www.runningwildpress.com. Educators, librarians, book clubs
(as well as the eternally curious), go to www.runningwildpress.com.

Paperback ISBN: 978-1-960018-93-9
eBook ISBN: 978-1-960018-89-2

For Erin
Hey

PROLOGUE

JUNE 10, 2006, OREGONIA, OHIO

"Wow," my mom said again, wiping tears from her eyes. We stood with my dad in the empty hallway, taking a beat before we opened the double doors and I walked down the aisle. "I just can't believe my baby girl...."

"... farted like a truck driver in her wedding dress?" my dad cut in.

"A truck driver?!" my mom retorted. "I was going to say earthquake!" Her body shook with laughter.

"You guys done?" I fixed them both with what I hoped was an annoyed look, but found it near impossible to pull off stern with four feet of tulle attached to the top of my head. "You try wearing shapewear all day and see what happens."

My mom hooked her arm through mine. "You've always had impeccable timing."

"We should go before I pass out," my dad said as he took his position on my other side.

"Glad to see you two getting along," I took a deep breath and squeezed them both close. "Okay, let's do this."

We were still laughing as we walked through the doors, a

sweet mandolin tune playing courtesy of a childhood friend's bluegrass band. I vaguely registered the friends and family, all turned in their chairs to watch me parade to the front. I focused on my fiancé, who, I noted thankfully, looked excited, albeit slightly uncomfortable, in his brand-new Men's Warehouse suit. I caught the eye of Erin, my maid of honor, who was giving me a "holy shit, this is happening" grin, which I returned with "I know, can you believe it?" crazy wide-eyes.

It was fitting that Erin was going to be up there with us. I mean, of course she would be, we'd been best friends since the moment we'd met playing light-as-a-feather at a seventh-grade sleepover; but really, she was the reason I was getting married at all. Without Erin, I never would have hiked the Appalachian Trail. And without the Appalachian Trail, I never would have met this wonder of a person that I was about to vow to love "til death do us part."

March, 2002, Chicago, Illinois

It all started with a phone call. I was, as I typically was in those days, stuck in Chicago traffic when my best friend, Erin, called from her house in St. Louis.

"Dude, I'm going to hike the fucking AT!" Erin blurted as way of a greeting. By AT, she meant the Appalachian Trail—an almost 2,200-mile hiking trail that runs from Georgia to Maine.

"What? When?" I asked, mentally screaming "MOOOOOVEEE" to the car in front of me.

"Next year, probably February or March." Erin was in the process of studying for the MCATs and was hoping to go to med school the following fall. She would be able to take the five months needed to hike the entire trail in the spring of 2003, assuming everything went as planned.

"That's really great, dude. I'm excited for you," I told her. We talked some more about her plans; me, inching along in traffic on my way back to my office in downtown Chicago; her, sitting on her porch in St. Louis getting ready to bike to the hospital where she was working as a nurses' aid.

When Erin finally got off the phone so she could get to work, telling me she had to go "wipe old-ass butts," I was still about five miles from the office, which meant probably another hour in the car. I was working for a non-profit based in downtown Chicago called Best Buddies where I would set up programs in area high schools to pair kids with and without intellectual and developmental disabilities in one-on-one friendships. I loved my job, but it required me to routinely travel out to schools in the Chicago suburbs, and I often spent hours at a time in my '86 Honda Civic that had no working stereo or air conditioner, driving out of and back into the city. The silence in the car gave me a lot of time to think.

I thought about Erin's plans. I decided I was jealous. The previous summer, right after I graduated from college, Erin, her older sister Cara, and I spent a month backpacking the Long Trail, a hiking trail that traverses the Green Mountains of Vermont, from the Massachusetts line to the Canadian border. It was my first long-distance hiking trip, and I hadn't been prepared for how hard it would be. Before that trip I was more of a summer camp counselor, car camping, day-hiking type of outdoorswoman, not a "carry everything I need for a week on my back and hike up and down mountains all day" type. Cara was a for-real outdoorswoman; a "moved to New Hampshire to live with her fiancé that she'd met thru-hiking the AT" kinda gal. I'd grown up idolizing Cara, and the chance to spend a month with her and Erin was a dream. But in the minutes after the three of us had reached the Canadian border and completed the Long Trail, but before I collapsed with exhaustion, I swore I would never do something like that again.

Spending that time with Cara and Erin had been magical in many ways. We'd laughed—so much—big, hard belly laughs every single day. And we'd met amazing people. There was the grandfather who had hiked the Long Trail every ten years and was out with his son and grandson for his 80th birthday, and the two sisters who had taken a train from Chicago to Vermont hiking with their six kids under 10-years-old that we nicknamed the Von Traps. And every day there was at least one moment when the natural beauty had overwhelmed me—like when I'd reached the peak of Stratton Mountain only to find it covered in vibrant purple and orange wildflowers. But every single day I was out there, I'd felt inadequate. I watched Cara, her feet so used to navigating the rocks and roots, she could practically skip over terrain that I stumbled through. I watched Erin, who wouldn't let herself quit until she got to the top of a climb, while I was stopping to catch my breath every few hundred feet. The mountains of the Long Trail get higher and more technical as you go North, so every day was harder than the last and every day was a negotiation with myself to "just keep moving." The hike had pushed me to my limits—and I'd been left feeling like maybe I wasn't strong enough physically or mentally for this kind of challenge. But now, it was almost a year later, the pain had faded, and the memories of the constant laughter, gorgeous vistas, and sense of satisfaction that comes with a task completed were all that remained.

Sitting there, in bumper-to-bumper traffic, I imagined myself in this same shitty car a year from now, probably staring at the same taillights, while Erin was off on a grand adventure without me. I couldn't just leave my job, or my boyfriend, or my friends in the city and disappear into the woods for five months, right? *Still,* I thought, *I would love to do something like that someday.* And maybe, if the cars had started moving, and I had made it back into the city, someday is where I would have left it. But I wasn't going anywhere fast, and pretty soon, I thought, "But... couldn't I go?"

After all, I loved my job—I routinely heard from parents and kids about the difference the program made in their lives—but I made a pretty meager non-profit salary and I was perpetually broke. I'd taken to cashing in the savings bonds my dad had given me to help pay off my student loans just to afford my rent. With no chance of a promotion within the small organization, I'd started thinking about applying to law school just so that one day I'd know the pleasure of a savings account. Plus, my boyfriend Kevin and I had already been long distance for almost a year, and we were making it work, right? Would me hiking for five months really be that different? And those friends in the city were kind of already moving on, too, weren't they? My roommate and closest friend, Bethany, was already spending most of her time out in the suburbs with her boyfriend, Joe, and they were bound to be engaged any minute.

So really, I thought, *what's stopping me?*

Without any idea of how I would make it work, still inching along in traffic, I called Erin back. "I'm coming with you."

And just like that, my life changed course.

* * *

Things seemed to just fall into place. I went from a 24-year-old with very little direction to a woman with a plan. Even though up until then law school was something I'd only given passing consideration, I bought a used test-prep book and two months later I was taking the LSATs. I'm a rule follower by nature, and I couldn't fathom doing something as "irresponsible" as leaving an adult job for something as frivolous as a life experience. It turned out law school was the excuse I needed to convince that side of my brain that it was okay to quit my job and hike. After all, I wouldn't just be flitting off to the woods for months on end with nothing to come back to, I was just taking a short break before I started my real life as a lawyer.

Kevin graduated from college in May and got a high-paying job with a big construction company in Tampa, Florida. When he suggested that maybe I should come live with him (rent free, no less) once my lease in Chicago was up in October as a way to save money before the trail, it seemed like a perfect solution to my money woes. Plus, Kevin reasoned, living together for a few months would be a perfect test run for what would probably be the rest of our lives. It made sense to me. Although I thought I'd take a job waiting tables when I moved and probably (definitely) make more than I currently was, by random chance the non-profit I worked for just happened to be looking for someone who could spend a few months planning the all-staff conference taking place in Miami in early February of 2003. I would work from Kevin's apartment and travel across the state every few weeks to work on the conference while I applied to law schools and prepared for the hike.

Erin made big changes, too, to make the trip happen. One week after sending me an email saying she thought she had met her "100% perfect boy," she left him and St. Louis to move back to our hometown of Dayton, Ohio, where she could live with her brother, Brian, and wait tables to save money.

Erin and I decided on February 23, 2003, as our start date. It was earlier than most, and we knew that meant we might run into some bad weather, but because we both would be starting school in the beginning of August, and the average thru-hike takes about five and a half to six months, we needed to get out as early as possible. February 23rd was the earliest I could leave my job, so that was the day we chose.

We planned obsessively. I spent hours researching every piece of hiking equipment, checking hiking message boards and customer reviews to find the lightest gear for the lowest price. I figured and refigured my gear list—the list of items that I would be carrying in my backpack—trying to balance the need to keep the total weight as low as possible, with my fear of not having everything I might need. Since it'd only been a few years since their own thru hike, we grilled Cara and her fiancé Chris about what to expect. When we'd hiked the Long Trail, Cara had told us what to pack and how to do everything, but now we'd be on our own. We read and reread every book we could find written about the trail. We poured over the guidebooks and Erin spent days sketching out a tentative mileage schedule. We knew most people about to hike the AT didn't plan their trip in as much detail as we did, but with us starting school in August, we needed to finish in early July. That gave us less than five months to complete the hike and meant we would have to keep a pretty quick pace.

"It's like a big puzzle," Erin told me during one of our near-nightly phone calls, "and just when I think I've got it figured out, I realize I didn't factor something in, like making sure we stop for the night near a water source, and I have to start all over. But I think I'm almost finished."

"Yeah, like I was thinking we should make sure we don't do mail drops on Sundays," I said, referring to the days we would need to go into towns near the trail to pick up supplies our family and friends would send to the local post offices.

"Fuck!"

It all happened so quickly, and the logistical Tetris fell into place so smoothly that it wasn't until I was in the car again, this time on my way to Florida with my cat named Cat, that I even stopped to think about whether this was what I wanted. It wasn't the hike; I was certain I wanted to hike the trail. The moment I'd told Erin I was coming, I'd become obsessed with the idea. Perhaps because I spent my early life moving around as an Air Force brat, I'd always had wanderlust. The more I read about hiking the Appalachian Trail, the more I came to see it as the ultimate wander. But the decisions to go to law school and move to Florida both came as a means of making the AT hike a reality and I couldn't be positive either would have happened otherwise. With my little Civic packed to the gills and Cat yowling to be let out of her cage before we even reached the Indiana border, I decided that it was too late for second thoughts.

* * *

When I arrived in Florida, Kevin and I realized living together wasn't what we thought it would be. Kevin and I had met the first day of residence hall counselor training in August, 2000. The previous semester, I'd studied abroad in Scotland and had an exhausting amount of fun. After running out of money somewhere in Italy, I'd repatriated and spent the summer temping for an evil insurance company and hooking up with a wide array of unsuitable boys. By the time I arrived at Purdue University's Harrison Hall to start residence hall counselor training at the start of my final year as a college student, I was primed to fall in love with a nice boy and Kevin was exactly that.

Kevin instantly felt like someone I'd known forever. He was sweet and fun, and perhaps most importantly at the time we met, was not part of the fraternity-stock of boys I'd dated in the past. Within a few weeks of meeting, we were a couple. I loved him, my friends loved him, my friends' boyfriends loved him. I adored spending weekends with his exceedingly normal, big Catholic family in Indianapolis, and he got along with my unconventional heathen brood in Ohio. My dad even declared that Kevin, who knew how to work on cars and fix things just like my dad, was the future son-in-law of his dreams.

When I'd graduated in May, 2001, Keith and I hadn't even considered breaking up, even though he had one more year of college in Indiana, and I'd be moving to Chicago to start my new job. Unlike a lot of couples we knew, we made the long-distance transition easily. On weekends I would visit him in West Lafayette and act like I was still in college, or he would drive to Chicago (where we would hang out with college friends and act like we were still in college). That was why, when I got to Florida and things between us were so hard, it caught us both off guard. Our relationship had always been easy.

Although we'd been together for almost 2.5 years at this point, this was the first time we'd lived together for more than a long weekend. I felt trapped, working at the apartment alone all day, not knowing another soul in Florida other than him. He felt overwhelmed, not used to dealing with another person's shit the minute he walked in the door from work. I was hurt when I found out that he hadn't told his mom that I'd moved in with him.

"It's just for now, Sally," he assured me. "You know how she is."

I did know how she was. I loved his mom and knew that as a devout Catholic she wouldn't approve of us living together. But still, I resented having to be quiet every time she called.

One night, after dinner grew cold while he went out drinking with his buddies, I exploded. "If this is what it's going to be like, I don't want any part of this life."

But as time went on, we began to figure out this new,

grown-up version of our relationship. I gave him more space, and he was more considerate of the fact that I was lonely without any friends. We spent a lot of time at the beach and entertaining friends who needed an escape from the cold Midwest winter. We went to bars in St. Petersburg where the average age of the patrons was 70. After one night of drinking, we made friends with an octogenarian couple who invited us to their RV to play Euchre, the ultimate Midwest card game. We picked out furniture for his apartment and built a coffee table together. We even laughed together in disbelief when we discovered that my cat named Cat had fleas and we'd have to wash every single piece of fabric in the apartment. We went to the weddings of several close friends, and started talking about how that might be us someday. And as I applied to law schools, I made decisions based on places we'd both want to live (yes to the Midwest, no to the West Coast). Kevin was supportive, excited, and even a little jealous of the AT plan. We both started talking about the hike as my last hurrah before the two of us settled into our life together.

CHAPTER ONE

DAY 1, GEORGIA, 2,169.8 MILES TO KATAHDIN

By the time Erin and I stood in the parking lot at the base of Springer Mountain, the Southern terminus of the Appalachian Trail, we had spent almost a year thinking about the trip. We were as prepared as anyone could be, but the time for planning was over, and now we just needed to take those first steps.

So why did I feel frozen in place?

We'd met up the night before in Dahlonega, Georgia. Kevin and I drove up from Florida, Erin got a ride down from Ohio with our friend Nicole, and my mom had driven over from her home in Clemson, South Carolina to see us off. The five of us had dinner and cheers-ed our new adventure. My mom fawned and fussed over Erin and I as if we were still 12, asking us over and over in her sweet southern drawl if we'd packed enough to eat and "are you girls really just gonna poop right there in the woods?" Afterwards, we'd all piled into Erin's hotel room for a pack explosion- what we called the phenomenon where you take everything out of your pack and marvel at how the contents can both fit into your small pack and blanket an entire hotel room. We wanted to go through our stuff, split up the things we were going to share and double check we had everything we needed. Somehow, despite our meticulous planning, we still ended up at Walmart at 10pm desperately looking for spandex shorts for Erin.

"How did I forget about chafing?" Erin had said when she'd realized she hadn't brought anything to wear under her hiking shorts. As a rule, long distance hiking and actual bare thighs do not mix. Not finding what she wanted, Erin had settled for full-length spandex pants which she cut off to shorts length. As she modeled them around the hotel room, one jagged leg slightly shorter than the other, she proclaimed, "I'm about to start a new fucking trend."

After a late, restless night, I hugged my mom goodbye a million times while she told me to remember "You. Are. Loved." adding, "Sweet Pea, you can call me to come pick you up anytime." Kevin and I drove in silence up the mountain to the parking lot where we'd start our hike. He hadn't talked much since we'd left the apartment in Florida the day before. In fact, as the time drew closer for me to leave, the quieter he'd become. The quiet made me nervous. A few nights before I'd left, I'd asked him if he was still okay with me leaving.

"Of course, I am," he'd assured me. "But I can be okay with you leaving and still wish you were staying, can't I?"

When Nicole and Erin got to the parking lot, we made small talk and took a series of pictures of Erin and I all bundled up with our packs on our backs and hiking poles in our hands. I was stalling; trying to figure out how to say goodbye. Kevin would be going back to his life, our life for the past months, alone, and I was walking into the woods without him. We both knew that as soon as I started walking down the trail, things would be different. At the very least, I wouldn't be moving back to Florida when I finished, I'd be off to law school in some yet-to-be-decided new town. Standing there in that parking lot, I was having a hard time balancing my sadness at leaving Kevin with the overwhelming excitement and nervousness I felt because the time had finally come, after almost a year of planning, plotting, thinking, obsessing about the trip, for us to start our hike.

It was the bitter cold that finally forced us to say goodbye. It had snowed the night before and the ground was covered, the trees still held a light dusting. From the parking lot we stood in, we knew we would have to hike about a mile South to reach the peak of Springer Mountain, the official starting point of the trail, and then backtrack through the parking lot to head North toward Maine, the direction we would be heading for the next months.

Kevin pulled me aside. "I love you, you know?"

"I know. I love you too."

"Be careful out there, and after this, promise you won't leave me for this long again."

"I'll be careful," I told him. He climbed into his Jeep, and tears stung my eyes as I watched him drive back down the dusty road.

"Dude! Let's go!" Erin said. I turned and looked at the trail up ahead. The canopy of trees formed a tunnel, looking like a secret passageway, inviting us to walk through and begin our journey. With Kevin gone, the sadness was there, but bubbling up next to it was an incredible excitement.

I bounced on my toes. "OH MY GOD LET'S FUCKING GOOO!"

Erin and I talked giddily as we walked. I could barely believe the thing I had imagined happening for so long was actually happening. Erin told me she heard that when you reached the top of Springer Mountain, you were supposed to take a small rock, and carry it with you the whole trip, to place on the top of Mt. Katahdin, in Maine, the Northern terminus of the trail. We joked about not being able to find a small enough rock, and being weighed down by the boulder in our pack the whole trip.

An hour passed quickly, but we still hadn't reached the top of Springer, so we were relieved when we finally spotted one of the mileage signs that often dotted the trail.

Erin reached the sign first and stopped. "Dude, you have got to be fucking kidding me."

"What?"

"This sign says Springer Mountain, 2.5 miles THAT way," she said, pointing in the direction we had just come from. "We went the wrong fucking way!"

CHAPTER TWO

DAY 1, GEORGIA, 2,168.5 MILES TO KATAHDIN

"Of course we did," I laughed, rolling my eyes like a teenager. For years, Erin and I had bumbled our way through one situation to another, and this turn was par for the course.

"Jesus, we are idiots. How many times did we look at that map?" Erin smiled as she pulled a trail map out of her pocket. It turned out, we were heading North, towards Maine. But in our giddiness to leave we forgot that we were supposed to have gone South out of the parking lot to reach the top of Springer Mountain, and then backtrack back through the parking lot to start the hike. On a normal hike, missing a peak wouldn't be a big deal, but we knew that missing Springer Mountain, the southern terminus, the very starting point of the Appalachian Trail, was different. For a year, we had looked at pictures of hikers, at the start of their journey, standing at the plaque that sits at the top of Springer, and we had imagined ourselves there a million times.

"So... what should we do?" Erin asked.

We had a choice, turn around and go back to reach the

peak, take our picture, and then retrace our steps—a move that would add more than four miles to our day—or we could keep moving. In what would become an all-too-common mantra, we simultaneously decided "Fuck it." I looked around at the nondescript patch of trees and trail that we found ourselves in, with nothing to distinguish it but a wooden mileage sign to the side of the trail, a far cry from the peak of Springer Mountain with what I imagined was a spectacular view of the North Georgia landscape. I pulled out my camera to take a picture of Erin as we deemed it "our Springer," and continued to hike North.

"We're not going to tell anyone about this, right?" I asked.

"Oh, hell no."

The rest of the hike passed quickly. The trail was fairly flat, and downhill, and we excitedly pointed out the scenery around us as we walked.

"Look," Erin pointed to the bushes that canopied the trail, "Rhododendrons."

"They're beautiful."

And they were; everything was. A light snow covered every surface, except the trail.

Every few minutes, one of us would say, "I can't believe this is finally happening" or "Dude, it's so on!"

Our plan was to hike about 8 miles that day. We knew, from our Long Trail hike, that trying to hike too many miles too soon could lead to injuries and fatigue. But we were so excited to be hiking that we walked quickly, and before we knew it, we had reached our destination, Hawk Mountain Shelter. All along the Appalachian Trail, usually every 5 to 10 miles, there are shelters for hikers to stay in. They are generally a three-sided wooden structure, located near a water source. Although in most sections of the trail, backpackers can pitch a tent anywhere along the path, many choose to stop at shelters because they provide water, a place to sit, and refuge from the weather.

The shelter was empty when we arrived.

"What time is it?" I asked.

Erin looked at her watch. "Shit... it's only 1:30. What do you want to do?" We were warm from walking, but it was very cold outside, and we knew that if we stopped for the day, it wouldn't be long before we'd need to get in our sleeping bags to keep from freezing. But we looked at the map, and the next shelter was another 8 miles down the trail, so we decided to stay where we were for the night.

As we suspected, within an hour of stopping, we were wearing every piece of clothing in our packs, and were buried in our sleeping bags. We played cards, cooked dinner, wrote in our journals, and were asleep by 7:00pm. That night I wrote "I think that, given some time, the full impact of what we are trying to do will set in, but right now it seems unfathomable that we are going to be hiking for five months."

The next morning, we woke at 7:00 am to slightly warmer, 35 degree weather. I repacked my bag, ate an energy bar, and we headed out. We planned to hike another low mileage day, about 8 miles, to ease ourselves into our new routine. The terrain was more challenging than the first day, and climbing mountains with 35 pounds on my back reminded me how hard hiking could be, and made me wish I was better prepared. In the months beforehand, after finishing a round of physical therapy for a knee injury, I hadn't been very active. I kept telling myself, "I'm going to be walking all day every day for the next five months, I can sit on the couch today." With my inactivity, on the day we started the trail, I was in the worst shape of my life.

As the day wore on, the sun came out, and the snow melted around us. At noon we climbed down a hill to a grassy area and creek. We decided to stop for lunch, and after looking at the map, realized that it was just over a mile to our destination for the night, Gooch Mountain Shelter.

"Let's just sit here for a bit," Erin suggested. We lay on our backs, warmed by the sun, for almost two hours. We would talk, and then fall silent, lost in our own thoughts. I thought about how peaceful it was by that creek, and how, for the first time in a long while, I felt completely calm.

Eventually, we made our way to the shelter. That night, we met some other thru-hikers. Erin and I started talking to a tall, lanky kid with early hints of a beard who told us his name was Mike, and a short-haired hiker with a mischievous grin who laughed when she told me she'd already adopted the trail name Lawn Ornament. Lawn Ornament and I gathered firewood, while Mike and Erin set to building a fire. The four of us, along with several other hikers who wandered in, sat on logs and rocks around the fire, cooking dinner. We took turns sharing bits of information about ourselves (Mike was 20 and taking a break from college, Lawn Ornament was from New Hampshire, the older couple across from me were excited to try out their homemade gear) and talked how we found ourselves attempting a thru-hike. I felt giddy, after spending a year of planning the hike with Erin, being with a group of who all shared this singular dream. At one point Lawn Ornament suggested we play a game.

"Hide and Seek?" Erin said with a straight face.

"Ring around the Rosey?" I chirped.

Mike chimed in, "Arm wrestling!"

"Sure!" Lawn Ornament laughed. "Erin, go hide, and Sally and Mike will arm wrestle while the rest of us sing Ring around the Rosey."

We eventually settled on a game where the first person names a celebrity and the next person has three seconds to name another celebrity whose first name starts with the first letter of the previous celebrity's last name.

"Jon Bon Jovi," said the hiker who sat next to me.

"Janet Jackson," I replied, confidently, confused when everyone laughed.

Mike turned to me. "Wait, do you think Bon is his middle name?"

"Isn't it?"

Erin cut in. "No, dude, she doesn't think Bon is his middle name. She thinks his first name is JonBon."

That night I wrote "It's been an amazing day. I'm tired, but I'm really happy."

And then, the next morning, the rains came.

CHAPTER THREE

DAY 3, GEORGIA, 2,156.3 MILES TO KATAHDIN

I woke up feeling stiff and sore and cold. The temperature had dropped dramatically, and the ground was frozen solid. No one talked as we packed our belongings; sleeping bag first, then clothes, then food and cooking gear at the top. The optimism and camaraderie from the night before was gone, erased by the dense gray fog that covered everything in sight. As we left the shelter, a light drizzle began to fall, and I pulled out the waterproof cover that would protect my pack, and my belongings, from the rain as I hiked.

Erin and I started out the morning walking together in silence, and soon, she pulled away, and I was left to shuffle along by myself. Having backpacked together before, Erin and I had agreed beforehand that we would each hike at our own pace, even if that meant we would be walking alone most days. As the slower hiker, I knew it would be equally frustrating for me to always feel like I was holding her up, and for her to feel like she had to slow her pace for me. But, despite what I knew, as the distance between us grew, I couldn't help berating myself, "You should be in better shape. You are not going to be able to do this. You can't make it out here. She's going to be waiting for you the whole trip."

The cold rain fell steadily, making the rocks and roots that covered the trail slick. I pulled the drawstrings tight on the hood of my rain jacket and tried to concentrate on putting one foot in front of the other. My mood grew darker as the day wore on. I was soaked with sweat and rain, and though I was exhausted from the climbs, steeper and more frequent than the days before, stopping to rest was not an option. As soon as I quit moving, my body heat dissipated, and within minutes, I was shivering uncontrollably. By the time I made it to the shelter that night, I was spent, emotionally and physically. Many of the same hikers we had met the night before were at the shelter when I arrived, and several straggled in soon after I did. We ended the day as we started it; cold, tired, and in silence.

The next morning, the fourth day of the hike, while the weather remained the same, cold and wet, the mood among the hikers was noticeably lighter. Everyone was excited because less than four miles from the shelter was Neel's Gap, where, right on the trail stood the Walasi-Yi Inn, which serves as an outfitter and hiker's hostel. With the warmth of a building with four walls and a roof calling us, even the steep climb over Blood Mountain passed without notice. A high percentage of those attempting to thru-hike the AT end their hike at Neel's Gap, some due to injury, but most because the trail just isn't what they thought it would be–it's too hard, too cold, too lonely. I had heard this statistic when Erin and I were still planning our hike and thought, "How could someone who set out to hike to Maine, quit after only 30 miles?" But now, thirty miles into my own thru-hike, I completely understood. It wasn't that the experience wasn't what I thought it would be–I had prepared for the weather, the physical pain, the solitude–it was that I wasn't sure that I was who I thought I would be.

When I'd pictured myself out here, I thought I'd be someone, like Erin, who was able to push through the hard parts, to make myself keep going when I was tired or sad, but I worried I wasn't. The feeling of inadequacy, of being both physically and mentally too weak to handle the constant discomfort of backpacking, that I had experienced on the Long Trail, was back, and I wasn't sure I'd be able to take five months of this feeling. I wasn't actually considering quitting, but I also wasn't as confident as I had been standing in the parking lot at Springer that I would make it to Katahdin.

Erin had waited for me at the Blood Mountain peak, which was covered in a dense fog, and we hiked down the mountain together. When we reached Walasi-Yi, all of the hikers took turns calling their families to give them updates, browsing the store for items they forgot, many going through their packs to send home unnecessary weight. I called Kevin, trying to sound more upbeat than I felt. In the comfort of the hiker's hostel, on a tattered thrift store couch, I took off my wet boots and examined the blisters that had sprung up the night before.

"Whoa! That's disgusting." A bearded hiker sitting next to me looked at my heels, and the blisters that with the rain had become quarter sized, gaping wounds. "You've got to take care of that shit, or you're not going to be able to walk."

I went to the outfitter and bought some antibiotic cream and large bandages, knowing that with the wet weather, and friction from my boots, it would be hard to keep the bandages in place. There wasn't much hope that the wounds would heal anytime soon, I just hoped to keep them covered as much as possible to stop the wounds from getting worse. An hour later, my heels bandaged, Erin and I agreed that we should get going. We had planned to hike another seven miles that day, and as nice as it felt to sit in the warm hostel, as tempting as a hot shower sounded, we weren't going to deviate from our schedule. Left to my own devices, I probably would have stayed, but Erin suggested we head out and I wasn't ready to tell her I was already having second thoughts. Of the twelve hikers who arrived at Walasi-Yi that day, only four of us left the building that afternoon; Erin and I, Mike, the thru-hiker we had met two nights earlier, and a section-hiker named Dan. Section hikers are people who hike a long trail in sections, for days or weeks at a time, sometimes over years; as opposed to thru-hikers, who hike a long trail in one season. Dan told me he only had two weeks off of work, so he was going to hike as far as he could before he had to go home.

With nothing to look forward to except another wet, freezing night, the last seven miles of the day dragged endlessly. When I finally arrived at the shelter, Erin announced that the roof leaked, so to be careful where I put my sleeping bag. Also, she told me, several people had written in the shelter log—the notebook found in most shelters for hikers to write in—that mice and bats frequented this spot. Listlessly, I cooked my dinner of Lipton Noodles, and then climbed into my sleeping bag, which I had covered with the garbage bag that usually lined my backpack, in hopes of waking up dry. As we lay there in the shelter, side by side, Erin, Mike, Dan, and I, played a game where you name as many bands as you can for each letter of the alphabet, trying to keep our minds off of what were truly miserable circumstances. We finally grew silent, but the rain continued to pound, mercifully drowning out the sounds of any mice or bats that may have shared our beds that night.

I woke up to Dan quietly cursing. "Fuck!" He hadn't covered the bottom of his sleeping bag like the rest of us, and he woke up to find that with the leaky roof, and the sideways rain, his bag was soaked through. "FUCK! I'm going to have to go back, aren't I?"

He looked desperately at us, hoping we would tell him

otherwise, but I knew he was right. The temperature was close to freezing, and the rain showed no signs of letting up. The next town was more than a day's hike away, and without a warm, dry, bag to sleep in at night, those conditions could lead to hypothermia, or worse. We said goodbye, and watched Dan head back towards Neel's Gap, knowing it would be that much harder for him to get back on the trail after this setback, and knowing that if we kept moving, we would probably never see him again.

I lingered in my sleeping bag, dreading putting on my wet hiking clothes, and not certain that I could face another day like those before. I re-bandaged my feet, and watched as Mike and then Erin left the shelter. Erin and I hadn't talked much since the rain started. I didn't want her to know how unhappy I was. She seemed so strong and confident, aware that the situation was miserable, but ready to face it nonetheless.

I reluctantly started walking, every step harder than the next. My gloves were still wet from the day before, and my hands were so cold, I could barely grasp my hiking poles. At one point, as the trail followed a mountain downward, I lost my footing and landed on my backside, hitting my knee on a rock. The knee instantly stiffened, and I struggled to continue walking. Our plan that day was to hike about 13 miles, but I knew there was a shelter after 6 miles, where we had tentatively agreed to stop for lunch. I thought that if I could just make it to the first shelter, Erin would be waiting there for me. I fueled myself on this notion, convinced that she must be as miserable as I was, or at least understand the pain I was in, and that once I got there, we could agree that we should stop for the day, instead of hiking the last 7 miles as we had planned.

Finally, after what seemed like hours, I saw the sign for the shelter. But as I approached the structure, my heart sank. There was no one there. Erin had already moved on, meaning that I would have to move on as well. But I couldn't. It had taken every reserve of strength I had to make it to this point, and I had no idea where I would find the energy to walk even one more step.

And so, I sat on the wood planks of the shelter floor, already shivering from the cold, and began to cry.

CHAPTER FOUR

DAY 5, GEORGIA, 2,129.7 MILES TO KATAHDIN

I sobbed so hard and long my stomach ached. I desperately searched for any way to change my situation, and found no solution. In a moment of weakness, I pulled a cell phone out of my pack, the cell phone that Erin and I had agreed we would only use in emergency situations, and turned it on with the thought that I could reach my Mom, or Kevin, anyone really, but saw, not surprisingly, that there was no reception.

I was in the middle of the woods, over seven miles from the next shelter, and 30 miles from any town. I sat there crying, hopeless, for a full half hour, until it finally sunk in that there was nothing I could do, I had to keep walking. Realizing this, that I had no other choice but to move forward, was oddly liberating. By having no options, I felt free. And then, as if someone else was controlling my limbs, I mindlessly searched through my pack for a dry pair of wool socks, which I put on my hands, loaded my pack on my back, grabbed my hiking sticks, and started walking.

Resigned to my fate, and with my socked hands now thawing, I was able to think about something other than my own misery. The rain still fell, and my feet and knee still ached, but a fog had lifted. I had hit rock bottom, and now I was moving on. If I was going to have to hike, and really, I had no choice, I decided I might as well try to have fun. I made up songs about the slippery rocks and tree roots that covered the trail, singing at the top of my lungs "Wet rocks and roots are not your friends. They will get you in the end."

By the time I reached the shelter, I felt like a different person. Erin and Mike were waiting there for me, Erin clearly worried, but not saying anything. They ushered me to the campfire that Mike had managed to start in the pouring rain. Erin told me that she had stopped at the previous shelter, but had been so cold and miserable that she had to move on.

"Today really sucked," she said, putting her arm around my shoulders.

"Tell me about it."

The next morning, we woke to something we hadn't seen in days, sunshine. It was perfect hiking weather; cool, but warm enough to strip off a few of the layers we had become accustomed to wearing. We were fortunate the conditions were so ideal, because the terrain was harder than any we had encountered, and we were attempting our longest day yet, 15.8 miles.

Around lunchtime I reached the base of a daunting mountain. I took my time to scramble and climb the boulders that comprised the steep path. When I finally made it to the top, I was rewarded by an amazing view of nothing but more mountains and valleys and trees as far as I could see. I was surprised to find Mike and Erin sitting on a rock outcropping, waiting for me. Erin later told me what I had figured, that they had been waiting there for about 20 minutes. She said that Mike had wanted to wait because he said that this was the kind of view you needed to share with someone.

We had now been hiking with Mike since our second

night out, coincidentally stopping at the same shelters each night, but after that day, we became a trio. Mike was goofy, and matched our energy. Erin and I are both the youngest of our siblings and so we loved the idea of taking on a little brother. Plus, Mike could start a raging fire out of nothing, in any weather, which we had come to learn was an invaluable asset.

We all decided that the next morning we would hike an easy 3.5 miles to Dicks Creek Gap where the AT crossed Highway 76. The town of Hiawassee, Georgia lay eleven miles down that road, and with it, a chance to resupply, make phone calls, and eat a warm meal. We reached the road quickly, eager to get to civilization, and were faced with the prospect of finding someone willing to drive three dirty, smelly, hikers into town. Hitchhiking is one of the central experiences of any AT backpacker. Most trail towns are too far to walk to from the trail, and so often, hikers have to rely on the kindness of others in order to get to town. Luckily, people who live near the AT are used to the sight of weary hikers sticking out their thumbs, begging for rides, and even a few are brave enough to stop. Erin and I had the advantage of being two of the relatively few women who thru-hiked that year, and probably seemed less threatening to many drivers. As time passed, we developed a routine where Erin and I would smile and wave and stick out our thumbs, and Mike would hide in the background until someone finally stopped.

That first day, standing on the side of Highway 76, we were fortunate to see the telltale signs of a ride, brake lights, and a quickly reversing car, within minutes. The driver was a Ridge Runner, the person responsible for maintaining shelters and the path, and providing support to hikers on certain sections of the trail. As we drove towards Hiawassee, he told us that we were the first thru-hikers he'd met that season, but that they expected record numbers to start their hikes in March and April. I liked that we were ahead of the pack.

Hiawassee is a tiny place, with a population of under one thousand people, but it seemed like paradise to us. Once in town, the first thing we did was go to the post office. In most towns near the trail, post offices will hold mail and packages for hikers. Like many hikers, we had asked our family and friends to send gear and goodies to post offices in towns where we planned to stop. For me, getting packages or mail was a nice treat, a way to stay connected with my people; but for Erin, arranging post office drops was essential. Erin had been diagnosed with Type I diabetes when she was 19, and her parents would ship insulin to her every few weeks along the trail.

After collecting a package containing a book and $20 from my dad, a little care package from Kevin and a card from my mom, we practically skipped across the street to an all-you-can-eat diner. As we chowed down on anything we could get our hands on—at one point I looked down at my (third!) plate of food and it was piled with gloppy mac n' cheese, fried hush puppies, a slice of pepperoni pizza, a ramekin of banana pudding, and a singular baby carrot—our perky teenage waitress pestered us with questions.

"So how much do y'all hike a day?" she drawled. When we told her, she exclaimed, "Goodness! I walked a mile yesterday, in order to get in shape for cheerleadin' and I'm still pooped!"

Her wonder at what we were doing, her announcement that, "Wow. I could never do what y'all are doing. That is just sooooo cool!" made me realize that she was right, despite my recent lows, this trip was a very cool thing.

We finished our meal, and after spending over an hour on three adjacent pay phones, talking to family, and in my case, Kevin, we stopped by the supermarket to refresh our food supply. In order to manage the weight of our packs, Erin and I had planned to only carry four to five days of food at any time, arranging our mileage so that we would arrive at a road crossing when we were running low. When we finished our shopping, we lingered in front of the market, drinking sodas and cracking jokes, knowing that the only thing left to do was find a hitch back to the trail.

Being in town is exciting. Leaving town... is hard. Your pack is heavy with your fresh resupply, your belly is full of greasy food, and the trail almost always climbs upward, away from town. On that day, my reluctance to return to the trail was intensified by the sores on my heels, which I discovered had only grown since I last checked them. Knowing that every step would cause pain made it hard to want to go back. I looked longingly at the rundown motel across the street from the market. I was just about to suggest to Erin and Mike that we get a room and a shower and a bed and a roof over our heads, when a pickup truck stopped and asked if we needed a ride.

Once back on the trail, which did, in fact, climb steeply from the road, I realized that my optimism, my feeling that this trip was a very cool thing, had vanished. I thought about the times I had felt happy over the past week, and realized they were few and far between. I started thinking that maybe thru-hiking just wasn't for me, maybe I really wasn't up for the constant discomfort, and that if I wasn't happy, maybe I should just quit.

That night, I made a deal with myself. I wrote in my journal "I started wondering today if I should quit. I'm hardly ever happy while I'm hiking, and I'm in constant pain. Today is March 1st. I've decided that I will give it a month, and if I'm still not happy, I'll leave the trail."

CHAPTER FIVE

DAY 7, GEORGIA, 2,099.9 MILES TO KATAHDIN

W hat I didn't know when I wrote that passage was that I had a more pressing concern, and his name was Falcon. Falcon, of course, wasn't his actual name, it was a trail name. Many people hiking the AT, or any long trail for that matter, adopt, or are given, a trail name, which they use during their hike. In fact, I never learned the real names of most of the people I met on the AT. Already, Mike had become Mike-nango, a combination of his name and his hometown in upstate New York, and Erin had become Sweet n' Low, a nod to her diabetes diagnosis (or, as we liked to say in honor of the classic Wilfred Brimley line, "diabetus"). I had not yet found a name that suited me.

Whatever his name, we knew Falcon was trouble from the minute he walked up to the shelter that night.

After he caught his breath, he zeroed in on Mike, saying, "That's an interesting stove you got there."

"Shit. A gear-head," Erin muttered under her breath, as I rolled my eyes and made a gagging gesture. Not much had changed since high school.

Gear-heads are a peculiar breed of hiker, one that, even in our short time on the trail, we had learned to studiously avoid. They are, generally, middle-aged white men, decked out with sparkling new equipment, who will talk about hiking gear until they are blue in the face. Falcon was no different. Like most gear-heads, Falcon only feigned interest in others' gear in order to pontificate about why his model of backpack/sleeping bag/water bottle/rain jacket was superior.

Although Erin and I had purposefully, and none-too-subtly, turned our backs to Falcon, leaving Mike alone to fend for himself, it wasn't long before he tried to engage us, too.

"Hey, what do you girls use to filter your water?" he asked, pulling his shiny new water filter out of his pack. Mike mouthed, "suck it, suckers" to Erin and I. Pay back.

Since all water on the trail comes from a natural water source- a spring, a river, in desperate times a mud puddle, it needs to be purified in order to avoid waterborne illnesses. Most hikers carry a water filter to treat their water. Erin and I used bleach. Two drops of bleach in a liter of water kills anything dangerous, doesn't affect the taste of the water, is light to carry, and most importantly, is safe to use. The method was uncommon in 2003, but certainly not unheard of. (One time, Erin and I collapsed in a giggle-fit when another hiker told us the joke, "What does Snoop Dog use to filter his water?" "BLEE-ACH!!")

"BLEACH!" Falcon screeched, living up to his name, "I've never heard of that! Are you sure that's safe?"

"Safe???" Erin said, "Well shit, Falcon, we never thought of that!"

Falcon, completely oblivious to the sarcasm Erin had so thickly laid on him, continued to quiz us about the bleach, and every other piece of gear we carried until I finally faked a yawn and told Falcon that we needed to turn in for the night. But my thought that we would find peace from Falcon in sleep was dead wrong. In addition to being a gear-head, Falcon was a world-class snorer.

Around 2am, without more than a few minutes of sleep, Erin and I simultaneously reached our breaking point. Half-delirious, Erin grabbed a hiking pole and began poking Falcon, while I stomped my foot on the shelter floor. This method worked to stop Falcon's snoring for about 2 seconds, and then we would hear a loud snort, and the racket would resume. Then, at 3am, out of the corner of my eye, I saw Mike pull out his knife. He shot an evil look at the still-snoring Falcon, and then plunged the blade into the corner of his foam sleeping pad. I watched as he cut two small squares of the foam, which he then stuffed into his ears.

"Ear plugs," Mike told us, and laid back down. Erin and I followed suit, but found that they did little to dampen the sound.

In the morning, I peeked an eye out of my sleeping bag, and saw Falcon cheerfully stirring his oatmeal, asking a bedraggled Erin, "How did you sleep? I didn't snore, did I?" Erin is a redhead, and can live up to her fiery reputation. I feared for his safety.

Mercifully, Erin did nothing more than grumble, "just a bit" and pull her bag back over her head to catch a couple more minutes of sleep.

Somehow, we managed to drag ourselves out of the shelter, and sleep walk through the day, buoyed by clear weather and the excitement at crossing our first state line.

After a week on the trail, we had made it to North Carolina.

CHAPTER SIX

DAY 9, NORTH CAROLINA, 2086.2 MILES TO KATAHDIN

The next morning, I woke to find the water in my water bottle frozen solid, a fitting reward after another snore-filled night courtesy of Falcon. Erin had audibly groaned the night before when we saw him amble up to the shelter where we had stopped for the day.

"How far are you all going today?" I heard Falcon ask Mike that morning as I tried to psyche myself up to leave my warm sleeping bag.

"Ummm, not sure... what about you?" Mike answered, being intentionally vague about our plans, in hopes we wouldn't have to endure another sleepless night.

Once I was satisfied that we would be hiking farther than Falcon, I quickly finished my morning routine—pee, brush teeth, pack, breakfast—eager to get hiking to generate some body heat. As the morning wore on, the sun came out, thawing the trail, and boosting my spirits. Even the two big climbs, over Big Butt Mountain, about which we made endless ass jokes, and Albert Mountain, at the end of the day did little to dampen my mood. I reached the top of Albert Mountain, after what was the steepest climb we had encountered so far, and once again found Erin and Mike waiting to share the view with me. We walked together the last half mile of the day, laughing about day hikers we'd come across wearing jeans and smelling like soap. Already, only nine days in the woods, we'd come to think of ourselves as apart from people who were just out for an afternoon. The sun was fading as we got to the shelter, so to beat the cold, we quickly went through our evening routine–pee, unpack, get water, cook dinner, get in sleeping bag.

Although the scenery was constantly changing, most days on the trail were routine–sleep, eat, hike, eat, sleep. That was why in-town days always stood out. Our 10th day on the trail was especially eventful because that day, we were going into Franklin, North Carolina, which would be the first place on the trail that we would get a shower, wash our clothes, and sleep indoors. I was beyond excited. The 10 miles we had to hike to get there felt like nothing–I was practically skipping along the trail that morning, filled with visions of pizza and beer and a pillow.

My euphoric state was broken when, out of the corner of my eye, I saw a bearded man wearing a black poncho and carrying a camouflage backpack come running towards me from a side trail, yelling and waving his arms to get my attention. I looked around for signs of Erin or Mike, and, finding that they were far ahead, I suddenly realized how completely vulnerable I was out there. I was still miles away from the nearest road, and I hadn't seen another person all morning. If this man wanted to hurt me, there was not much I could do except try to outrun him, and quickness wasn't my strong suit. My heart pounded as he approached me.

"Are you a thru-hiker?" he asked me. As he got closer, I realized what I thought was a poncho was actually a garbage bag that he'd cut holes in for his arms and head.

"Trying to be," I answered tentatively, trying to pick up my pace.

As he walked along beside me, I watched as he brushed crumbs from his scraggly beard. He told me that he was a psychologist studying people who attempted to thru-hike the Appalachian Trail, and so he was trying to track people down at the beginning of their hike to fill out a survey. He then wanted them to fill out another survey at the end of their hike, wherever they got off the trail, to see what the difference was between someone who completed their thru-hike and someone who got off the trail somewhere short of Maine.

Still eyeing him wearily, I took his survey with the promise that I would mail it to him from Franklin and hurried down the trail. When I reached Erin and Mike at the road crossing, I told them about the guy and asked if they were stopped, too. Neither of them saw him, and I never ran into another hiker who had either.

It was 11am and pretty soon after we stuck our thumbs out, a pickup truck stopped to give us a hitch into town. It wasn't until we had loaded our packs in the back that I noticed the rebel flag sticker on his rear window, not an uncommon sight in the South. Erin and I slid in the extended cab and Mike sat up front. The driver, a big guy in a muscle shirt and cut-off jean shorts, introduced himself, asked, "Hey, have y'all heard this one?" and proceeded to tell us a string of racist jokes. Erin and I sat there slack jawed while Mike mumbled, "No, I don't think I've heard that one before."

"Well," I said as the pickup pulled away, "I'm not sure how to feel about that."

"I guess in his case it was hate, not heritage," Erin said.

I nodded, adding, "Love the ride, hate the racist?"

Our driver had dropped us off at the Franklin Motel where we rented a hotel room and took turns taking long, hot showers.

We grabbed lunch, and then headed to the Franklin County Library. Libraries were always a first stop in any trail town, because they have computers with internet access. The three of us sat in the library for over an hour, reading emails from friends and sending out updates of our progress. I cherished the connection, but was amazed by how separated I already felt from the outside world.

In a mass email to family and friends I wrote:

The trip so far has been a little bit of everything. We have had a variety of weather- from freezing cold rain to 50 degrees and sunny and so far we've survived so I think that's a good sign. My emotions run the spectrum, too. On Sunday, we crossed the Georgia/North Carolina line and today we cruised past the 100 mile mark... I think I'm getting the hang of this stuff.

The scenery is ever changing- one minute I'll be walking through a pine forest and the next I'll look up and I'm under a canopy of rhododendrons (sp?). There have been some really tough mountains but on a clear day, the reward of an amazing view far outweighs the effort it took to get up there. My biggest complaint is probably the state of my feet...lots of blisters that make it painful to walk. But hopefully I'll be getting a handle on that with a trip to the pharmacy!

*I think about everyone a lot (I've got lots of time to do that now, in between wondering what the lyrics are to Ice, Ice Baby and "how the *&^* could I have only walked 2 miles?"). I hope everything is going well!*

That night, after running errands and gorging ourselves on pizza and one beer apiece (we worried about being dehydrated the next morning), we lay in our beds watching mindless television, thankful to be out of the cold and rain that fell steadily outside. The bed and pillow were a vast improvement over the hard uneven floors of the shelters I had become accustomed to sleeping on, but still, I had a hard time falling asleep. When I did fall asleep, I woke up every hour and stared at the digital clock. My mind raced, worrying about the rain and the next day's hike. It was as if subconsciously I couldn't let myself get too comfortable, knowing that the next morning we would be back in the cold and the rain.

CHAPTER SEVEN

DAY 11, NORTH CAROLINA, 2064.2 MILES TO KATAHDIN

W orrying about the next day's hike had become a bad habit. I would pour over the elevation maps and trail descriptions, the mountains growing larger and the climbs steeper in my mind each time I looked at the maps. I would obsess over the mileage, fearing that I wouldn't be able to hike as far as we had planned. As usual, the next morning I found that my concerns had been overblown, and my sleepless night, spent fretting over the cold and the rain, was for naught. The morning started out foggy, but soon the sun was shining, and the temperature rose to a balmy fifty degrees.

About halfway through the day, I reached the peak of Wayah Bald. It was always a bit disorienting to find development on top of a mountain, and as I emerged from the woods, I was met with the site of a parking area, toilets, a paved walkway, and a stone lookout tower. Dripping sweat, after having just spent over two hours hiking up the side of the mountain, I felt a bit defeated seeing a fresh smelling couple strolling hand in hand from their car towards the peak.

When I reached the tower, I dropped my pack and climbed

the steps to the top, where I found Erin and Mike talking to a small woman with two long pigtails. She had breezed by me on the trail earlier while I was taking a break with a quick, "Everything okay, hon?" I disliked her instantly.

"This is Happy. She thru-hiked a couple of years ago and is out hiking for a couple of weeks," Erin told me through gritted teeth. It seems I wasn't alone in my opinion of this woman. Apparently, for the fifteen minutes before I arrived, Happy told Erin and Mike and anyone else who would listen about all the things we were doing wrong on our hike, and how when she thru-hiked, "things were just so much better."

"Fucking know-it-all. I hope we don't see her again," I grumbled to Erin when we finally started hiking again that afternoon.

"You can count on it."

The first person I saw when I got to the shelter that night was, of course, Happy, this time foisting her views on a couple in their early sixties. When they finally politely, yet firmly, extracted themselves (Happy moved seamlessly on to another unsuspecting hiker), the couple introduced themselves as Doc and Virginia Creeper. I loved them instantly. Doc told me that he and Virginia had met only five years earlier at an Appalachian Trail conference, had fallen madly in love, and were recently married. Doc was attempting to thru-hike and Virginia was joining him on several sections of the trail.

That night we were packed into the small shelter like sardines, eight of us in a space designed to sleep six at most, when the wind picked up and hail started to pound the tin roof.

"Oh, this is so not good," Happy told us all. "If it starts lightning, we're total goners. When I thru-hiked, I knew two people who got struck by lightning. So not good."

"We'll be alright, there are plenty of tall trees around," Doc said, giving me a knowing smile.

"I guess...."

Though no one got much sleep that night, we all survived, and over the next two days Erin, Mike, and I hiked over an endless stream of peaks and valleys, gladly walking further than Happy, but sadly also Doc and Virginia Creeper. At one point, I hypothesized that the trail builder was a sadist, and asked Erin, "Why else would they put the trail right up the side of a fucking mountain, only to go right the fuck back down, and then right the fuck back up another one?" The trail in the Southern part of the Appalachian Trail is known for its numerous steep climbs and descents. Instead of following ridge lines, much of the trail in the South crosses ridges, which means hauling yourself, and your pack, up and down tall mountains, all day long.

At the end of the second day, I came across Erin sitting on a rock, crying. Next to her was a sign for a spur trail, indicating that it was just a 1/10th of a mile to the shelter where we were staying that night.

"I'm exhausted," she told me through her tears. "Nothing's wrong, I just can't stop crying." I knew what she meant. At the end of most days, not only was I physically spent, but I was at the bottom emotional reserves, too, leaving little barrier to hold back whatever raw emotion that came bubbling up. It was why we laughed so hard our stomachs hurt at anything remotely funny, but also why the tears were so quick to flow.

"You know what we need?" I said as I helped her back to her feet, "Risa."

The next day, Mike, Erin, and I hiked twelve miles in record time to get just that. We reached Fontana Dam before noon that day, where we had arranged to meet my mom, Risa, and spend the night at the Fontana Village Resort, which rented rooms at a discount to hikers. It was just what we needed. My mom took all three of us to lunch, immediately welcoming Mike like he was one of her own. It was how she had always been. When I was younger, she was always gathering random neighborhood kids for cookie making or craft parties. Every Christmas Eve, anyone who didn't have anywhere else to be was welcome to join the feast at Risa's home. She made sure our house was the one all of our friends wanted to hang out at. On that visit, she fussed over our injuries, ferried us to do errands, and told us over and over how proud she was of us.

In the morning, she pulled me aside and asked me if I wanted to go home with her; she was worried about the state of my feet, and my knees, which had mysteriously swelled overnight.

"Honey, y'all could just come with me for a couple of days and rest and I'll bring you right back here when you've mended."

"No, I'm okay, I promise," I said, almost as much to convince myself that it was the truth. While taking a few days off and being cared for sounded wonderful, I knew I needed to keep moving. It was a surprise to myself to find that I actually wanted to keep moving. Fontana Dam was the entrance to the Smokies, one of the most beautiful parts of the trail. In fact, it was a hike in the Great Smoky Mountains National Park with my dad almost ten years prior that had introduced me to the Appalachian Trail, and I was excited to be in familiar territory.

At the entrance to the park stood a ridge runner, keeping a record of the hikers that entered. While Mike, Erin, and I stood there talking to him, another hiker walked by.

"Trail name?" the ridge runner asked him.

"Turbo," the hiker, a young guy with shoulder-length brown hair and a beard, answered, and kept walking without even glancing in our direction.

Erin and I rolled our eyes at each other, assuming that the

hiker adopted this trail name as a reflection of his attitude about hiking–full speed ahead.

The ridge runner then asked each of us for our trail names, writing them in a notebook. When he got to me, he asked, "Do you have a trail name?"

As I had countless times before to the same question, I answered, "Nope, not yet."

"Well, there you go," he said, "your trail name is Not Yet."

And with that, I became known to the trail community as Not Yet.

CHAPTER EIGHT

DAY 15, NORTH CAROLINA, 2007.5 MILES TO KATAHDIN

We said goodbye to my name-giving trail runner and headed up the steep trail and into the Smokies. Right away, the trail was more populated than any before it. It was March 9th and spring break was in full swing. I took particular pleasure in easily passing a group of loud college age men, loaded down by their too-full packs. It was tangible confirmation that even though most days I still felt slow and out of shape, I was actually getting stronger.

That night, Erin, Mike, and I, as well as a few other thru-hikers, sat around a fire with four spring breakers. They were full of questions about thru-hiking, and Erin and I lapped up the attention, eager to make what had been a pretty rough few weeks seem more glamorous. I noticed that Mike seemed unusually moody.

"What's going on?" I asked him.

"I fucking hate thoughtless hikers," he grumbled, pointing to one of the spring breakers who had tossed an orange peel on the ground in front of the shelter. "They're fucking dangerous."

"Maybe he just doesn't realize..."

"Then he shouldn't fucking be out here!" Mike said as he picked up the peel, tossed it in his garbage bag, and stomped off.

Erin caught my eye and I gave her a little shrug. Mike wasn't wrong that food left lying around would bring animals, and the Smokies were known for their abundance of black bears. By now, it was second nature to us to make sure no trace of food was left around the shelter, any food prepared had to be eaten, and all wrappers, food scraps, and cooking instruments went into our food bags. In most shelters, we hung the food bags from strings at the front of the structure, meant to prevent mice from chewing through them. However, in areas with a known bear population, we hung our bags from trees or poles designed to keep the food out of the bears' reach. Because the Smokies attract so many visitors, the park also attracts animals who are conditioned by humans' tendency to leave food out. And while most backpackers, whether they are thru-hikers or just out for a weekend, understand the importance of keeping a clean campsite, there are always a few who don't know, or worse, don't care. So, while Mike's concern was certainly understandable, his anger seemed uncharacteristic.

Even sunshine and clear skies the next day didn't do anything to change his outlook. I reached the shelter that night and didn't see Mike anywhere. I realized that I hadn't seen him all day, which was unusual.

"Where's Mike?" I asked Erin, who had arrived before me.

"He took off. He said he wanted to get away from people, so he was going to try to make it to Clingman's Dome tonight." Clingman's Dome was another five miles up the trail.

"What's his deal?"

"I don't know," Erin said, "but his attitude sucks, so it's probably for the best."

I had to agree with her. I looked around at our shelter-mates, and saw that we'd be spending the night with a group of obnoxious 50-something year old men, and a couple of frat boys, just the type of hikers to send Mike into a rage.

Erin pointed to the shelter, where the men were busy spreading out the contents of their massive packs, bragging about their past adventures, and trying in vain to start a fire, and whispered, "I've dubbed it the Tool Shed."

"Holy shit," I laughed, "you're not kidding. Hey! Do you think it scares the frat boys that they are glimpsing their future... here's you in 30 years?"

"Let's show them how to make a fire." Erin and I gathered wood, and quickly started a blazing fire.

Total. Badasses. I wrote in the margins of Erin's journal. Just like we'd passed notes all through middle school and high school, Erin and I had taken to writing little notes in the margins of each other's journals when we wanted to have a private conversation in a crowded shelter.

"Thanks..." one of the men said, "I was just about to do that."

Between the chorus of snores and the howls of coyotes throughout the night, neither Erin nor I slept well that night. The next morning, we woke extra early and quietly gathered our stuff while the Tool Shed continued to snooze.

"What time is your mom supposed to meet us?" I asked. "Seeing your mom and my mom in one week, it's like Bring Your Mom to the Trail week up in here!"

"Mom-a-polooza?" Erin asked.

"Mom-pocolypse?" I countered.

"No." Erin shook her head. "She'll be there at noon."

"We better get a move on," I said as I buckled the hip belt to my pack. We were meant to meet Erin's mom at Newfound Gap, a parking area that crossed the trail about halfway through the Smokies, and we would need to do twelve miles before noon. From the gap, Erin's mom would drive us to her family's lake house in Tennessee where we would spend two nights, including our very first zero day—our first full day without hiking.

We hiked along at a fairly fast clip, which proved harder to maintain the closer we got to Clingman's dome. Clingman's dome is the highest point on the Appalachian Trail, at 6643 feet, and even in March, the trail at that altitude stays covered in snow and ice. Several times throughout the morning, Erin and I found ourselves flat on our backs, unable to keep our footing on the slick iced trail.

"Do you think Mike will be there?" I asked Erin as we walked gingerly, trying to avoid falling yet again. Mike had been invited to come with us to Erin's lake house.

"I don't know; he didn't say anything about it before he took off yesterday."

We managed to reach the parking lot at Newfound gap a few minutes before noon, and though it was crowded with tourists who would never make it further into the park than the lookout spot in the parking lot, we had no trouble finding Erin's mom, Cathy, who has the same flaming red hair as Erin. Next to her stood a sheepish-looking Mike, who had decided to join us after all. After sweaty hugs from Erin and I, Cathy piled the three of us into her Dodge Neon.

"Okay, you three," she said as she started down the windy road to Gatlinburg, "let's get you home."

CHAPTER NINE

DAY 17, TENNESSEE, 1,967.2 MILES TO KATAHDIN

We were headed to the Nealon family lake house, about an hour North of Gatlinburg on Norris Lake, and to Erin and I it really was like going home. In eighth grade, Erin's family took the two of us on a spring break trip to Norris, which Erin and I had prepared for by using puffy paint to decorate matching boxer shorts with phrases like "Spring Break Tennessee" and "Homies 4EVA" and "Anti Sweat Leaf" (in eighth grade we had very firmly bought into the no drinking, no drugs, no sex mantra being drilled into us by teachers and parents). It was on that first trip that Erin's parents found the land where they would eventually build their house, and through the years we spent countless weekends and holidays roaming the nearby hills and splashing in the lake. The lake house had become one of my favorite places to be, because, at over thirty minutes to even the nearest convenience store, there was nothing to do there but relax.

After spending almost two and a half weeks in the woods, it was a bit of an odd choice to take our first day off at a house surrounded by the woods, but the lake house suited us perfectly. The three of us wanted nothing more than to lay around, eat home-cooked food, watch TV, check our email, use the phone, and maybe drink a beer or two. I spent a good deal of my time talking to friends and family, and of course, Kevin. I talked to my two closest friends, Bethany and Hadley, who were both recently engaged and in the throes of wedding planning, full of news about dresses and venues and engagement parties. It was my first realization that while I had withdrawn from society, life was continuing on for those I loved, and I felt a twinge of sadness for what I was going to miss over the coming months. The rest of my time, I alternately laid on the couch in front of the TV and sat on the deck playing board games, always with something edible within inches of my mouth. By the time we headed back to Gatlinburg I was, for the first time since beginning the hike, fully rested.

We had resupplied our food the day before, but decided to stop in Gatlinburg at an outfitter called the Happy Hiker before driving up the mountain back to Newfound Gap. After picking up a few odds and ends, a fuel canister for Mike, a new water bottle for Erin, we stood outside while the store owner took our picture. Like several outfitters and hostels along the trail, the Happy Hiker took photos of thru-hikers who had made it to that point and hung them along the rafters. We looked at past years' photos and found one of Cara, whose trail name had been Supergirl, taken during her thru-hike in 1999, and imagined finding ourselves there in several years.

As we were heading out the door, Erin started giggling uncontrollably.

"Wha..." I started, but then looked to my right and instantly realized the source of her laughter was a giant sign for a restaurant called the Burning Bush.

"Oh my god, you guys have to get a picture," I told Erin and her mom.

"You girls are so bad," Cathy chided, but still posed for a picture of the two redheaded women in front of a Burning Bush sign.

Still laughing, the four of us packed back into the little Dodge Neon and headed up the winding road. On the left we passed four hikers we recognized from the Happy Hiker, thumbs out, looking for a hitch back up the mountain. Erin and I gave them a wave and a look saying "sorry, we totally would but we can't," a look we had seen and resented many times ourselves from passing motorists. It was nearly 11am when we finally reached Newfound Gap, and the parking area was already crowded with cars. We were finishing up our goodbyes and taking a few final pictures when a van pulled up behind us and the four hikers from the road filed out.

"Dude, you guys totally gave us the shrug off," laughed one of the hikers from the van, a good looking guy around our age with a scruff of brown hair and the customary hikers' beard.

"We were in a Neon! There was no room!" Erin protested, laughing along with him. He introduced himself as Pilgrim, a shorter guy with a big grin and even bigger calf muscles as Sugar High, Pilgrim's best friend from home, and a stocky, bearded man and beautiful, willowy woman with two-brown braids as Lucky and Sparrow, a couple from Tennessee. We all stood around chatting before we started up the trail. Pilgrim charmed us with his story of his mission to collect "flair" from every state, showing us the battery powered NASCAR radio that was his Tennessee memorabilia, and Lucky laughing about all the trail names he considered and then rejected, like "Notgonnamakeit."

We came across the four of them several times throughout the day, and fell into a comfortable rhythm of teasing and joking. They felt like instant kindred spirits, serious about hiking, but ultimately wanting to have fun. I was disappointed that night when I headed down the side trail to the shelter and ran into them walking the other way.

"Are you guys heading on?" I asked. It was almost dark, and the next shelter was at least another five miles.

"Yeah..." Sparrow told me, wistfully, "Lucky and I have to get off the trail for a couple of days for a wedding and we need to get through the Smokies the day after tomorrow to meet my parents."

"Ahh... well, be careful, it's pretty icy out there. I hope to see you guys again. Happy hiking."

"Yeah, we'll see you up the trail," she said, a common refrain among hikers.

"Just make sure to give us a ride next time," Sugar High teased.

I watched as they headed up the trail, sad to see them go, and then turned and made my way down to the shelter.

The day had been long, but good, not filled with the angst and dread that usually accompanies returning to the trail. And it wasn't just the thrill of meeting new people, but also the extraordinary beauty of the Smokies. Much of the trail that day followed a very narrow ridge, allowing sweeping views of lush green mountains on either side. I had spent all day alternatively scared I would fall down the mountain and amazed by where I found myself. And now, I sat on the shelter steps cooking my noodles and watching the sun go down and the sky turn a pinky orange, thinking how content I was. Cold, but content.

Eventually, one of the men staying at the shelter–there were a group of Michigan alum out for their annual get together–came and asked me about the little stove I was using. Instead of buying expensive propane backpacking stoves, Erin and I had made stoves out of soda cans (a trick we learned from Cara, the source of all our backpacking knowledge). We would prop our little hiker's pots up on tent stakes over the stove, which we fueled with denatured alcohol readily available at hardware and grocery stores. The technique was fairly common among backpackers, who were always looking for ways to shave weight and save money, but was a source of interest for hikers out for a day or weekend, who seemed fascinated by our homemade gear. By the time I had finished my demonstration, which included some smack talk about Michigan football on my part (I went to Big Ten rival Purdue), and I had eaten my noodles, the sun had completely set.

The next day we were reminded why the Smokies were so named, as a thick fog covered the mountains most of the day, making it impossible to see more than a hundred feet ahead. Much of the trail was covered in patches of ice and snow and as I struggled to stay upright, I thought about Pilgrim, Sugar High, Lucky, and Sparrow, trying to make their way in the dark the evening before. By the time I reached the shelter that night, the fog had lifted, but I was exhausted from my many falls and near wipeouts. I was relieved to see only Mike and Erin waiting for me, rather than the crowds we had come to expect in the Smokies. Soon, we were joined by a ridge runner, who told us he was responsible for maintaining the section of the trail and its shelters from Newfound Gap to the northern end of the Smokies, which we would cross the next day. The four of us played cards, deciding that the losers had to collect firewood for the evening. Throughout the game, as the ridge runner talked, I couldn't help but stare at his abnormally large teeth. I wasn't the only one who noticed, because in the morning, Erin elbowed me and pointed to a toilet bowl brush poking out of the ridge runner's pack, and whispered, "Do you think that's his toothbrush?"

After hiking a couple of miles that morning, Erin and I came upon Mike sitting on a rock, reading his trail guide, waiting for us. All of us carried "The Thru-Hiker's Handbook" an AT guide created by a former thru-hiker named Wingfoot. The Handbook contained mileage logs for the entire trail, as well as descriptions of amenities, lodging, and even hand drawn maps of the towns along the trail. Although it wasn't always 100% accurate, it was an invaluable resource, and one we pored over every night, trying to figure out where we wanted to go the next day, and where our next resupply stop would be.

"Wingfoot says there is a store called Mountain Mamas about a mile off the trail at Davenport Gap where we can get burgers," Mike told us. "We should go. It says the owner will give us a ride back up to the trail."

We flew the five miles down to the gap, propelled by visions of hot food, and had hiked over seven miles by 10:30 in the morning. About a quarter mile after leaving the trail, we saw a handwritten sign reading "Mountain Moma's Store" with an arrow pointing down the winding asphalt road.

"Do you think her name is actually Moma?" I asked, pronouncing it like the MOMA. "Or did they misspell mama?"

"That Moma, she can't spell for shit, but she sure can cook!" Erin twanged.

"I hope she can cook... I'll be pissed if we walk a mile out our way for nothing," added Mike, voicing what we all felt. Like many thru-hikers, we hated to walk anything that wasn't a "trail mile," and usually only the promise of food or shelter would lure us off the trail, and even then, we would try to hitch a ride for even short distances, often waiting much longer for a ride than it would have taken us to walk. It was very rare for us to take any of the many side trails that led to spectacular over-looks or waterfalls along the trail (VERY rare). It was an awful feeling to realize you had veered off the trail somehow and needed to backtrack. We were happy to hike, but only if it meant forward progress.

After twenty minutes on the road, we spotted a small

wooden cabin, and out front on picnic benches, sat Pilgrim, Sugar High, and Sparrow. Lucky was loading his pack into the back of a car driven by an older couple.

"Are you guys taking off?" I asked as we approached, remembering that he and Sparrow were headed home for a wedding.

"Yeah, dude, we'll be back on the trail in a couple of days. It sucks, I don't know if we'll be able to catch back up with these guys," Lucky said, nodding to Pilgrim and Sugar High.

After a round of hellos and goodbyes, we watched the four of them climb into the car. Pilgrim and Sugar High were being dropped off at the trailhead, and I was excited to learn that they planned on hiking to the same shelter where we hoped to hike to that evening.

"Hey, this is kinda like payback. Later!" laughed Pilgrim as they took off back up the winding road, leaving us standing in front of the store. We left our packs outside and opened the door to Mountain Momas (the sign above the door also had an O), instantly overwhelmed by a combination of cigarette smoke and home perm. The building was divided into two sections, a small convenience store on one side, and a deli counter with several booths on the other. On the deli counter side were two older ladies, one sitting on a folding chair while the other rolled her hair in tight rows of curlers. Both had long skinny cigarettes dangling from their mouths.

"Let us know when y'all are ready and we'll fix ya whatever you want!" shouted the woman in the chair, who I assumed was Moma, with a raspy country drawl. We quickly looked over the menu–every single item was fried–put in our orders and rushed outside for some fresh air.

"Dude, do you think the burgers are seasoned with perm solution?" Erin whispered to me.

Our food was delivered by the beautician, who told us, "If

y'all want a ride back up the mountain, you're going to have to
wait for Mama's perm to set." Even though we had no idea how
long that would take, and we had eleven miles still to hike, we
told her we'd wait. I quickly ate my french fries and chicken
sandwich that was so drowned in mayonnaise I doubt I could
have tasted home perm if it had been there. We stood around
literally kicking rocks until an hour later when Moma/Mama
came out in a housecoat and slippers, tight gray curls covering
her head.

"Come on and get in my van and I'll take y'all back up the
hill. Yous might need to move some things around to all fit,"
Moma told us, cigarette still dangling from her lip.

We shifted around a mound of junk and Erin and I situated
ourselves in the back, while Mike slid into the front seat. Erin
and I were always more than happy to volunteer to squeeze in
the backseat of a car, or sit in the open bed of a pickup truck,
because the person in the front had the job of talking to the
driver, and often, it was a struggle. Erin and I smiled to
ourselves as we listened to Moma's constant stream of chatter
and Mike's polite murmurs back. With one last waft of home
perm and smoke, Moma dropped us off at the trailhead and
sped back down the mountain.

We started back up the trail, now officially out of Smoky
Mountain National Park, and I instantly fell behind the other
two. My stomach felt like it had a brick in it and my muscles
were tight from sitting around. The trail changed, too. Where
in the Smokies the trail was well maintained and always scenic,
this portion of the trail was rocky and if it's possible, ugly. The
trail was a series of switchbacks that looked as if it was recently
dug, with exposed roots, loose rocks and dirt strewn all down
the mountainside. We'd crossed under I-40 and the unwelcome
sounds of trucks and cars accompanied the climb. I shuffled
along, my mood darkened. I felt queasy and was upset when I

realized that because I had forgotten to refill my water at the store, I was now completely out of water. Behind me, I heard voices, and turned to see a long line of teenagers gaining on me. I stepped to the side of the trail to let them pass, annoyed with myself that I was moving so slow. My stomach lurched. I waited until the group was out of sight, put my hands on my knees, and vomited, tears streaming down my face as I muttered to no one, "fucking Mountain Moma."

CHAPTER TEN

DAY 21, TENNESSEE, 1,931.2 MILES TO KATAHDIN

T hen, taking a deep breath, I told myself to suck it up, and started walking again. By this point in the hike, the turn-around time between despair and resolve was little to none. I could have a nervous breakdown one minute and be laughing the next, knowing that I quite literally had to keep putting one foot in front of the other. Within ten minutes I had reached a small stream trickling down the side of the mountain and I stopped to fill my empty water bottle.

"Hey," a voice called from behind me. I turned to see a tall, thin hiker with bright blue eyes, wearing running shoes and carrying one of the smallest packs I'd seen. We chatted while we both got water and he told me his name was CT.

"Hey, I've heard about you!" I told him. "You're the guy who hikes, like, 30 miles a day, right?"

I'd found the AT hiking community operated a bit like a very poorly organized spy network. You'd pass a day hiker going the other way who'd tell you a story about a thru-hiker he'd met two days ago, at lunch you'd read something that hiker had written in the notebook at a shelter, and later that night you'd meet someone who had hiked with person for a day or two. Through these little tidbits, you could start to piece together hazy pictures of who was on the trail and where.

CT laughed kindly, and said that was him, that he was trying to finish quickly. "It gets a little lonely, though, I never get to really meet people, you know?"

"Yeah, you just breeze right past them... PEACE!"

He took off ahead of me, turning to yell back, "peace!" and I knew that would be the last I'd see of him. Erin and I had yet to hike 20 miles in one day, and doing thirty seemed near impossible.

Finally rehydrated and feeling inspired, I pushed myself to finish the day strong. It was amazing how instantly different I felt when I had water or food. I could go from my legs barely moving and a foggy mind to energized and clear headed with a gulp of cold water and a peanut butter cracker. When I got to the shelter, which lay in a grassy valley, Erin, Mike, Sugar High, and Pilgrim sat at a picnic table talking.

"Look who else is here!" Erin said, pointing to the shelter.

I turned to see Doc and Virginia Creeper, the sweet older couple who we had met a week earlier. The seven of us gathered around the picnic table to cook dinner, conversation flowing easily as we talked about ourselves and our hikes. After dinner Pilgrim challenged me to a "foot off" and we removed our bandages to show off our respective foot injuries–his, a rash that covered most of both feet, and mine, gaping heel wounds that still refused to mend. I won, hands down, and Erin declared that the whole thing was, "fucking disgusting."

That night, as we lay in our sleeping bags, talking and laughing like old friends, I thought about CT, making this trip by himself, and knew I wouldn't want to do it that way, no matter how impressive the physical feat.

The next day, Erin and I stuck close together. We talked

about Doc and Virginia Creeper, who we both had fallen in love with that morning when, still in their sleeping bags, Doc had leaned over to kiss Virginia and whispered "hey stinky" to which Virginia had responded with a girlish giggle. They were hiking South for a couple of weeks (while we were forever headed North), so we knew we wouldn't see them for awhile. We giggled about how we thought Pilgrim was hot and Sugar High was sweet. "Just like us," Erin said.

"Wait? Which one am I?"

"Isn't it obvious?" she laughed.

The day passed quickly, and by 2pm we were at the shelter. Mike and Sugar High sat swinging their legs off the front.

"We've got a proposition," Mike said, looking at us expectantly. "We think you guys should hike to the next shelter with us. It's ten miles...but that would mean we'd get into town early tomorrow." The next day was March 17th and the night before the five of us had decided we'd stay in Hot Springs, NC, a town right off the trail, to celebrate St. Patrick's day.

"Since when did Mike become a 'we' with Sugar High and Pilgrim?" I asked Erin after we'd sent the guys on their way, telling them there was no way in hell we were walking another ten miles and that we'd see them the next day.

"He just needs some dude time," Erin said, rolling her eyes. And apparently, we needed some girl time, too. It was the first night the two of us had been alone in a shelter together and we passed the time gossiping and laughing, talking in a language only the two of us could understand.

At one point I asked Erin, "do you think Pilgrim and Sugar High call each other by their trail names? Because I'm sorry, I just can't call you Sweet n' Low."

"Nah, dude," Erin said, suddenly very serious. "When you're best friends you don't need names, you're just like... 'Hey!'"

It was quiet for about two seconds before we simultaneously burst out laughing, both of us rolling on the shelter floor. We'd recover, start talking about something else, and then one of us would say "it's just like... Hey!" and we'd lose it again.

Later, after the sun was down, we lay side by side in our sleeping bags.

"Erin?"

"Yeah?"

"Thanks for making me do this."

A few minutes later, "Erin?"

"Yeah?"

"Did you touch me or did a mouse just crawl across my head?"

CHAPTER ELEVEN

DAY 23, NORTH CAROLINA, 1,913.25 MILES
TO KATAHDIN

"Dude... my hands are in my sleeping bag."
After a restless night spent paranoid about what might be crawling around the shelter, but with no additional sightings, Erin and I woke early, excited to finally get to Hot Springs. Chris, Cara's fiancé, had told us that once we reached Hot Springs we were officially thru-hikers. We had also heard about a bed and breakfast in the middle of town called Elmer's that was supposedly very accommodating to thru-hikers. Luckily, the terrain was mostly flat and downhill and we arrived in Hot Springs in time for lunch.

Elmer's turned out to be better than advertised; a warm, beautiful Victorian home full of musical instruments and books and home-cooked vegetarian food that, because the owner had hiked the AT, allowed dirty, messy thru-hikers to stay for next to nothing. Erin and I settled into our room, thrilled to each have our own bed and a door that shut, took showers, and headed down the two block main street. After loading up on a greasy lunch that instantly had me clutching my stomach and running for the bathroom, we hit the post office, laundry, grocery store, and outfitter. It wasn't until we returned to Elmer's that we realized we hadn't seen Mike, or Pilgrim and Sugar High, since we'd arrived. We asked around and Turbo, the hiker who had passed us on our way into the Smokies, told us that they were doing "work for stay," an option that several hostels along the trail offered to hikers low on cash to do handy work in exchange for room and board. Erin and I had both saved enough money working in the year before we left to comfortably get us through five months of hiking, but those guys, recent college graduates (or, like Mike, on a break from college), were always low on cash.

Mike popped his head in our room an hour later to let us know he had made it back, and shortly after the three of us headed down the street to the one bar in town, the Paddlers' Pub. Earlier that day I had bought new army green, zip-off hiking pants, pleased because I seemed to have lost some weight, so those and the long sleeve hiking shirt I usually slept in became my "going out" clothes. Mike was bubbling over with stories from his night spent with Pilgrim and Sugar High, and of his day spent working for Elmer. We ordered beer samplers and proceeded to offer cheers for each new flavor.

"To becoming real mother fucking thru-hikers," Mike proposed.

"Real mother fucking thru-hikers!" Erin and I echoed as we raised our glasses.

Not long after we'd finished our samplers, we spotted Pilgrim and Sugar High sitting at a booth with a hiker I'd never seen before. They motioned us over and we all squeezed in.

"I'm See Blue," said the stranger in a gravelly voice, offering me his hand.

It was clear right away that See Blue was not the run of the mill thru-hiker. Thru-hikers generally come in three varieties: 20-somethings trying to stave off the real world for a bit longer, the recently retired who are realizing a life-long dream, and the perpetual wanderer. See Blue was none of these. He was in his mid-thirties and had been a tow truck driver in North Carolina before selling his business and starting his hike. I could instantly picture him in the front row of a concert screaming, "Hell yeah, brothers! FREE BIRD!!!!" He was tall and wiry with a mess of dirty blonde hair, a full set of false teeth that he proudly took out for a laugh, and an ever-present cigarette dangling from his lips. Within minutes he had told us all about the love of his life, Roxy, a 22-year-old hairdresser he'd left at home, and ordered the table a round of shots.

After the shots, the rest of the night was a blur. At some point Erin wrote on the backs of all of our hands "19.6"—a reference to the distance we were supposed to hike the next day and a reminder not to drink too much—a reminder I promptly chose to ignore. I was having too much fun to think about how I might feel the next day. Although the bar was packed for St. Patrick's Day, the six of us made ourselves the center of the action, laughing loudly, teasing each other, making friends with the regulars, and just generally acting like fools. Erin, Sugar High, and I started an impromptu dance party, persuading as many as we could to dance like assholes with us to Britney Spears or Justin Timberlake. The other guys bellied up to the bar, which is where we left them at 11:30pm when Erin finally convinced Sugar High and I that it was time to leave.

"Mike really likes hanging out with the guys, huh?" I gossiped to Erin as we teetered down the street. Erin, who had wisely cut herself off around 9pm, walked the rest of the way to Elmer's while Sugar High and I stopped at the bank of pay phones. After several miss-dials, I correctly entered Kevin's number while Sugar High called his longtime girlfriend, Jen.

"Hello?" answered a sleepy voice.

"Keeeevvvviiiinnn! Happy St. Patty's Day!" I shouted drunkenly into the phone in an embarrassing attempt at an Irish accent.

"I thought you were going to call before dinner," Kevin said in a flat voice. I had called while we were running errands earlier but he was at work, so the conversation had been brief.

The reception on the pay phone was not very good. "What? Oh, right, I just, totally got busy..." I trailed off and then laughed when I caught Sugar High raising his eyebrows at me.

"Okay, well... why don't you just call me in the morning. I was already asleep and I can't hear you very well." The same flat voice.

"Ummm... we're heading out really early, so I don't think I can. But I'll see you in a few days, right?" We had made plans for him to drive up to Erwin, Tennessee, the next town we'd be stopping in, to visit for two days.

"Yeah, see you in a few days. Just...call me when you get into town. Good night."

"Wait, Kev...?" The line was dead. "Shit." I muttered, staring at the receiver. I caught Sugar High's eye, and we both burst into beer soaked giggles. "Holy shit, I think I just got hung the fuck up on."

"Sorry Not Yet," he said as he steered me back towards Elmer's.

We sat on the back porch for over an hour talking about the struggles of leaving someone at home while we were on this journey and about what we thought the future held for our respective relationships. Sug (as we had started calling him) was sympathetic and easy to talk to, the kind of guy who girls loved to be friends with. We talked in low voices until, around one in the morning Pilgrim came stumbling around the corner, having just left the bar.

"I think I just did a shot of wheatgrass," he slurred.

"I'm pretty sure that doesn't have alcohol in it," Sug laughed.

"I thought it tasted funny," giving me a sly grin. The three of us finally headed to bed at one thirty, and I was asleep within seconds of my head hitting the pillow.

The next morning, Erin woke me up at 6:00am. I groaned and looked at her, remembering the 19.6 miles, and pulled the sheet back over my head. When I finally stumbled out of the room, I ran into Pilgrim, dressed in only his boxer shorts, looking like I felt. He grunted at me, scratched his head, and went into the bathroom.

Twenty minutes later, Erin and I were on the porch tying up our boots when Sugar High popped his head out the front door. "Hey guys, I don't think we're going to make it out for awhile, so I just wanted to say goodbye and I hope we catch up with you soon."

We exchanged hugs and reassurances that we would all meet up again within the next few days. We looked around for Mike, decided that he was probably staying back with the other boys, and then Erin and I pounded fists, which still had "19.6" scrawled on the back of them, and headed off. My head pounded from too little sleep and too much beer. Soon enough, E pulled away from me, and I trudged up mountain after mountain by myself, constantly fighting my hangover. I thought about my conversation with Kevin, and realized how frustrating our conversation must have been for him; for that matter, how frustrating every quick phone call over the last three weeks must have been. He was planning to meet me in a few days in Erwin and I hoped that once we were face to face things would be smoothed over. I replayed the previous night in my head, smiling at the memory of Erin, Sug, and I dancing and Mike, Pilgrim, and See Blue commandeering the bar. I tried to imagine Kevin in that scene, but couldn't quite make him fit.

Towards the end of the day, it started drizzling, a constant mist that soaked through my clothes but never quite turned into rain. With about two miles to go I was completely spent, with no idea how I would make it the rest of the way. This was the farthest I'd ever hiked so even under ideal conditions it would have been a struggle. In a daze, I made my way up the last steep climb to the shelter, crawling hand over foot at times to propel myself forward. I had thrown my pack off and dramatically collapsed on the floor of the shelter before it registered that there were lots of other people there. I spotted several thru-hikers, including See Blue, who sat at the picnic table smoking a cigarette and writing in his journal.

"College group," whispered Erin, nodding to the six people I didn't recognize.

"How far did you guys hike today?" asked a girl from the group.

"Oh my god, that's amazing... I could never hike that far!" she exclaimed after we told her.

"I didn't think I could either," I said, still sprawled out on the shelter floor. Not hungry, but knowing I had to eat, I begrudgingly cooked dinner and was already in my sleeping bag when we heard someone coming into camp.

"MIKE! Shit dude, we didn't think you were coming!"

Mike flopped down next to me, looking as exhausted as I was. "Come on... I couldn't leave you two."

CHAPTER TWELVE

DAY 24, 1,880.5 MILES TO KATAHDIN

Over the next three days, Mike, Erin, and I covered the distance to Erwin, Tennessee. Towards the end of a long, hard, second day, I emerged from the woods to find myself on top of a grassy bald enveloped in thick fog. I fought my way across the summit as the wind whipped around me, at times so forceful it was a struggle keeping my balance. And then, as I was about halfway across the bald, I heard something that made me stop in my tracks. With the wind causing the fog to swirl surreally, I listened as the voice on the small armband radio I carried told me that the United States was officially at war with Iraq. Tears rolled down my cheeks, and I finished the final miles to the shelter in a daze. Having grown up in the Air Force, I thought about the military families dealing with this news, and my heart broke. At the same time, after being on the trail for only a month, it was eerie how disconnected I felt from the outside world. I felt almost as if what I was hearing was happening to another country- I couldn't, or didn't want to, wrap my mind around the reality. When I shared the news with Mike and Erin, we marveled over how lucky we felt to be where we were.

Later that night, I discovered that one of my toenails had fallen off. "Great," I said, in a lame attempt at a joke, "first the war and now this!"

However, when we woke the next morning, our minds were solely focused on getting to Erwin. We planned to take a zero day there, which would give us some much needed rest and allow me to spend time with Kevin, who would be arriving from Florida that evening. I was anxious to make amends after the drunken St. Patrick's Day phone call. Even though we hadn't been able to talk much in the past month, I had kept up with his day-to-day in the letters he wrote me each night and then sent, along with candy or other supplies, to whichever post office we were set to be at next. The letters were always very sweet and supportive, but I could tell that he was struggling with my absence.

The day's hike was hard, but we finished by 2:30pm and soon got a hitch into the small town with a woman and her young son, who seemed both nervous and excited about picking up backpackers. With a wave, they dropped us off at Miss Janet's, a hikers' hostel famous among the AT community for the owner's kindness and generosity. Sitting on the porch were two dark headed hikers, who introduced themselves as Firewood and Merlin. Because up until then, Merlin was ahead of us on the trail, I had read his entries most nights in the trail registries- the notebooks kept at each shelter where hikers can sign in and write about their hike. Given the terse tone of Merlin's entries I wasn't surprised that I found him a bit abrasive ("a real asshole" is how I phrased it in my journal that night). Firewood, on the other hand, was soft spoken and helpful, telling us that Miss Janet was out for the afternoon shuttling some hikers around, but would be back by 5pm.

Thanking him, we left our packs on the porch and headed down the block to get something to eat. Mike had read that there was a place in town with amazing burritos, but when we got there, we found a sign on the door reading "Closed—Gone to Bristol." We saw similar signs at several other businesses in town, and learned that because so many people in Erwin, including shop owners, were at the NASCAR race in nearby Bristol, Tennessee, most of the small stores in town had closed for the weekend. We finally found an open Sonic and settled in for a snack of fries and onion rings.

As we were walking back to Miss Janet's I heard someone yelling my name. I turned and saw Kevin leaning against his silver Jeep. My heart soared as I ran and jumped into his arms. When we finally untangled ourselves, I whispered in his ear, "I'm sorry about the phone call."

"I'm sorry, too," he replied, squeezing me tight. And then laughing, "Darlin', you stink!"

"What? I showered, like, five days ago!"

Hand-in-hand, we made our way back to Miss Janet's, where we met Miss Janet herself and found that she was exactly as advertised. She helped Kevin and I search for a local hotel, and then when we realized that because of the NASCAR race all motels within a 30 mile radius were booked, she made room for us at the hostel. Once we were settled, Kevin asked Erin and I if we were hungry. We looked at him like he was crazy.

"Dude," Erin told him earnestly, "we are ALWAYS hungry." Like most hikers, after a few weeks on the trail, we had developed an insatiable appetite. Hauling a heavy pack up and down mountains from sunup to sundown burns an incredible number of calories, and it was nearly impossible to carry enough food to replenish our bodies each day. When we were in town, the amount we ate was equal parts amazing and horrifying. Mike, who had seemed irritable all day, decided to stay at Miss Janet's while Kevin, Erin, and I drove a half hour to eat our weight in food at an Outback Steakhouse.

Not surprisingly, we woke up hungry the next morning, too, and Miss Janet fixed us all a breakfast of biscuits and gravy and eggs. Kevin spent most of the day shuttling Erin and I around, Mike, once again opting to hang back with the other hikers at Miss Janet's. We had gone to the grocery store, lunch, done laundry, caught a matinee of the movie "Old School," and were heading back to the hostel when we spotted two familiar figures walking down the street.

"Can you pull over?" I asked Kevin, as Erin and I hopped out of the Jeep to greet Pilgrim and Sugar High. "You guys made it!!" The four of us excitedly talked over each other, recounting the four days since we last saw one another. They told us that they had tried to leave Elmer's to catch up with us the morning after St. Patty's day, but were too hungover to hike, and so ended up staying there another night. They had just checked in at Miss Janet's and were on their way to Sonic when we stopped them. After several minutes, I realized I had left Kevin sitting by himself in the Jeep.

"Oh shit, guys this is my boyfriend, Kevin. Kevin, Pilgrim and Sugar High, the guys I told you about?"

Graciously, Pilgrim walked over to shake hands with Kevin, saying, "Hey man, Not Yet told us all about you. How was the drive?"

When we all got back to the hostel, Miss Janet announced that everyone was going to the local Mexican Restaurant for dinner, and that we should be ready in an hour. Kevin and I tried again to find a hotel for the evening, and once again, struck out. As we were getting ready to go, Miss Janet pulled out a box of clothes from Goodwill and encouraged everyone to pick out an outfit, knowing it would be fun for all of us to wear something other than our hiking clothes.

She pulled Erin and I aside, "You girls should wear some of these dresses to dinner... it'd be nice to feel like a woman for an evening, huh?"

Outfitted in oversized dresses, but with high spirits, we piled in the back of Miss Janet's van with ten other hikers, including See Blue, Mike, Pilgrim, and Sugar High. We filled three booths at the restaurant, and ordered an enormous array of food and several rounds of beer. While the rest of us talked excitedly, telling trail stories, and comparing experiences, Kevin was quiet.

"Hey," I said, squeezing his arm, "are you okay?"

"Yeah, I'm fine..."

"What?"

Looking around at our boisterous group, Kevin lowered his voice, "It's just... I wanted to spend time with you, ya know?"

CHAPTER THIRTEEN

DAY 28, TENNESSEE, 1,832.2 MILES TO KATAHDIN

And I did know, I had missed him so much during the long weeks on the trail, but I also felt a twinge of annoyance. This was the kind of easy camaraderie I had pictured the countless times I had dreamed of the trail over the past year. I knew that when Kevin left the next day, these were the people that I would be hiking with and eating and sleeping next to for days to come. I wanted him to understand why I needed to be out there, and thought that if he could have a true "trail" experience, he'd feel closer to me when he was home. I didn't understand why my usually affable boyfriend couldn't just have a good time. I thought about earlier that day, while Kevin slept, when Miss Janet had asked me how the visit was going.

"Good... I think."

"It's hard to have someone visit," she said gently, pouring me a mug of coffee. "I've seen it a million times when a hiker's boyfriend or girlfriend comes out to see them. Remember that while you've been out here having all of these intense experiences and making all of these new, male, friends," she raised an eyebrow, "he's been sitting at home missing you. He's probably a little jealous. Just be sensitive, you've got a good guy there."

Remembering Miss Janet's advice, I swallowed my annoyance, kissed Kevin on the cheek and apologized. "I know, babe, I'm sorry, we'll have all day tomorrow. I promise."

Miss Janet had offered to slack pack us the next day, so after another hearty breakfast she shuttled Mike, Erin, Sug, Pilgrim, Kevin, and I twenty miles up the trail so that we could hike south back to her place. Slack packing meant that we could hike without our heavy packs, still move along the trail, but sleep in a bed again that night.

Soon after Miss Janet dropped us off, the rest of the group broke away from Kevin and I. For a thru-hiker, hiking without a pack brings a special freedom. Without the extra thirty-five pounds weighing me down, I felt like I could run up and down the mountains, which is exactly what the rest of the crew was doing. Kevin, while not out-of-shape, didn't have the stamina the rest of us had acquired over the past month, and so he and I slowly made our way through the woods. After about three miles, Kevin asked to take a break.

"Of course!" I said, forcing myself to stay cheerful even though I was getting antsy by how slow we were walking and worried about how far in front of us the others must be. That morning, Miss Janet had offered to pick Kevin up at a road crossing 10 miles into the hike, but he had refused, figuring he could finish the full twenty miles the rest of us had planned. I had encouraged him to reconsider, thinking that twenty miles might be a struggle, but he insisted he wanted to try.

"Okay, honey," Miss Janet told him, slipping me her phone number and telling me to bring Kevin's cell phone, "Just in case he changes his mind."

I found two tree stumps and took out a package of crackers

from my jacket pocket. "Here, eat these, they'll give you a little energy."

After a few minutes, I noticed Kevin staring at me, "You're not tired at all, are you?"

"Well... no... not really."

We started hiking again, over, what seemed to me, fairly easy terrain. Every 15 minutes or so, Kevin needed to stop and catch his breath, and I became increasingly nervous that he was physically not going to be able to hike the full twenty miles. About six miles in, I finally told him that we needed to call Miss Janet and see if she could pick him up. I was scared I would hurt his ego, but to my surprise, he agreed right away. When we reached an open field, I punched Miss Janet's number into Kevin's cell, only to find that there was no reception.

Kevin looked panicked, "What are we going to do?"

"Well..." I said carefully, "I guess we'll just take it slow and keep hiking. I don't know what else to do."

The further we hiked, the more worn out Kevin got. And the more worn out he got, the more irritable he became. He started snapping at me, "You don't pick up your feet at all when you hike."

"Really? Well, it hasn't hurt me so far..." Still trying to keep the cheer in my voice.

"It looks so weird. I'm surprised you don't fall more. You should try picking up your feet."

Finally, I'd had enough. "LOOK. What is your problem? I know you're tired, but you complain that we aren't spending enough time together and the minute we're alone all you do is bitch at me. What is it, Kevin?? What?" Tears streamed down my face.

"I'm sorry," he said, tears in his eyes, putting his arms around me. "It's just...it's been really hard without you. And, I come out here and you're having all this fun and it doesn't seem like you've missed me at all. And...and now I'm just frustrated with myself that I'm so tired and we're not even halfway finished. And I don't know..."

"What?"

"Well... it sucks to have your girlfriend be in better shape than you are." He looked down at me sheepishly.

I started laughing, "Kevin... all I've been doing for the past month is hiking, of course I'm going to be a stronger hiker at this point. I totally sucked at the beginning!" I gave him a playful rib poke. "I mean, I wasn't as slow as you, but I totally sucked."

The tension cleared, we started walking again. I tried several more times to call Miss Janet, but could never get a signal. The cell reception in the mountains is spotty in the best circumstances, and in 2003 it was practically non-existent. At the pace we were going, I feared it would be well after sundown before we finished. Eventually, we came into a clearing and spotted a parking area, which I figured was the 10 mile point.

Just as I was saying, "Maybe we can find someone to give you a ride into town," I spotted Miss Janet's van in the parking lot. I felt a rush of relief.

"I thought maybe I should just come on anyway... just in case," she drawled, giving me a wink. Erin and Sug climbed out the back of the van, handing Kevin and I both donuts and orange juice.

"Sug and I decided we'd wait here, so you'd have someone to finish with," Erin told me as we hugged like we hadn't seen each other in weeks. "Mike and Pilgrim are long gone."

I thanked Miss Janet and said good-bye to Kevin, who was going to try to find us a hotel room for the night, and then Erin, Sug, and I started back up the trail. My mood was infinitely lighter and we hiked almost twice as fast as Kevin and I had.

"We were starting to worry... it was taking you guys so long," Erin confided.

"Yeah, dude, he was really struggling."

"Poor guy."

I decided to chalk the weirdness with Kevin up to his exhaustion and the strain of our time apart. Besides, I was having too good a time with Erin and Sug, the three of us telling stories from our past, and making up ridiculous scenarios for our future. We were practically running down the trail, even 16 miles into the day, and I marveled at how strong I felt. I told Erin and Sug about the pact I had made with myself at the beginning of March, when I decided that I would give the trail a month, and if I was still miserable, I would quit.

"I didn't know that," Erin said quietly.

I shrugged, "I didn't want you to know. But, like, I can't imagine quitting now! We've come too far!"

"But does having Kevin here make you want to go home... even a little bit?" Sug asked, probably thinking about his own girlfriend he'd left back in New York.

"No. Not even a little bit," I said emphatically. "I mean, look, I miss him so much. Every day I miss him. But this is a once in a lifetime thing, and he'll still be there when I get home."

"Good!" Erin said, putting her arm around me. "I wouldn't let you leave me anyway."

We arrived at our pick-up point, still in a great mood and feeling surprisingly energetic for having just finished a 20 mile day. We used a payphone to call Miss Janet, who in turn called Kevin. Miss Janet told me that Kevin had crashed as soon as he got in the van, but that he'd found us a hotel room and wanted to come get me. Miss Janet arrived first with her van full of hikers to pick up Erin and Sug. It was getting dark, so they decided to wait with me until Kevin got there. Ten minutes passed and the hikers started getting restless; they were on their way to dinner when Miss Janet stopped. After twenty minutes, we started to worry.

"Just go ahead," I told them.

"No, honey, why don't I bring you back to my place and you can call Kevin from there," Miss Janet offered. Then looking at the hungry van of hikers, she added, "I'll just drop these guys off first."

I was climbing into the van when the headlights of Kevin's Jeep appeared. Kevin looked frazzled, so I said a quick goodbye to Miss Janet and the hikers and got in the Jeep.

"I got lost," he mumbled, "I've been driving around this fucking town for 30 minutes."

I touched his hand. "Well, you've got me now. Come on, let's go back to the hotel."

An hour later we were content, laying on the ratty motel bed, an empty pizza box sitting on the floor. We watched TV and made small talk, laughing like we always did at the ridiculous reality show contestants. He talked about his job and told me stories about our cat named Cat. As we turned off the lights, my head resting comfortably on his shoulder I said, "I'm really glad you came."

"Are you?"

"Yeah, I really am. And I'm sorry things weren't perfect. I just, I guess I just wanted you to feel a part of this."

"But darlin', I'm not a part of it. This is your thing." He kissed the top of my head. "And that's okay. I guess it's just hard knowing that tomorrow you'll be back out there and I'll be driving home where the only thing waiting for me is a flea-bitten cat."

"Only a few more months and I'll be all yours."

"You promise?"

"As long as you get rid of those fleas."

The next morning, after a tearful goodbye, I watched from the sidewalk as Kevin's Jeep drove away. Erin walked down from Miss Janet's porch and put her arm around me. "You okay, babe?"

"Yeah... I'm just a little sad." I said, wiping my eyes. *And relieved*, I thought guiltily. I felt relieved to see him go.

CHAPTER FOURTEEN

DAY 30, TENNESSEE, 1,813.1 MILES TO KATAHDIN

Even though we were getting back on the trail that day, none of us seemed in any hurry to get going. Erin and I spent the morning hanging around with Turbo, who was taking a zero day at Miss Janet's.

"Dude, Turbo," said Erin, after realizing how delightfully goofy he was. "We thought you were going to be a cocky hiker boy when we heard you say your name was Turbo going into the Smokies. Like 'look at me, I'm Turbo, I'm super fast.'"

Turbo looked up from the bursting at the seams pack that he was unsuccessfully trying to shove a big bag of Skittles into. "No! So whatsit... uhh, the name's a joke because I'm kinda slow and, you know, I carry a huge pack."

"Jesus, Turbo, are you really going to carry that whole bag of Skittles?" asked Sug, eyeing the family sized bag.

"Dude, go big or go home."

Unlike Turbo, most hikers were obsessive about how much their pack weighed. Each item that went into the pack was scrutinized for its usefulness and discarded if it wasn't a necessity. Even needed items were altered to shave ounces-toothbrush handles got sawed off, extra straps on backpacks were cut, all food packaging was removed before it went into the pack, book chapters were torn out and left behind after being read. Some of the choices seemed ridiculous (Erin and I carried a deck of miniature cards instead of a full-sized deck to save weight), but the weight of the pack made such a difference in how far and long you could hike, that to us, it made perfect sense to carry only the bare minimum. With full food and water, my pack weighed between 30-35 pounds, a decent weight for most hikers. And there are some backpackers, known as ultra-lighters, who, through a system of special lightweight gear, multipurpose items, and packing only the absolute essentials can whittle their full pack weight down to 15-20 pounds. When Turbo started the trail, his pack topped 60.

Once the group of hikers heading back up the trail had piled into the back of Miss Janet's van, someone pointed out the map of the AT taped on the ceiling.

"I put that there so that thru-hikers realize how far they still have to go. This thing's a marathon, you know, and you guys are just at the beginning."

I placed my finger on the dot marked Erwin, TN, and each of the hiker's eyes traveled the distance up the map to Katahdin, Maine.

"God... and here I was thinking I was a badass for hiking 350 miles," I muttered, my eyes fixated on the more than 1,800 miles we still had to hike.

It was noon by the time Miss Janet dropped us at the same spot she had the day before, only this time we would be heading North and there would be no warm bed to sleep in at the end of the day. I said goodbye to Miss Janet, and started up the trail. The melancholy from Kevin's departure hung over me as I lugged my abnormally heavy pack on the steep climb up to Roan Mountain. I tried not to dwell on the negatives of the visit, but I couldn't help but feel unsettled. During the day while I hiked, I replayed the weekend, chiding myself for not being more understanding of the situation I had put Kevin in and resolved to be more attentive.

It was already dark when I reached the shelter, and I was in no mood to talk. Luckily, the large group we were traveling with now made it hard to spend much time in my own head. In addition to Pilgrim and Sug, we were keeping pace with a couple of stoners, Nasty and Shaman, an old hippie named Vagabond, Firewood, and a sweet, devoutly Christian couple called Mawee and Pawee. Erin told me that Mike had pushed on to the next shelter with See Blue. We both agreed that it was for the best. From the minute we arrived at Miss Janet's three days earlier, Mike had barely spoken to either Erin or I.

"He's probably sick of us. We have been together every day for the last month." Erin whispered once we were tucked in our sleeping bags.

"Well, I'm certainly sick of him," I retorted. "He's acting like... like..."

"Like a 20-year-old boy?"

"Well... yeah." I conceded.

Since our second day on the trail, the three of us had been a team, and not that Erin or I would admit it, but both of us were hurt by Mike's disappearance.

By the next morning, my mood had improved. The sun was shining and no one was in a hurry to get on the trail. I'd never been a morning person, and I always resisted the rush to get out of the shelter in the mornings (but I always did it because the other option was to sit around shivering). We took our time eating breakfast and re-packing our bags, and I finally got a chance to take in the view that I had missed by arriving after sundown the night before. Erin, Sug, Pilgrim, and I started our day hiking together, falling into an easy banter, posing questions like the hiker favorite, "what would be your perfect meal?" Any angst over Kevin or Mike had vanished and I felt a giddy excitement to be on the trail. We spent the day hiking over a series of grassy balds, allowing unobstructed views of the mountain ranges that surrounded us. At one point Erin and I stood at one peak and could look North to see Sug and Pilgrim on the next peak. We waved like idiots, excited to be out in the open, under the warm, clear skies. The majority of our time on the trail was spent hiking under the cover of forest, catching only glimpses of the sky when we reached a summit once, maybe twice, a day. To have unlimited views and sun gave the day a magical twinge and made me feel free and happy and almost nostalgic, wanting to hang onto this precise feeling forever.

Around noon, we spotted an old barn in a field a couple hundred yards off the trail. I checked the guidebook and figured that this was the Over Mountain shelter–a barn that had been converted into a shelter several years back. Erin and I walked down to have lunch and found Sug, Pilgrim, Nasty, and Shaman already there.

"Let's go outside," Pilgrim suggested after we had eaten. The six of us lay in a row on the grass in front of the barn, letting the sun warm us, for over an hour. Every once in awhile someone would speak and we'd joke for a few minutes, but mostly we lay in comfortable silence, each soaking up the moment. It felt amazing to be there, to have nothing to do the rest of the day but walk in a landscape that most people would never be lucky enough to experience, for once to be warm enough to linger and close our eyes, and not have to hurry along to generate body heat.

"This is it," Erin said, arms folded behind her head, eyes closed to the sun, "This is all I wanted."

Eventually, we left the spot, rested and content, and set to climbing one last steep bald. I loved that while distance grew between us–Pilgrim first, then Sug, then Erin, and me, as usual, bringing up the rear–I could still see each of them, little dots making their way up the long climb. After making it to the top, the rest of the day's hike was downhill, and I made it to the shelter for that night in good time. I was surprised to find Mike and See Blue building a fire, I had figured they would have hiked further than us that day.

"Hey!" Mike called out. He told me that he and See Blue had stayed at the barn the night before and so had made it to this shelter before lunch. "There's a road crossing a couple tenths of a mile up the trail from here, so See Blue and I decided to hitch into town and pick up beer and hot dogs for everyone."

"There's beer?" I asked, thinking that after having the perfect day, this was too good to be true.

"There's beer," said Mike, as he put a cold Busch light in my hand.

We spent the night roasting hot dogs (just the buns for me since I had long ago given up beef and pork) and drinking beer, telling crude jokes, and laughing at Nasty's antics. Nasty, a tall, goofball of a guy, and you never knew what nonsensical phrase would come out of his mouth next. Noticing that he had smoked three cigarettes in a row, he quipped "I'm smoking like a bitch out of water!" Erin and I doubled over in laughter when Nasty, searching frantically through his bag, muttered to no one in particular, "where is it? where is it?" and then pulled his hands out the bag, with his pointer fingers and thumbs looking like a shooter's, and said with a smile, "ahh, here it is... the old fart gun," letting one rip.

Tears rolled down my face. "I totally wasn't expecting that!"

"It was just... so well timed." Erin giggled.

As we finally all settled into our sleeping bags, the fire still crackling, I wrote in my journal "by far- my favorite day on the trail."

CHAPTER FIFTEEN

DAY 32, NORTH CAROLINA, 1786.1 MILES TO KATAHDIN

The next morning, I lay in my sleeping bag thinking that after a month as a thru-hiker the only thing I knew for sure about what lay ahead of me was that I couldn't know what lay ahead of me. I could pore over elevation maps and read guide books to get a sense of the terrain, but uncontrollable factors like the weather, the state of my body, the weight of my pack, my ever-changing mood, or the company I kept, could transform a seemingly easy day into an epic one, and an insurmountable distance into a walk in the woods. While the day before was magical, I knew I couldn't count on the feeling carrying over, and I would have to take the day as it presented itself. And as so often happened, that day presented itself with a cold, drizzling rain, and legs that felt like tree trunks. For all the beauty of the previous day, this day's landscape was unforgiving, a series of sharp climbs and steep descents that made my still open wounded heels sting with pain. The big group, so boisterous and carefree the night before, was that evening crammed into a too-small shelter, silent and collectively moody.

The following day was an improvement simply because I

woke with a sense of purpose. Erin and I had a plan; we would hike six miles to the Kincora hostel that was set several tenths of a mile from a road crossing, pick up the packages that were hopefully waiting for us there, get a ride into town to resupply our food, and then get back on the trail for another 10 miles of hiking. We knew that some of the other thru-hikers would choose to stay at the hostel overnight, if not longer; the lure of a dry bed and hot food too much to pass up. So, when Erin and I arrived at the cozy hostel around 10 am, we weren't surprised to hear Nasty, Shaman, Vagabond, and several others making plans to stay the night.

But then Mike took us aside and told Erin and I, "I'm gonna stay, too. The owner said he'd slack pack us tomorrow if we would do some trail maintenance today. Why don't you guys stick around?"

"You know we can't do that, Mike," Erin said quietly. Mike knew that Erin and I were intent on sticking as close as possible to the schedule we had set for ourselves, and that we were worried about falling behind this early in the trip and not being able to summit before our schools started at the beginning of August. Erin and I had agreed that we would stay on course unless an irresistible opportunity or obstacle presented itself, and Kincora, while a lovely hostel, was not irresistible.

"Alright," Mike said, turning away. "I'll just have to catch up with you in a few days," not mentioning how hard it could be to make up that distance.

Back on the trail after completing our errands, I thought about how tenuous the connections we made often were. We shared intense experiences with the people we met, and while friendships were instantly forged, they were also easily discarded. One of the few codes of the thru-hiker is "hike your own hike." Everyone has their own philosophy of how to attempt a thru-hike. Some people believe you need to hike every inch of the trail with your pack on, others think it's okay to take short cuts here and there; some want to cram as many miles as they can into a day, others feel you aren't truly experiencing the trail if you don't take your time. To reconcile these differences, most hikers believe that if you want to do your own thing–hike the miles you want, stop when and where and how often you want–you've got to let everyone else do their own thing, too. Of course, like anything where strong opinions are held there are some who can't help espousing their views, but for the most part hikers tried to be respectful of each other's choices. Although we couldn't foresee circumstances where it would happen, even Erin and I had made a pact that we would split up if it was the only way we could each finish the trail happy. So even though we had spent almost a month solid with Mike, and thought of him as our sometimes annoying little brother, when he told us he was going to stay, and we said we wanted to go, neither side protested.

We hiked for several miles along a river, passing a gushing waterfall, and then made a laborious 2000 foot climb up a flat topped mountain. From the North side of the peak we could see Watauga lake, but it was several more miles before we finally wound our way down to it. We crossed a road to get to the lake, excited because we knew we were now close to our shelter for the night. The trail climbed away from the shoreline, and we followed a serpentine brook until I spotted the three-sided structure and picnic bench. To my surprise, the shelter was empty. Sug, Pilgrim, and See Blue had left Kincora before us, and we had made plans to meet at the Watauga lake shelter at the end of the day.

"Do you think they kept hiking?" I wondered aloud.

"That sucks, I thought they said they were stopping here."

Both bummed that we had now lost our entire crew, we set about our evening chores in silence–unpacking sleeping bags and pads, fetching water, pulling out food bags, and setting up stoves. I was finishing the last bite of my mac and cheese with tuna when I heard a commotion coming from behind the shelter. Erin and I tentatively peaked our heads around the wooden side, and simultaneously shrieked.

"See Blue!!! Pilgrim! Sug! Wha... how did you get behind us? Where have you been?"

"Ladies," came See Blue's gravelly voice. By way of explanation, he pulled two beers from his pocket and handed one to each of us, then lit a cigarette and opened a beer for himself. Pilgrim and Sug talked over each other.

"We got to the lake really early, so we hitched into town to get some beer," Pilgrim explained.

"Yeah, but Pilgrim ate too much at the McDonalds and we had to sit around for awhile until he didn't feel like he was going to explode."

"Well, yeah, but then it took forever to get a hitch back," Pilgrim retorted, and noticed me staring at the bunch of firewood sticking out of his pack. "Oh, on the way up here, we stopped to get firewood."

"And Pilgrim jacked me in the face with a log," Sug laughed, pointing to a small trickle of blood square between his eyes.

I giggled, "Jacked... face... log."

"Here," grunted See Blue, tossing Sug a beer. "That'll fix ya."

And like that, our spirits were back up. With a fire blazing in the fire ring, the five of us played drinking games like "would you rather" and "boxers or briefs." Later, tipsy from the beer, smoking a bummed cigarette, I watched Erin trying to dry the pants she was still wearing in the fire and thought about how much I liked being around these guys.

"Thanks for showing up," I blurted. "We thought you'd left us."

"Nah... we wouldn't have done that." See Blue soothed. I caught Erin's eye, thinking that it probably wasn't true, but that it was nice to hear anyway.

We stuck together over the next two days hiking long and challenging 23 and then 18 mile days into Damascus, Virginia. Pilgrim and Sug tried several times to convince Erin and me to stick around town the next day and take a zero, but even though we'd been hiking for eight days without a break and wanted to stay with those guys, citing our schedule, we told them we couldn't. While See Blue checked into a motel and waited for his girlfriend, Roxy, to arrive, the rest of us headed to the hostel in town and then went for dinner and drinks at a diner owned by a former thru-hiker. Like all the time we'd spent with Pilgrim and Sug, this night was fun and effortless, like hanging out with friends we'd known for years. Towards the end of the night, Pilgrim and I stood outside, giving our ears a break from the laughably bad band and doling each other small insights into our lives, I started feeling wistful that if he and Sug took a zero day while we hiked on, we might lose them like we had lost Mike.

"You sure you guys don't want to stay tomorrow?" Pilgrim asked.

"No... but we probably shouldn't..."

Back inside I clumsily tried to broach the subject with Erin, wanting to see if she would consider changing our schedule, but then abandoned the thought, convincing myself that it was wrong to mold our hike to anyone else.

I woke the next morning to Pilgrim whisper-yelling, "Holy shit!"

"What the fuck, dude?" I moaned and pulled the sleeping bag up over my head.

"Not Yet, you've got to see this."

"No."

"Dude.... seriously."

"Fine," I said, not bothering to hide my annoyance. I climbed out of my bag and trudged to the window. "Holy shit!"

And there we both stood, mouths agape, looking at the foot of snow that had magically blanketed the ground overnight and the large white flakes that showed no signs of stopping.

"Well then," I said, after a few minutes of stunned silence, "A zero day it is."

CHAPTER SIXTEEN

DAY 37, VIRGINIA, 1,713.7 MILES TO KATAHDIN

S oon, Erin and Sug were awake too and marveling at the snow. The hostel, an old house maintained by a church, had no heat and so by 7 a.m. we were sitting at the diner, eating breakfast. By 10 a.m. we had checked our emails, made phone calls and played two games of Taboo. By 10:30 a.m. I was so antsy that I pushed my chair from the table where the four of us sat in bored silence and announced that "I'd be back."

Because we went to the grocery store, post office, and laundry when we arrived in town the day before, there wasn't anything I needed to do, but I needed to do something, so I trudged through the snow to the only thing open: the Dollar Store. On the two other zero days we'd taken in our five weeks on the trail, the first at Erin's lake house and the second at Miss Janet's with Kevin, maybe because they were planned, I'd been able to relax and enjoy the much needed downtime. But for some reason, as I aimlessly wandered the aisles filled with plastic trinkets and past date canned goods, I couldn't shake my restlessness. I'd grown used to the forward momentum of the trail, of never staying in one place, of every day making concrete progress towards our ultimate goal of Maine, and this day off felt more like a roadblock than a break.

After a half-hour of browsing, I stepped back into the snow carrying three fun-sized bags of Cheetos and a $10 Walkman. In addition to my armband radio, which actually picked up a radio station about a quarter of the time, I also carried a portable cassette player, and one or the other was almost always on when I hiked alone. I heard comments from some hikers, mostly those out for a day or a weekend, who felt listening to anything but the sounds of nature ruined the experience. But after five weeks alone with my thoughts, I was ready for some background noise. Erin's brother Brian made us a bunch of mix tapes and we carried two or three at time.

Musicians like Bob Dylan, the Flaming Lips, Snoop Dog, and Weezer, interspersed with the voices of David Sedaris, Mitch Hedberg, and Chris Rock, became the soundtrack of my hike. I walked through the woods, singing at the top of lungs "I got bitches in the living room gettin' it on and, they ain't leavin til six in the mornin' (six in the mornin')" or laughing out loud to Mitch Hedberg's joke "My friend asked me if I wanted a frozen banana, and I said 'no, but I want a regular banana later, so... yeah.'" There were times when the music seemed to be the only thing propelling me up the mountains. And when the perfect song came on at the perfect time–like Shawn Colvin's cover of "This Must Be the Place" on the top of a cloud-covered clearing in Tennessee–the two became forever linked in my mind, so that any time I heard the song, I would be instantly transported back.

I made it back to the hostel and was greeted by Erin, bundled in her sleeping bag, writing in her journal with gloved hands.

"Hey, See Blue stopped by. He wants us all to go out to dinner tonight to meet Roxy."

"Oh, cool, I'm interested to see what she's like." Roxy was See Blue's girlfriend who had driven up from Raleigh, North Carolina for a visit. Roxy was See Blue's favorite topic of discussion, and it was obvious to anyone who spent more than three minutes with him that he was smitten with her. The two of them had been holed up at the motel in town since we'd arrived, making dinner the first time we'd meet her.

Between napping, reading, and another trip to the Dollar Store for more Cheetos, I somehow passed the afternoon. That night, Erin, Sug, Pilgrim, and I walked into the restaurant and were instantly greeted with hugs by a small 22-year-old woman with a giant smile.

"Oh my god, you guys, I've heard so much about you!" Roxy squealed, and then said the thing that instantly endeared her to the thru-hikers in us, "Come on, let's eat, I'm paying!"

We spent the evening stuffing ourselves with pasta and trading stories. Roxy entertained us with tales about her and See Blue, asked about each of our lives off the trail, and even seemed interested when we told and retold our hiking stories.

At one point I leaned over to See Blue and squeezed his arm. "She's great," I whispered, thinking, *"Why wasn't Kevin like this?"*

"I know." See Blue answered, never once taking his eyes off her.

The snow had stopped coming down at some point that evening, and although it was still there, a full foot and a half, the next morning we all decided that we should get back on the trail. See Blue headed off first, in no mood to talk after his tearful goodbye with Roxy, and after breakfast, Erin and I followed his footsteps up the mountain, leaving Sug and Pilgrim at the hostel saying they'd get started after running a few errands. The hiking was slow, making the sixteen-mile day seem like at least twenty. The trees lining the trail were bent over from the weight of the snow and Erin and I were constantly running into branches, only to have a shelf of white powder dumped on our heads and down our backs. About two miles from the shelter, I noticed the distinctive imprint of Sug's boots.

"There is no way they could have gotten in front of us!" Erin decided. But when we got to the shelter, along with Sea Blue and a thru-hiker couple named Eric and Kristy, sat a grinning Pilgrim and Sugar High.

"What the hell, dude?" I asked, completely confused.

"Yeah, we met this guy, Lonewolf, when we went to breakfast and he told us about a shortcut out of town," Sug explained, telling us how the Virginia Creeper trail, primarily used as a bike path, basically bypassed the mountain we'd spent the day climbing up and over, and cut miles off their hike. Where I had noticed Sug's bootprints was where the Creeper met back up with the AT.

"Seriously?" I said, trying to get the last of the snow out of my soaked shirt.

"Before you get angry, we brought a present," Pilgrim said as he pulled out a water bottle filled with pinkish liquid and handed it to me. "Peach moonshine from Lonewolf."

Before the trail, I never would have dreamed of drinking some stranger's homemade moonshine, but home rules no longer applied, and so I took a big gulp.

"Shit! Well... that will certainly warm you up."

The next morning, April 1st, the snow was still on the ground, but the temperature had risen dramatically. We hiked along in the snow in t-shirts, following the footprints left by Eric and Kristy, who had left before sunrise, telling us they were being picked up by a family member at a road crossing a couple miles from the shelter. We walked in a line, See Blue first, then Pilgrim, Sug, and Erin, with me bringing up the rear. We reached a clearing and See Blue came to a sudden stop.

"The footprints stopped," See Blue yelled back.

"That must be where Eric and Kristy got picked up," Erin said.

I caught up to the others and saw beyond the footprints and tire tracks lay a sea of pristine white snow, and understood the problem. We'd lost the trail.

CHAPTER SEVENTEEN

DAY 39, 1695.6 MILES TO KATAHDIN

"Oh, ha ha, I get it," Erin said at last.

"Get what?" I asked, scanning the field of powder in front of us, and the forest beyond for any sign of the trail.

"60 degree day? A foot of snow on the ground? And now we've lost the trail?" She looked at our blank faces expectantly. "It's April Fools' Day, bitches!"

We then took turns telling "Yo mama" jokes in honor of mother nature's twisted sense of humor while See Blue forged ahead, looking for the trail.

"Look like you're lost," I commanded, snapping a picture of Erin, Sug, and Pilgrim giving their best "where the fuck are we" faces. See Blue waved us forward, having found the trail at a nearly indistinguishable break in the trees.

"How'd you find it?" Sug asked.

"White blaze," See Blue grunted, pointing to a nearby tree marked with a rectangle of white paint. The whole of the Appalachian Trail is marked every so often with white blazes, painted on trees or rocks or wooden posts, making the AT a very easy trail to follow. AT hikers get so used to blindly following these white rectangles that thru-hikers joke that at the end of their hike they'll catch themselves following the white paint lines down the middle of a road.

The snow made walking a chore, and I spent so much of the day concentrating on following the deep footprints in front of me that I almost forgot to look for one of the unique features of that area of Virginia--wild ponies. We were stopped for lunch at a shelter on Thomas Knob, all inordinately worn out from the twelve miles we'd hiked and deciding whether to hike on or call it a day, when Erin spotted one, "PONY!" She rushed over to where it stood and then immediately doubled over with laughter.

"What?" I called, too tired to get up from the picnic table.

Now laughing so hard she could barely talk, she finally spat out, "This pony has the biggest... the biggest... shlong... I've ever seen!" and then, "Come take a picture!"

After confirming that the pony was indeed "hung like a horse," we begrudgingly kept hiking, Erin motivating us, as she usually did, to stay on schedule, and as a reward that night we drank the rest of the moonshine.

The next two days were sunny and in the 70s, making me theorize that the snow had just been a fucked up side effect of the 'shine. We hiked two 20+ mile days, deciding to push on to Atkins, Virginia on the second day in order to make it to the post office before it closed. I noticed that the five of us–See Blue, Pilgrim, Sug, Erin, and I–were now making choices as a group–how far to go, when to stop, when to push on–rather than just randomly ending up at the same place. In college, most of my male friends had been frat boys. Sug, Pilgrim, and See Blue were unlike guys I knew, and yet their company felt completely natural and familiar. Sug and Pilgrim were like Erin and my male equivalents, all inappropriate jokes and silliness, and See Blue had become the groups' older brother. The more I got to know them, the more I liked each one. I knew it was a precarious bond between the five of us; after all, we hadn't seen Mike in days, but one that felt real and important nonetheless.

In Atkins, we decided to all pile into a dingy motel room just a few feet off the trail at a road crossing, where we could shower and make phone calls, rather than hiking on to another shelter. The others had made a beeline for the Dairy Queen nearby and I was putting on my sandals to follow them when I heard an angry rap at the door. I opened it to find the motel owner stomping his foot impatiently.

"I counted five of you in this room!" he yelled at me. "You have to pay extra for five in the room."

"Whoa, buddy... there were five of us here when I checked in. The person at the desk didn't say anything. I'm happy to pay the extra, but there's no need to yell," I said evenly. My calm surprised me. Although normally a laid back person, I tended to get instantly defensive and sarcastic when confronted. Maybe it was the two beautiful days I'd just spent in the woods, or maybe I was just worn out from the hiking, but I found I couldn't summon up my normal outrage.

Later, we all sat in the room watching TV and eating our Blizzards, the door open to let in the fresh air. After spending so long outside, it felt claustrophobic to have four walls around us.

"Holy shit!" Sug yelled. "Dog!"

"Wha... oh shit!" We looked over to see Sug corralling a large dog that had wandered into the room.

Seconds later the motel owner appeared at the door. "Oh, sorry... come here puppy."

"Hey. I'm not paying for that dog, too!"

CHAPTER EIGHTEEN

DAY 42, VIRGINIA, 1,638.4 MILES TO KATAHDIN

The next morning, I walked into the motel room, coffee in hand, and was almost knocked out by the stench.

"Jesus, is this what we smell like to other people?" Then, noticing Erin on the phone, I mouthed, "Oh, sorry...."

I propped the door open as Erin hung up. "Dude, that was my sister, she's going to meet us in Perrisburg and slack pack us!"

Having Cara visit was the best of both worlds; having the comfort of home combined with someone who understood exactly what we were going through. For sisters born four years apart, Cara and Erin are exceptionally close. Cara had served as a de facto older sister for me, too. On the surface, Cara is sweet, thoughtful, caring. And she is all of those things, but underneath lies a strong, reckless streak that I've always envied and tried to emulate. Hiking the AT four years after she had, we were now literally following the path she blazed for us.

But three days later, it was a cheerless bunch of hikers that Cara picked up in a diner parking lot on a country road 26 miles outside of Perrisburg, Virginia. It's hard to pinpoint exactly what happened that left us at what we would remember as one of our lowest points on the trail (so low, in fact, that Erin sent a group text seven years later saying "P day tomorrow... Perrisburg," to which Pilgrim responded "sigh (repeat indefinitely)"). The first day out of Atkins started with all of us well-rested, clean, upbeat. We spent an hour during lunch lounging in the sun and dipping our feet in a nearby stream. But then, as we finally got back to hiking, Erin mentioned that her knee felt stiff from sitting around so long and was "kinda bothering" her. I could tell, from her labored gait and the tears that sat at the corners of her eyes when we finally reached the shelter that night, "kinda" was an understatement.

"Where's the water?" I asked an unusually subdued Pilgrim and Sug, who had arrived at the shelter well before we had. See Blue was already laying in his sleeping bag, back turned toward the wall, humming to the Blue Oyster Cult blaring in his headphones.

The first thing we did at the end of each hike was re-fill our usually empty water supply. It was the last chore before we could rest for the night, and we wanted to get it over with as soon as we could. Erin and I both carried a one liter Nalgene bottle that we filled at night for cooking and rehydrating, and a 2-liter Platypus water bag fitted with a drinking tube that clipped on our pack for hands free drinking while hiking (after puncturing her water bag during our hike of the Long Trail, Erin declared that she was going to "buy myself a yellow 'pus," a quote Cara and I never let her live down). Shelters are usually built within a tenth of a mile from a water source, which is why Erin and I simultaneously groaned when a woman I'd never seen told us this one was almost a half mile away. The last thing we wanted, at the end of a hard day, was to walk more.

"Have fun!" she yelled after us. I caught Sug's eyes mid roll.

"I don't think she means that," Erin mumbled.

The woman, and her male companion, turned out to be former thru-hikers, usually a welcome addition. People who hike the trail tend to feel an intense connection with it and those who come after them, and were known to be the bearers of all sorts of "trail magic," from beers left in streams to bags of Little Debbies tied to a high tree branch in the middle of the woods to offers to stay in their homes. These two, however, seemed to revel in discouraging us; telling us every negative detail of their hike several years earlier.

"I got bone spurs so bad, I can barely hike now. You'll probably get them, too, what with those boots you're wearing," the woman said, nodding in my direction.

"Oh, and the bears were so bad our year. I bet they are even worse now."

And in the morning, as we prepared to leave in the pouring rain, "You better watch that ridge you're walking today, it's full of iron and you might get struck by lightning. Two people got struck the year we hiked."

"I would rather be struck by lightning than stay here," said See Blue under his breath, taking off his headphones for the first time since we'd arrived.

Though we tried to shake it off, it was as if the wear of the last month had formed a crack, allowing the couple's negativity to seep in. The rain soaked us through and over the next day both Pilgrim and I came down with wicked sinus infections. We would lay in the shelters, neither of us able to sleep, trying and failing to suppress our coughing and blowing.

On the second day, I woke up unable to breathe out my nose. Thankfully, I found out we would hike past a road crossing with a nearby grocery where I could stock up on decongestant. I was so focused on getting medicine that I nearly passed by a cooler full of sodas in the middle of the trail. I stopped to open the lid, but as I read the note taped to the top, I felt as though I'd been punched in the stomach.

"In memory of Ted "Soleman" Anderson," the note read in bold letters.

Before I began my hike, in an effort to prepare myself as much as I could while sitting in front of a computer 9 hours a day, I joined an online group of potential AT hikers. People discussed their start dates, the gear they wanted to bring, their hopes and fears about embarking on a five to six month walk in the woods. One of the leaders of the group was a guy who called himself Soleman. Hiking the AT was one of Soleman's lifelong dreams, and his enthusiasm for the trail was contagious. He lived only a few hours away from Kevin and me in Florida, and we commiserated about trying to get in shape in our flat surroundings. In December, I wrote on the message board that I couldn't find the lightweight camping pot I was looking for and a few minutes later I received a message from Soleman, "I've got two. I'll send you my extra! No need to send money, just pay it forward." Ted "Soleman" Anderson had died suddenly at the end of February at age 56, just a week before he was set to begin his thru-hike.

I sat on the cooler for a long time, crying for a kind man I had never met, for his family, and for his unrealized dream.

When Cara picked us up the next day, after walking miles in the cold rain, I felt a relief that only family can bring. I was hopeful that rest and a warm bed would breathe much needed life into our collectively weary bones, and give us all a renewed determination to continue on.

I was wrong.

CHAPTER NINETEEN

DAY 45, VIRGINIA, 1,575.4 MILES TO KATAHDIN

The night Cara picked us up we went through the motions of town. We gorged ourselves at a Chinese Buffet, made phone calls, did laundry, shopped for food. Later, the boys walked over from the hostel they were staying at to the dingy motel room Erin, Cara, and I shared, and we all drank beer and watched as Syracuse beat Oklahoma in the NCAA championship game. Nobody mentioned how late it got, or that we had 26 miles to hike the next day. I needed a break, mentally and physically, from the trail and it was nice to imagine us as just a bunch of friends watching a basketball game, even for a few hours.

I spent most of the night alternately trying to suppress my coughs and tossing from the weirdness of being in a bed as opposed to a shelter floor. At one point in the night, Erin woke up from a dream laughing uncontrollably, having no idea why. Between my exhaustion and everyone else's stalling, we didn't start hiking until after 10am the next morning. Cara was slack packing us, so we left our packs in the hotel room and she drove us back to where she had picked us up the day before. We were to hike the 26 miles to Pearisburg and spend another night there before saying goodbye and hiking on. The day out of Pearisburg was the day we all learned that slack packing could be both a blessing and a curse. It is amazing how light and fast you feel hiking with nothing when you are used to 35 pounds on your back. But what we chose to ignore with our late night and late start was that we still had a marathon's length of mountains to climb before the end of the day.

Cara hiked the first three miles with Erin and I, listening sympathetically as we complained, assuring us that what we were going through was completely normal.

"As crappy as it could be, Chris and I still talk about the trail at least once a day, even four years later. And I know we'd both love to be out here with you guys," Cara told us.

We felt good as we waved goodbye, encouraged by her enthusiasm. We felt good until about noon, when it started to pour and we realized we still had twenty miles to hike. And then everything fell apart. Objectively, there was no reason this day should have felt harder than any other, especially because we weren't carrying packs. But the collective weariness had taken hold and every mile felt like two, and the cold rain soaked me to the core.

I started crying as I stood at the base of what turned out to be the last big climb of the day, seriously believing that I couldn't keep hiking. I cried when Erin and I reached the motel and she turned to me with tears in her eyes, saying "Let's never talk about this day again." I stopped crying long enough to eat almost an entire pizza, but started crying again as I lay in bed, once again unable to sleep. I cried as we stood at the hostel with the boys the next morning and waved goodbye to Cara.

I was standing outside trying to compose myself enough to hike when See Blue came and stood beside me.

"What's going on?" he asked.

I sighed. "Nothing," I said, shaking my head and wiping my face.

"Yeah," he agreed, and lifted up my pack and placed it on my shoulders.

It was late when we finally got going. We had discovered a scale in the hostel and took turns weighing ourselves and our packs. In the weeks since we started hiking, I had lost over 20 pounds. We decided to hike only six miles that day. We needed a bit of an easy day, but we all decided it would be best to get ourselves clear of Pearisburg and the dark cloud that seemed to sit over it for us. I listened to Bob Dylan's "Hurricane" over and over as I crossed a river and willed myself up the mountain. As soon as Dylan sang his last, "he coulda been the champion of the world," I would rewind to "pistol shots ring out in the barroom night..." and start the story again. Sometimes it was the most random thing that got me through a day. After at least eight times through, I came upon Pilgrim sitting on a large rock staring out to the fields below.

I took off my pack and sat down beside him. "You okay?"

He sighed. "I'm just so fucking tired. We're not even a 1/3 of the way finished with this fucking trail and I'm already so fucking tired."

I nodded, but didn't say anything. I couldn't let myself voice the doubts I constantly carried with me, especially now, after the sickness and weather and injury and, as Pilgrim had put it, the being so fucking tired all the time. My drive to keep putting one foot in front of the other was so fragile that saying anything out loud might mean I wouldn't make it, and more than anything; more than sleep and warmth and hot meals; I desperately wanted to be a person who could finish this thing I had started. Even though I felt weak and weary, I wanted to be strong and determined.

So I listened as Pilgrim talked. Like me, he was wrapped up in his own struggles and worries. Eventually, we moved on and talked for almost an hour about our families and our ideas of what life would be like when we got home until we fell into a companionable silence.

"Should we leave the rock?" I asked after a few minutes.

"UGHHHHHHHHHH!" Pilgrim yelled in exaggerated frustration, grinning maniacally and hauling his pack over his shoulders.

In minutes, we were at the shelter with the others, boiling water for dinner, trying to stay warm in our sleeping bags.

The next morning the fog hung in front of us so thick that I could barely make out See Blue's figure 20 feet after he set out from the shelter. Pilgrim hadn't moved all morning despite the flurry of activity as the rest of us went through our morning routine—pee, pack, eat, hike. Sug just shrugged when we asked what was going on. As Erin and I were grabbing our hiking poles, Pilgrim stuck his head out of his sleeping bag, looked out at the fog and proclaimed, "I'm not fucking hiking today." It was what I wanted to say many mornings, but had never considered that it might actually be an option.

"I guess we're not going anywhere today," Sug shrugged again, obviously used to his friend's mood swings. "We'll catch up."

Looking over my shoulder as Sug climbed back into his sleeping back, I worried about losing our friends, worried that Pilgrim's impulsive decision not to hike might change every-thing. As I walked, the fog turned to pounding rain, which turned to driving sleet.

"What else are you going to do?!" I screamed to the sky, not giving a thought to how ridiculous I must look. "Seriously, Mother Nature! What the hell else are you going to do?!"

Two minutes later, as I reached the shelter where See Blue and Erin sat huddled in their bags, I got my answer. The sleet suddenly and silently turned to snow.

CHAPTER TWENTY

DAY 49, VIRGINIA, 1,485.1 MILES TO KATAHDIN

Two nights after the snow, I lay on a cot in the garage of a man I didn't know, staring up at a poster of a naked woman draped over a motorcycle. I took a sip of my Natty Light and smiled, content for the first time since before the sickness and mess of Pearisburg.

The day after we left Sug and Pilgrim in their sleeping bags vowing not to hike, Erin and I had made our way, slipping and stumbling, through three inches of slushy snow covering a ridge trail made of rock. I fought to stay upright, my soaked boots rubbing against my once again open heel wounds. My poles slipped constantly from my sock covered hands (I had learned in our first week that only my wool socks kept my hands from stiffening with the cold). Every so often we would see "this sucks" written in the snow, an encouraging message from See Blue, walking a few minutes ahead of us. And even though the snow melted by the end of that day, "this sucks" was still the thought most frequently running through my head when we walked up to the Four Pines hostel; home to the garage cots, naked lady posters, Natty Lights, and Joe Mitchell, one of the nicest hostel owners we would meet on the trail.

"Which one of you is Erin?" Joe had asked us when we arrived. There were few women on the trail and so his guess that one of us was Erin was not a stretch. He was leading us to the back of his sizable property, which included a house and dirt bike track situated a few minutes walk down a road that intersected the trail. "Your mom called, wanted to make sure you got this package... it's insulin and I understand how important that is."

It turned out Joe was also a diabetic and had worried about Erin ever since her mom had called wanting to know if we'd made it there yet. Her mom knew we'd planned to stay at Four Pines because every couple of weeks, we tried to update our families and friends about what towns and hostels we thought we might stop at. That way, they could send supplies, like Erin's insulin, or luxuries, like books or CDs. My dad made a habit of sending a book with a $20 bill as a bookmark and a box of band aids for my feet to every place we stopped. Kevin always sent cooking fuel and sweet letters, along with candy or Cheetos. My mom wrote me encouraging notes, Erin's brother sent mix tapes, and my brother sent brownies. Every post office or hostel was like a mini-Christmas, a connection to home, a reminder that people other than us were invested in our journey.

"How about a beer, ladies?" We had entered a huge garage housing ten cots, a card table, radio, shower and toilet in one corner, and a refrigerator filled with beer.

"It's not much..." Joe trailed off.

"It's perfect," Erin and I agreed, meaning it.

We talked to Joe and drank beers while his kids zoomed around on four wheelers outside. Joe told us that we were some of the first thru-hikers he'd seen, but that later in the season the garage would be filled past capacity every night.

After See Blue arrived and we'd all taken showers, Joe offered us the keys to his old pick-up truck so that we could drive into town, three across in the front seat, to eat at a nice family style restaurant called the Home Place. For several hours, we feasted on $10 all-you-can-eat fried chicken, mashed potatoes, green beans, corn, biscuits, coleslaw, and peach cobbler, stopping only to grunt about how good the food was or to ask the patient waitress for more.

Laying in our cots the next morning, bellies still full, Erin and I re-evaluated our planned mileage. We'd been hiking 20-plus mile days fairly consistently, but we were both tired, so decided to cut back on the long days for a bit while we let our bodies heal. Besides, we both hoped that our low mileage would give Sug and Pilgrim the chance to catch up. We hadn't talked about it much because the fluid nature of the trail meant that people came and went all the time—we had learned that after we lost Mike—but to me, our little group felt incomplete.

As we rearranged our miles ("Okay... so we can do 17 instead of 20 today, and 18 tomorrow, not 22. We'll just make those miles up in a week or so."), I experienced a mental shift. I realized that I'd been dreading hiking. Every day for awhile, I'd gone to sleep worrying about the next day's itinerary, and I'd woken up fearing what was to come. Just remembering that I had control over how far we were going and where we'd stop, and that I could say "look, I need a break," reminded me that what we were doing was a choice, not a job.

And when my mental fog lifted, thankfully, so did the weather. We left Four Pines and Joe that morning, comfortable in our shorts and t-shirts, marveling at the cloudless sky. My body felt good, rested, healthy, probably properly nourished for the first time in weeks. We reached McAfee's Knob, one of the trail's most photographed overlooks around lunch time, finding it swarmed with day hikers. Until then, I hadn't realized it was a weekend. I sat on the rock formation jutting out over rolling Virginia farmland far below, occasionally answering the questions of people curious about thru-hiking, but mostly soaking up the sunshine, and I felt something I hadn't in too long-gratitude.

CHAPTER TWENTY-ONE

DAY 55, VIRGINIA, 1,383.8 MILES TO KATAHDIN

F ive days later, Erin and I sat alone together in a shelter for only the second time since the beginning of the trail.

"It's going to be weird sleeping without See Blue mumble-singing Blue Oyster Cult all night," Erin said, throwing a pebble at a tree. We both felt guilty. The day before, caught in a sudden shower of freezing rain, Erin and I had stopped for the day short of our planned destination without telling See Blue. With his long legs, See Blue was a fast hiker and always the first one out in the mornings. When we'd arrived at a shelter, shivering and unwilling to walk another mile, the other hikers there reported that he was long gone. We had no idea how far ahead of us See Blue was, or when we'd see him again.

"You think he'll wait for us to catch up?" I asked.

"Like we've waited for Pilgrim and Sug? Or Mike?"

"Right." Separating from See Blue was another illustration of how unpredictable trail life was. When Mike, and then Sugar High and Pilgrim had decided to stay behind, Erin and I had hiked on, not willing to change our schedule, and I doubted that See Blue would alter his full speed ahead mentality for us even though he had become like an older brother to Erin and I.

The three of us had spent the five days since the sunny afternoon on McAfee's Knob hiking through the rolling mountains of Virginia. After the dramatic peaks and gaps of Georgia, Tennessee, and North Carolina, Virginia's landscape was a welcome change. Instead of hiking up and down mountains, in Virginia the trail largely follows ridgelines and meanders through pastures. Thru-hikers spend more trail miles in Virginia than any other state, almost 550 miles. In the early days, we would long to be in Virginia, joking that it must be like a paved highway all the way to West Virginia (it wasn't). It was a milestone to get to Virginia, and would be a milestone to get through it.

During those days together, See Blue, Erin, and I had spent an equal amount of time hiking North and exploring Southern Virginia trail towns. We resupplied at a gas station in Daleville, Virginia and caught a hitch in the back of a pick-up truck sporting multiple confederate flag stickers into the charming town of Buchanan where the owner of a Christian bookstore/50's café bought us all lunch. We spent a night watching hours of Friends reruns in a rundown motel in Glasgow, a town notable only for the dozen full-sized fiberglass dinosaurs stationed throughout the sparse town center. We had also hiked almost 100 miles and had scaled the last peak over 4000 feet until we reached New Hampshire. See Blue introduced cocktail hour to our routine, surprising us by packing in wine and marshmallows one night, prompting Erin and I to stock our own "mini-bars" with little bottles of liquor. We discovered that See Blue slept naked inside his sleeping bag ("you gotta let your shit breathe, girls"), a revelation that amused us to no end, as did his tendency to hum out loud to whatever heavy metal song was playing on his Walkman. We had settled into a comfortable trio, happily dividing camp chores, picking up the slack for whoever was feeling especially tired on a given day.

Now, with See Blue miles ahead, Erin and I both grew silent as we sat, legs swinging from the edge of the shelter, tossing rocks at the trees and looking out into the woods that had become our home.

"Wow. We're, like, alone," I mused.

Erin stared at me for a full ten seconds and then the sides of her mouth curled into a smile and her nostrils flared with suppressed laughter.

"Wow. You're, like, fucking deep."

"And you're, like, a fucking asshole," I laughed and shoved Erin's shoulder, causing her to tip over, making us both laugh harder.

CHAPTER TWENTY-TWO

DAY 56, VIRGINIA, 1,383.8 MILES TO KATAHDIN

The next morning, we were slowly gathering our things, long past autopilot on our morning routine, when Erin announced that it was Easter.

I hadn't even realized it was a Sunday before Erin said it, and now I wondered aloud if we should somehow mark the occasion. It seemed important, not out of religious obligation, but as a way to inject some normalcy into lives that were becoming more detached from the "real world" every day. I had gone to church as a kid, and had tried on variations of Christianity over the years, most notably my stint as a "kinda Catholic" during my years at Chaminade-Julienne Catholic High School, but nothing had really taken. And while Erin had grown up Catholic, she wasn't overly concerned with the ceremony of faith. During her time at a Jesuit university and for the years afterward she had focused her energy on social justice, working to make good in her community and the world, but she didn't care whether she made it to church on Sunday. It is one of the things I admire most about Erin; she is a person of action, not pretense.

"I could hide your candy bars around the shelter like an Easter egg hunt, if that will make you feel better," Erin teased as we headed out.

The day was pleasant and we spent the morning hiking together, talking about faith and telling stories about Easters growing up. I told her about how I was 11 before I finally realized there was no Santa Claus and that while I sat crying to my mom (who I now know was thinking "How can this kid be so smart and yet so dumb?") about my late revelation, I looked up at her and said, "wait! Does that mean there's no Easter Bunny, too?"

Around lunch time we walked down to a shelter for water and a rest, and ran into Flashback, a section hiker we'd been hiking around for a couple of weeks. Section hikers generally hike the entire trail in several hiking seasons and Flashback was out for a month, completing as much as he could before he had to get back to a job and his wife and children. Erin and I both really liked him, having felt an instant kinship the day we found him climbing back up a ravine after tumbling off the trail because he was lost in thought. He handled himself with much more humor than I had the time I'd lost my footing going down a steep trail and then cried to Erin that I had "fallen off the fucking mountain!"

We hadn't seen Flashback in a couple of days and it turned out he was being slack packed by the owners of a bed and breakfast right off the trail called the Dutch Haus. He told us that the owner was picking him up at the end of the night, and that it was not only Easter, but also his birthday, so he thought we should stay the night at the Dutch Haus and celebrate with him. Erin and I agreed to go and were secretly relieved when he insisted that it be his treat. By thru-hiker standards, we had both saved a decent amount of money to hike the trail, but the

Dutch Haus, at a mere $25 per hiker a night, seemed beyond what we should be spending.

The rest of the day flew by, even though the hiking was challenging. Flashback told us that the Dutch Haus stay included a home-cooked breakfast and dinner as well as complimentary laundry. We completed 22 miles and were picked up by the B&B owner, Earl, on a road a few miles north of the Priest mountain summit. As he drove, Erin asked Earl about how he and his wife had come to open the B&B in tiny Montebello, Virginia and I looked out the window at the passing landscape, thinking of how amazing a hot shower would feel.

Earl had just driven into town when I saw something out of the corner of my eye.

"STOP!" I yelled instinctively, and then seeing a startled Earl, "Sorry, do you mind waiting here for just a minute?"

Erin saw what I did and screamed with delight.

Sitting outside the post office were Pilgrim and Sugar High.

CHAPTER TWENTY-THREE

DAY 56, VIRGINIA, 1361.8 MILES TO KATAHDIN

It was only a little over a week since the day outside of Pearisburg when Pilgrim woke up refusing to hike and Erin, See Blue, and I had set off into the fog without them, but the four of us greeted each other like it had been six months. I had halfway convinced myself that we would never see them again and yet there they were, as if we had planned all along to meet up outside of the post office in this tiny Virginia town.

Conscious of Earl and Flashback waiting for us in the car, Erin told the guys to meet us at the Dutch Haus when they finished their errands. Within ten minutes of arriving at the bed and breakfast, Erin and I were shown to our room, given fluffy bathrobes and told to leave our laundry outside the door of our room, "Don't you worry, we'll take care of it...we've seen worse!"

I had just finished the long, hot shower I had daydreamed of when I saw Pilgrim and Sug walking towards the house. I opened the window and shouted down at them, "I'M BLOW DRYING MY HAIR!"

They gave me a confused thumbs up, obviously not as

taken with the novelty of a hair dryer as I was. On the trail I would often go a week without combing, let alone washing my hair, so the hair dryer was a luxury.

Erin and I met the guys on the front stoop and learned that they had come into town about eight miles behind where we had stopped for the day. They decided that instead of staying the night at the Dutch Haus with us, they would go back out onto the trail that evening, hike those eight miles so that we would all be starting out at the same place the next morning.

"What have you been up to since we saw you last?" I asked. "I thought you guys would have caught us days ago. We were going pretty slow."

It turned out that hours after we'd left them in Pearisburg, Stitch, a guy we'd hiked with on and off in North Carolina showed up at the shelter with another thru-hiker, Ben. Stitch and Ben were going into Blacksburg, Virginia the next day so that Ben could get off the trail to visit his girlfriend in Madison, Wisconsin, and Sug and Pilgrim decided to go with them. The four of them drank wine, ate cheese, and chatted up Virginia Tech girls all day.

Erin looked at them with fake anger. "So while we hiked in the snow that day, you guys were lounging on some college quad? That's fucked up!"

"Yeah," Sug said, "and it was awesome! You guys would really like Ben."

Pilgrim chimed in, "He's kinda like me, but super laid back."

"So... not like you at all?" I joked.

Pilgrim told us that Ben and Stitch had been hiking thirty-mile days, something none of us had attempted yet.

"Yeah, Ben doesn't hike super fast or use hiking poles, he just puts his head down and hikes all day. He said he's lost like 30 pounds since starting."

I pictured a friendly, short, chubby guy with a hiker's beard and decided I'd probably like him, but knew that if he'd be off the trail for a week to visit his girlfriend, we'd most likely never meet.

"Since we took those two days off, we've had to hike big miles to catch up to you guys," Sug told us. In the past when we'd hiked with them, we'd never really conceded that we were staying together as a group on purpose and so it surprised and pleased me to know that they had worked to catch up with us. It felt like maybe our friendships weren't as fleeting as many on the trail had turned out to be.

After an hour, the guys took off for their nighttime hiking adventure, and Erin and I went inside, still in our fluffy bathrobes, to eat dinner with Flashback. We had a lovely dinner and I was sad to learn that this would be the last time we saw him, because he was leaving the next day to go home to his family. While we drank wine and cheers'ed Flashback's birthday and successful section hike, I thought about all the snapshot relationships I'd collected on our hike and was even more grateful that Sug and Pilgrim had caught up to us.

The next morning, after finding our freshly laundered clothes sitting outside our door and eating a delicious home-cooked breakfast, Erin and I waved goodbye to Flashback and Earl from the trailhead. We found the shelter where Pilgrim and Sug had slept and woke them up, deciding to end the day about 25 miles up the trail, just on the outskirts of Shenandoah National Park. This part of the AT in Virginia defied the picture of an easy, downward slope that I'd carried with me through the earlier states. The day started out with a rough climb up a mountain that had three false summits. False summits are as annoying as they sound; just when I'd think I was at the peak of the mountain, I'd turn a corner and see that there was more climbing to do. It had been awhile since Erin and I had hiked over 20 miles in a day and by the last four we were trying to find anything to distract us from the pain our bodies were experiencing from the constant ups and downs. My Walkman was, yet again, broken, so Erin would sing out loud as she listened to a tape and I would sing along. We discovered that "Southern Cross" was a great motivator, and sang "How many times I have fa-allen!" at the tops of our lungs as many times as it took us to reach the shelter.

The four of us had the shelter to ourselves that night. Pilgrim introduced the concept of "AT gym", reasoning that while our legs were getting super strong, our arms and abs were not, so we should do sit-ups and pushups at night. "Let's just get super ripped!"

Even though everyone was exhausted from the day, we all joined in.

"Hey, should we hike through Shenandoah together?" I asked at one point, trying to seem casual, but still surprisingly shy to ask other hikers, even ones who had become true friends, to adjust their schedules to ours.

"Of course," Sug answered without hesitation.

"Yeah. Cool," I said, as if I had completely expected his answer.

The next day, the four of us set out for Shenandoah National park, expecting to see the Blue Ridge parkway, crowds, wildlife; but not knowing that this would be one of the most eventful sections of our hike.

CHAPTER TWENTY-FOUR

DAY 58, VIRGINIA, 1,326.2 MILES TO KATAHDIN

Before entering Shenandoah, we had one more pit stop. Sug talked us all into making another unscheduled stop in Waynesboro, Va. It was a fairly tough negotiation with Erin and I pointing out that we had just stayed the night at the Dutch Haus, Pilgrim and Sug countering with an offer to pay for a motel, and Erin and I immediately agreeing.

Checking our guidebook, we learned that Waynesboro is the home of the Fishburne Military School, an imposing campus in the middle of town, and, more interesting to us, an all-you-can-eat pancake house. After checking into a Days Inn that by any other traveler's standards might rate a disappointed "it's just a place to sleep" but elicited cheers from me for the tiny complimentary bottles of shampoo and lotion, we headed into town. Because we had just resupplied and done laundry at the Dutch Haus, after stuffing ourselves on pancakes, we were at a loss for what to do and resorted to loitering in front of the post office trying to look menacing to the straight-laced military students.

"Hey!" Erin said suddenly. I could practically see the light bulb go on over her head. "Let's get drunk!"

And so we did.

Armed with a case of beer and an extensive collective catalogue of drinking games, we took to our room at the Days Inn on a mission. Several hours later, having drunk enough beer and eaten enough pizza for two men, I found myself in the bathroom on the phone with Kevin.

"I'm so glad you're having fun. I miss you," Kevin told me, sounding like he meant both things.

Pilgrim peeked his head in and I could hear Erin and Sug's laughter from the other room. "Hey, sorry, I need to make a quick call whenever you're done and then I volunteered us to go get more beer," he whispered, shutting the door.

I finished up my call and handed off the phone and privacy of the bathroom to Pilgrim. Kevin and I had talked regularly since his visit in Tennessee and there was almost always a package or sweet letter waiting from him at post office drops. The first couple of phone calls after Kevin went back to Florida were the definition of fine. Nothing was wrong, per se, but it felt like our happy balance was slightly off. Our conversations lacked their usual ease and always left me feeling like I should apologize, although I wasn't sure what for (leaving? being happy?). I was relieved that things seemed like they were finally back to normal. Ten minutes later, a suddenly somber Pilgrim and I walked the two blocks to the gas station for beer none of us needed.

"Who were you talking to? Everything okay?" I asked, the alcohol making me think it was okay to pry into the life of someone usually so private.

"Yeah, it's dumb. Just this girl," He mumbled. And then, apropos of nothing, "I know you guys probably think I'm just this small town guy."

"What are you talking about?" I was genuinely thrown. I saw Pilgrim as smart, artistic, complex; the opposite of what I thought he meant by "small town." Not knowing what else to say, I blurted, "Dude, I'm from Ohio!"

Pilgrim looked at me for a second and we both laughed and moved on to some other beer-fueled topic. But as I hiked the next day, the relative easiness of the Shenandoah trails making it possible to ponder something more than "not another fucking climb," his remark stuck with me. It struck me that my decision to hike the trail, although I had never articulated it, was in part because I wasn't happy with who I felt I'd become. At some point, maybe during college, I'd begun thinking of myself as dull, directionless, as someone with nothing much to add. I looked at Erin, who had (and has) such a spark about her that people couldn't help but instantly love her, and I wished for some of her vibrance instead of feeling like the dumpy sidekick. As I hiked through a nondescript patch of woods, it occurred to me, honestly for the first time, that maybe like Pilgrim, my self-image was skewed. I was, after all, the same person who had, on a whim, decided to take stand-up comedy classes, and had spent the last several months I'd lived in Chicago performing at comedy open mics around the city. I resolved to spend more time thinking about who I was, who I wanted to be and about how to go be her.

CHAPTER TWENTY-FIVE

DAY 59, VIRGINIA, 1,306.2 MILES TO KATAHDIN

S henandoah National Park is one of the most populated sections of the trail due to its proximity to Washington DC, its accessibility, and many amenities. Shenandoah is beautiful, but the Appalachian Trail doesn't travel through many of the most scenic parts of the park. Instead, the AT follows closely along Skyline Drive, a winding road that cuts through the middle of Shenandoah, the trail crisscrossing the drive 30 times in 101 miles. In entering the park, it was the amenities that excited us. We read that all along the trail there were camp stores, restaurants, and even a lodge, and pictured ourselves eating our way through the relatively easy stretch of trail.

Our second day in the park we were up early, partly because it was a cold morning, partly because we had spent the night with a group of noisy high school aged kids and were eager to put some distance between us and them, but mostly because we read that there was a campground with a store seven miles up the trail. The four of us hiked together, and it wasn't until we were several miles into the day that I realized, for the first time, that I wasn't struggling to keep up with the group. I'd felt myself getting stronger with each passing week, judging my progress on how easy it became to pass day and weekend hikers, but I consistently lagged behind Pilgrim, Erin, and Sug. It wasn't something new; I'd been slow my whole life. I was always one of the slowest kids in the 15 years I'd played soccer and softball; I'd resigned myself to being the slowest hiker early in the trip. And up until that point, I had been the slowest. I'd become accustomed to arriving for lunch or at shelters to find everyone waiting for me. I tried to not let it bother me, but the truth was, the truth I'm not sure I would have admitted to myself, was that every time I was the last one in, part of me was right back to being the embarrassed kid at soccer practice. If I had thought about it at the time, I would have realized how liberating it would be to not have to carry that self-imposed label anymore.

But my thoughts at that moment were not focused inward but to where they were ninety percent of the time I was hiking: on food. Which is why, when we arrived at the campground and found the store was not yet open for the season, we treated the disappointment with all the maturity of small children denied their favorite toys. It didn't matter that we had food bags full of the same packaged foods the store would probably sell, there was a magic in buying and eating food you didn't have to carry up and down mountains. We set back out onto the trail, mentally and probably literally kicking at the dirt. Soon, though, we crossed paths with a woman hiking the opposite direction who told Erin about a park restaurant and store a mile off the trail that we hadn't known about and our faith in the universe was restored. Not only would we be getting food, but we'd be getting hot food and indoor plumbing and at that time in my life I'd have been hard pressed to think of something I valued more.

A half hour later, Pilgrim, Sug, and I sat in a booth happily eating high school cafeteria grade hamburgers, when Erin emerged from the women's restroom.

"Dude, don't go in there," she whispered in my ear. "Someone stopped that shit up."

I laughed, knowing exactly who "someone" was, holding up my hand for a high five. Even if Erin and I hadn't been friends since the seventh grade, her comment would have felt completely normal at that point in the hike. The frequency and openness with which backpackers talk about their bodily functions would make even the least squeamish in the "outside world" blush. When you have no privacy and limited facilities, where and when you choose to do your business is a source of constant concern and completely open for discussion. I could have pinpointed without hesitation the daily poop schedule of every person in our group and thought nothing of it (once in the morning was preferable, so you could get it out of the way at a privy).

I had already taken to calling the park the Shitendoahs. Eating town food more often was throwing off my routine and making me thankful for the increased access to restrooms and privies that being in a populated part of the trail provided. It was common knowledge in our little foursome that I was proudly making use of every privy I passed.

We finished our meal and walked into the adjacent gift shop. I grabbed Erin's arm and pointed out the caution tape that now blocked the entrance to the women's restroom.

"What did you do?!" I giggled.

She just shrugged, continued looking at the candy selection and asked with a straight face, "What kind of fudge should I get?"

Erin and I stood at the counter to make our purchases (chocolate for me, rocky road for her) and overheard one young, disgusted looking employee telling another, "It was like a baby's arm. Who DOES THAT?"

When we finally recovered our composure, Erin said thoughtfully, "It's a rare thing to overhear a stranger talking about your shit. Is it weird that I feel kinda proud?"

"Oh my god. This really is the Shitendoahs!"

In any other context, the baby's arm incident would have become a highlight, a story that I told friends over drinks to make them laugh (to be fair, I still trot it out fairly often). But it quickly became a footnote to our time in Shenandoah, because the next day, one of us almost died.

CHAPTER TWENTY-SIX

DAY 61, VIRGINIA, 1,284.8 MILES TO KATAHDIN

We sat in the shelter on the morning of April 25th looking at the trail guides, trying to figure out our mileage for the day. The four of us, but mostly Pilgrim and Erin, who Sug and I deferred to when it came to mileage planning, decided to do 24 miles with a stop for dinner at mile 20 at Big Meadows- a lodge and restaurant in the national park. I felt really strong as we set out that morning. Pilgrim and I hiked ahead of Erin and Sug, Erin complaining that her knee was bothering her a little bit, something that was happening more and more frequently despite Erin's insistence that nothing was seriously wrong. When Erin's sister, Cara, had thru-hiked she'd developed a stress fracture on the top of her foot about halfway through her hike. She'd visited a doctor who told her to stay off it for a couple of weeks. She'd agreed and then immediately laced up her boots a little tighter and kept hiking despite the pain. I couldn't imagine Erin stopping for anything less. It made me think twice when I felt like complaining about my blisters that would never heal.

After a stop for lunch, the four of us set off together. I

confessed to the group that sometimes when I hiked alone, I would think about what I would say in a submission tape for the Real World.

"They should do a Real World: Appalachian Trail," said Pilgrim.

I laughed. "Can you imagine anything more boring? So... they're still walking..."

"What? We're fascinating."

"Yeah, but we go whole days without talking to each other except at meals," Sug pointed out.

"And I doubt anyone is as interested in poop as we are," I said.

"Speaking of..." Erin said and motioned to me that she was going to take a pit stop.

Pilgrim, Sug, and I walked on, hammering out the logistics of Real World: AT ("They'd have to get some super fit camera men."). In the middle of our discussion on whether we would make more of an effort to clean ourselves if cameras were on us all the time, we came across a man with a huge walking stick, hiking in blue jeans. We chatted with him for a few minutes, discovering that he had thru-hiked years earlier. I looked over my shoulder several times, thinking Erin should have caught up with us by then.

"Hey, if you see a girl with red hair coming this way, will you tell her we'll meet her at Big Meadows?" I asked the blue jeaned hiker, knowing that we weren't far from our dinner stop and figuring she would catch up there.

Within 30 minutes we had reached Big Meadows, a complex consisting of several buildings with a bar, gift shop, restaurant, and hotel rooms. All three of us headed straight for the bank of payphones that were located inside the building near the Tap Room. I spent twenty minutes talking to Kevin, and then went to look for Erin, thinking she was probably in the gift shop. I ran into Pilgrim walking back into the main lodge.

"Where's Sweets?" he asked, referring to Erin by her trail name.

"What do you mean? I just got off the phone, you haven't seen her?"

"No, I'm worried. She should have been here a long time ago."

I could hear the panic in Pilgrim's voice and I knew he was right, she shouldn't have been more than five minutes behind us, but I wasn't worried. Erin has a horrible sense of direction. Almost every time we'd come up a path from a shelter, she'd head the wrong way down the trail and I would just wait silently until she'd realize that I wasn't behind her, then she'd yell "fuck!" and turn around. I figured that she had taken a wrong turn or ended up in the wrong building. Pilgrim said he and Sug would look around while I talked to the people in the lodge about where else she could have gone. A woman at the gift store told me that there was another store about a mile away that Erin could have gone to if she'd veered off the AT onto one of the many side trails that run through the park. I was feeling pretty confident that this was what happened and asked the woman to call down to the other store and ask them to look around for a red headed thru-hiker.

"Sorry, honey," the woman said, as she hung up the phone.

"Wait? She's not there?" I stammered and the woman shook her head apologetically, "Okay. Thank you for checking."

I walked outside to look for the boys and a light rain started to fall. A small knot formed in my chest, worried for the first time. I didn't really believe that anything bad had happened, still thinking that Erin was lost, but I knew now that we would need to go back out to look for her. It had been over an hour since we'd seen her. Pilgrim and Sug found me, having had no luck, and we hashed out a plan. Sug and I would backtrack up the trail, and Pilgrim would stay at the lodge in case Erin turned up there.

Pilgrim couldn't contain his worry, "Be careful, you guys, it's starting to get dark."

"I'm sure she's fine," I reassured him, zipping up my raincoat. I felt a flash of annoyance, picturing Erin stubbornly walking the wrong way without me behind to redirect her.

Just then, a car stopped in front of us, and Erin popped out of the passenger seat carrying a six-pack of beer missing two and a gift shop bag full of half-eaten candy. The driver, an older man in a fleece jacket, opened the trunk and pulled out her pack and hiking sticks, setting them on the sidewalk. He gave Erin a quick wave and drove off.

"What. The. Fuck. Dude!" I yelled, feeling a mixture of relief and anger.

"Dude. You don't even know," she said, a smile on her face but giving me a look that shut me down immediately.

I walked over and hugged her, while Pilgrim and Sug gathered her stuff and ushered us inside. And then the story came pouring out. Erin had stopped to pee on the side of the trail, "and I guess I passed out, because the next thing I knew, this mother and son duo wearing matching American flag track suits were standing over me, shaking me, asking, 'HONEY, HONEY, WHERE ARE YOU GOING?' in like, a crazy southern accent and I thought I was hallucinating, but she kept saying "Where are you going?" and I was just like 'I'M GOING TO MAINE!', and that was the point when I realized I was lying on the fucking trail with my fucking pants around my ankles."

Erin hadn't known, but the site where her insulin pump connected to her body had been disconnected all day, meaning she had received no insulin, sending her blood sugar sky-rocketing. On top of that, she was super dehydrated, having run out of water earlier in the day but not wanting to take the time for a refill. When she squatted, those conditions combined to overwhelm her system and she'd passed out "MID FUCKING PEE!" "Team USA Hiking", as Erin referred to them, had helped her to a road crossing and pointed her in the direction of a store, Erin thinking it was the one where we were supposed to meet. Erin had sat on the side of the road, given herself some insulin, drank some water, and then brushed herself off and walked down the road to the store.

"We called down there!" I exclaimed, not quite knowing what else to say.

"I don't know, dude, I must have been on the phone or something. I thought I was waiting on you guys, since I walked down the road. I was just hanging out, eating Doritos and Twizzlers, drinking beer. When I came back in after using the phone, they told me you'd called down and that guy gave me a ride up here."

When we finally stopped laughing (each time we'd stop, someone would yell "I'm going to Maine!" and we'd fall out all over again), Sug looked at E and said, "Jesus. Let's get a drink." He led us all towards the Tap Room.

We had just ordered food and were well on our way to getting drunk, when it finally hit me.

"You could have died!" I blurted.

"I know," Erin said quietly.

After Erin's diabetes diagnosis at 19, she'd had several serious incidents as she learned manage the illness, including a very scary stay in the ICU in December of her sophomore year. In the early years, her blood sugar was constantly fluctuating as she figured out how much insulin to give herself for certain foods and how much she could exercise without her blood sugar going dangerously low. A few times, she'd had seizures from her blood sugar crashing. Once, she'd had a seizure in her sleep and was saved by a group of hot firemen who worked at the fire station next door.

Now, at 24, Erin was much more adept at anticipating and managing her blood sugar. There are endless inconveniences and worries that accompanied backpacking with diabetes—carrying extra food and supplies, her insulin pump periodically being ripped out from her body by her backpack, having any one of her sensitive pieces of equipment malfunction from the constant wetness—all of which happened to Erin at one point or another. Erin treated these events as non-emergencies, as annoyances she expected to deal with, and so I adopted that attitude as well. She was diligent about checking her blood sugar and recalibrating her insulin while we hiked and before this day, she hadn't had any notable issues.

Now, Erin broke into a big smile and raised her glass, "To Team USA Hiking!"

"Team USA Hiking!" we echoed. I smiled back at Erin. She was so incredibly tough that most of the time I forgot that she was diabetic, but I promised myself right then that I would never let her get behind me again.

"So..." Erin said with a wink, "We don't really have to hike any more today, do we?"

CHAPTER TWENTY-SEVEN

DAY 61, VIRGINIA, 1,284.8 MILES TO KATAHDIN

E ven though we had planned to hike four more miles that night, looking around our table at the Tap Room, it was clear that none of us was walking another step. We were all caught up in our relief and the warmth of the booze, and wanting to connect with each other in the way drunk people do. I told them about my biggest relationship regret and a guy I thought I'd probably never get over (Erin giving me a look and whispering, "you never told me that."). Erin talked about meeting and leaving behind a guy in St. Louis and her fear that she'd never have a chance to see what could come of it (me giving her the same look). At one point, Erin and I stumbled to the front desk and rented a hotel room for the night (at almost a hundred dollars, it was the most expensive room we had or would rent during our hike) and then stumbled back to the bar for another round. Before we finally went to bed at the late, for us, hour of 11pm, Pilgrim and Sug convinced Erin and I that we should hike 33 miles the next day and we were drunk enough to agree.

I woke up the next morning feeling, not hungover—our

bodies were so efficient by then that alcohol didn't have much of a lasting affect—but nervous. We had hiked plenty of days over twenty miles, but for some reason, thirty seemed like a ridiculous distance to walk. Pilgrim and Sug had done it in the days when we were apart, telling us that the of hikers they'd met, Ben and Stitch, were routinely doing 30+ mile days.

"They're not \fast hikers. They just hike long days."

The night before, Pilgrim had made it seem like an adventure. He'd broken the day into three parts—we'd hike 9 miles in the morning to Skyland, a Shenandoah restaurant on the trail where we'd have an early lunch, and then 18 more to a picnic area with vending machines and toilets where we'd stop for dinner, and then an easy 6 to the shelter. I found the prospect easier to consider when it was presented that way. I'd only think about the section in front of me and then pretend like the next one was a new day. But even though we easily finished the first leg, we arrived at another Shenandoah restaurant not yet open for the season.

"Okay, let's just go," Erin said, always the one ready to face the task head on, while I usually dragged my feet.

"No," Pilgrim said firmly. "We're going to figure this out."

"Dude. It's closed. Let's go."

Pilgrim didn't budge, head down, looking through the thru-hikers guide. We stood there in the parking lot, packs on, waiting for him to make a move. Finally, he said, "Okay, the book says that if we hike 4 more miles there is road crossing, and then 11 miles down the road is an all-you-can-eat buffet. We're going to get a ride down there and have lunch."

It made no sense. Once we got to the road crossing, we'd have 20 miles still to hike, but none of us questioned him. Within an hour, we'd done the four miles and Erin had talked a young couple finishing up a day hike into driving us to the restaurant. And then, at the restaurant, we lingered, acting like we had nowhere to be. By the time we'd found a ride back up to the trail, it was 2pm. Erin sat up front talking to the older gentleman she'd found to drive us, while Sug, Pilgrim, and I sat squeezed in the backseat grumbling to each other about how full we were.

"Why are all these cars parked along the side of the road?" Erin asked.

The man replied, "Oh, those are truffle hunters."

"Ah," Erin murmured and caught my eye in the rearview mirror. I shrugged.

"It's big business up here, people looking for wild truffles," the man continued, "it's illegal to do it on federal land, but they still do."

Back at the trail, I was strapping on my pack and I felt Sug looking at me. "You thought he was talking about chocolate, didn't you?"

"What? No..." I said, laughing along with the others, realizing I didn't get it, but not wanting to ask what we were laughing about. It reminded me of the time when Erin and I were in high school, hanging out in our friend Amy's kitchen. Erin picked up a meat tenderizer and announced, "This is what we beat the meat with at my house!" Amy and I laughed, and Erin continued, "You know, pound the ground," causing Amy and I to literally roll on the floor with laughter. Finally, a clueless Erin asked, "Wait. Why is this so funny?" which only made us laugh harder.

Even though it was late in the day, I felt good about the rest of the hike. In my mind, we only had fourteen miles until we reached our dinner stop. The four of us hiked together, laughing and taking pictures as Sug hand fed one of the thousands of deer in the park a leaf. I didn't even think about the remaining miles until around 6pm, when the sun started to go down, and the temperature dropped, and we were still over two miles from our dinner stop.

It was at 7pm, with the four of us huddled between two vending machines, eating candy bars and drinking sodas, watching the rain fall in the dark, when I finally asked, "Ummmm... how are we going to see the trail?"

"Headlamps!" Sug answered, flicking his on and shining it in my eye to illustrate his point.

We lingered until 8pm, waiting for the rain to stop (which it did, turning first to a fine mist and then to a thick fog), the 28 miles we'd already hiked and the late night finally wearing on our muscles. We started hiking and quickly realized that in the dense darkness, our headlamps were almost useless. Pilgrim's light was the brightest, so he led, the rest of us following along so closely that I could touch Erin's pack in front of me. The hiking was tortuously slow, our moods swinging from slap happy song singing ("Night hiking, deserves a quiet night.") to deeply depressed silence. It was during one of these silences that I ran into Erin's pack, not realizing the three in front of me had stopped.

"Oh my god, oh my god, oh my god," Erin repeated in a low voice. I followed the weak beam of her light over to the right.

"HOLY SHIT!" I was looking at hundreds of eyes looking back at me, shining in the darkness.

"It's deer," Sug told us in an unsure voice.

"Go, go, go!" I urged, not wanting to find out who we were sharing the woods with.

It was almost midnight when we finally reached the shelter, finding that it was almost full with a group of sleeping high school kids. We silently unpacked and squeezed our sleeping bags into the space.

"Hey," Pilgrim whispered, "we have something for you guys...for finishing your first 30 mile day."

And then he and Sug each pulled out a bottle of beer from their packs and handed it to Erin and I.

"No way," Erin said, sounding as touched as I was. "This is the best."

It was such a sweet gesture, and a perfect end to an epic day. Had I not been so tired, I might have cried. Instead, I took a sip of the beer and passed the bottle to Sug.

"Oooooooh!" I whispered. "Like a mushroom truffle!"

CHAPTER TWENTY-EIGHT

DAY 63, VIRGINIA, 1,232.5 MILES TO KATAHDIN

The next day was our last in Shenandoah, and if I thought the shenanigans the park had provided this far were over, I was wrong. About 11 miles into my day, I was walking down a hill when I spotted Erin, ten feet off the trail, barely concealed behind a rock, squatting with her pants around her ankles.

She looked up to see me, and not realizing the headphones I wore were off, yelled, "MY ASS... IS... EXPLODING!"

What she did not take into account was that it was a sunny, Saturday afternoon, that we were two miles from a road, and in one of the most popular parks on the trail. So maybe she could have anticipated, but definitely did not know that at the moment she was looking at me, yelling about her ass exploding, I was locking eyes with an attractive man in his mid-twenties hiking up the trail from the opposite direction who was also within earshot (and eyeshot) of her pronouncement. He gave me the slightest bemused smile and carried on up the trail, mercifully being careful not to look too long in Erin's direction.

"Dude. We all hear you. And see you," I told Erin when I stopped laughing.

"Jesus. Of course, it had to be a hot guy. There was no time to find a better place, it was behind that rock or in my pants!" Erin was finishing up her business when a family with two young children passed by, making no qualms about staring at Erin in open horror.

"What?" she barked.

That image of Erin behind the rock, yelling at me about her ass, to this day makes me laugh almost as hard as the day it happened.

That night we stopped at a shelter about six miles past Front Royal, Virginia, still laughing about Erin's ass explosion incident. Sitting on the picnic bench out front were two men and a woman in their mid-forties who introduced themselves as Just Ducky, Soft Serve, and Snake. Just Ducky and Soft Serve were a married couple who'd started the trail a week before Erin and I, and I'd followed Soft Serve's entries in the trail registries eagerly, her neat scrawl detailing the experience of the only other woman thru-hiker we knew of. It was a bit like meeting a celebrity, where you know so much about the person and feel an instant kinship before realizing they know nothing of you. The three of them turned out to be lovely people and we spent the evening laughing about our collective misadventures and talking about future plans. Erin made everyone campfire brownies and Just Ducky provided peanut butter for frosting.

We said our goodbyes the next morning, the four of us planning to hike further than the three of them that day. The day was beautiful and the 25 miles passed uneventfully, but still, a collective melancholy had set in by the time Erin, Sug, Pilgrim, and I sat silently in the shelter that night. Partially, we were worn out from the stretch we had just hiked called "the Rollercoaster" that lived up to its name. We'd been told that the trail maker had purposely routed an unnecessarily difficult series of ascents and descents and I felt it in my aching feet. And partially, at least for me, was the realization that in a day the certainty of our little group would be up in the air again.

We were now in the home stretch into Harper's Ferry, West Virginia, the symbolic halfway point of the trail (the actual halfway mark is another 70 miles away in the middle of the woods in Pennsylvania). I was conflicted about finishing the roughly 25 miles to get to Harper's Ferry. Harper's Ferry had been our interim goal for so long that it seemed surreal to finally be so close. It would mean that we were finally out of Virginia and we would be able to check in at the Appalachian Trail Conference visitor's center as official thru-hikers (the ATC is headquartered in Harper's Ferry). But also, it was where Pilgrim and Sug would be leaving the trail for a few days to stay at Pilgrim's sister, Jen's house.

We got into our sleeping bags early that night, and had all been asleep several hours when a sound woke everyone and caused a chorus of, "WHAT THE FUCK WAS THAT?"

Awake now, I saw whatever it was zip across the front of the shelter again, rustling the leaves as it ran into the woods.

"Jesus, was that a coyote? A fox?" I whispered.

"It sounded like a velociraptor," Erin answered, voice shaking.

"Damn it. I have to pee, but no way I'm leaving now," I said eventually.

The animal never reappeared, but none of us slept well after that and in the morning we decided that the 25 miles into Harper's Ferry we'd planned wasn't happening. I wasn't too disappointed, since that meant we'd all have an extra day together. We hiked 4 miles to Snicker's Gap and then a mile down the road to eat lunch at a restaurant. After lunch we decided to try to hitchhike back up to the trail, in keeping with our policy of no extra miles unless it leads to food. The first car that stopped was a white haired man who introduced himself as Don Maloney. As he drove, he told us how he had retired to the area and started a woodworking shop with his wife, Harriet.

"If you want to see the shop, it's just up the road at our house and you can walk through our woods to get back to the trail from there," Don offered.

I was already completely charmed by Don, and I could tell by how readily the others agreed to go to his house, that they were, too. In most other contexts, I would laugh at someone who told me they'd hitched a ride from a stranger and then had willingly gone to their house. I would joke that it's the beginning of every awful slasher film. But on the trail and with Don, the situation seemed perfectly normal.

We were lucky we'd lost our real world hesitation, because the visit to Don's house became one of my favorite memories of the trail. He introduced us to Harriet and the house they'd built together. He showed us his studio, where he handcrafted gorgeous bowls and other pieces from the woods on their property. Erin, especially, was delighted when he showed us the Guinness he kept on tap in the shop. Don was a storyteller, entertaining while showing us how to use a lathe. It was several hours before we reluctantly agreed that we should get going, but not before Erin had ordered a bowl, made from wood found along the Appalachian Trail, as a wedding present for Cara and her fiancé, Chris, whose wedding we'd be going to in a month.

It was a perfect way to spend a last day with our friends.

The next day, we passed the 1,000 mile point, made it to Harper's Ferry in the morning and checked in at the ATC. We were the 13th-16th thru-hikers to make it there that season, and Erin and I were the 2nd and 3rd women (we later found out that Ducky and Soft Serve had hiked through the night to pass us because Soft Serve had wanted to check in as the first woman). We lingered at lunch with the boys until they finally had to go to meet Pilgrim's sister.

"I'm so sad," I blurted while I was hugging Sug for the 8th time.

"We'll see you guys again. It's definitely going to work out," Sug told me, ever the optimist.

I honestly didn't see how it would happen, but I nodded my agreement. They would be slack packing for several days from Jen's house, doing bigger miles than we could with our packs and then we each would be getting off the trail for various reasons (Erin and I to go to Cara's wedding, Sug to a friend's wedding, and Pilgrim for his graduation). As I watched them walk down the street, I felt sure it was for the last time.

When they were gone, Erin and I walked down to the post office, Erin complaining for the first time that day about her knee hurting. It took awhile to sort through the packages we'd received—I got a big haul from Kevin, with candy and fuel and sweet notes; as well as boxes from both my mom and my dad—and by the time we started walking up the hill to check into a hotel, Erin's muscles had stiffened to the point where she could barely walk. Silent tears rolled down her face and it hurt to see how much pain she was in. We would walk a few feet, stop, she'd take a deep breath, and we'd start again. When we finally reached the hotel, I found Erin some ice, propped her up on the bed, gave her an inadvisable amount of ibuprofen, and cracked open a Corona. After two beers apiece, Erin felt in good enough shape to walk to the outfitter, where Erin bought new shoes and a knee brace, and I bought a belt to keep the pants up on my shrinking waist.

As we walked back through the lobby of the historic hotel, Erin said, "I got so used to having the boys around. It feels weird, right?"

"For sure. It's too quiet." I had the room key in my hand and was putting it in the lock when I stopped short. Stuck to our door was a note in familiar handwriting that read, "Ladies, I just got here. Let's go to dinner."

We'd lost the boys, but See Blue was back.

CHAPTER TWENTY-NINE

DAY 66, WEST VIRGINIA, 1,164.6 MILES TO KATAHDIN

See Blue, who'd gotten ahead of us the day before we'd found Pilgrim and Sug at the Dutch Haus, had been able to hike big miles through Shenandoah and Northern Virginia without us to slow his long legs down, but had spent a couple of days off in Harper's Ferry with his girlfriend, Roxy.

"You just missed her," he told us in his gravelly voice over dinner that night. He sighed deeply, his blue eyes focused on something beyond my head. "I'm glad you girls are here, I don't know how much longer I'd make it by myself."

I caught Erin's eye and she raised an eyebrow. See Blue often talked idly about leaving the trail if it got too hard to be away from Roxy, but I never saw it as a real possibility. I chalked his melancholy up to having just said goodbye, remembering how Kevin's visit had thrown me off for a few days, too. At some point, I'd stopped thinking about leaving as an option, even though in the first month of the trail I'd fantasized constantly of quitting. I'd been out of shape, constantly in pain, and mentally and physically spent in a way that I didn't know was possible. Home, laying on the couch with Kevin, was a comfortable place I'd often let my mind wander to as I cursed the trail and struggled to catch my breath; truly believing, every time, that I couldn't take one more step. But over the last few weeks, even though I was still constantly exhausted, frequently bored, and popping Ibuprofen in massive quantities to mask the hurt, I'd noticed that my daydreams were less about home and more about life after finishing the trail. I assumed it would be the same for See Blue once we got back in the woods.

It was 3:30pm before we set out the next day, and it didn't take long to see that See Blue wasn't the only one struggling. Even with the new knee brace, Erin was having a hard time walking. The first several miles out of Harpers Ferry, including the only two miles of the AT in West Virginia, are completely flat before the trail rises gradually in Maryland. So even with Erin's hobbling, we got to the first shelter quickly and I almost suggested we keep moving until I caught the visible relief on Erin's face as she took her pack off and sat down. I'd worn the same expression countless times myself, when I'd kept it together just long enough to get through the day and the notion of going any further would have shattered me. It turned out we had stopped in the exact right place, because a half hour after us, Just Ducky, Soft Serve, and Snake walked in and set down their packs on the picnic bench. Immediately, Just Ducky noticed Erin's knee brace, telling her he was a physical thera-pist, and got right to business diagnosing her problem (patellar tendonitis).

"This brace you bought is useless," he proclaimed, and proceeded to MacGyver a proper brace out of the one she got at the outfitter and a piece of the water tubing from her camel-back. Just Ducky hand-sewed the neoprene fabric of the brace around the tube into a band that would sit right below her knee and apply pressure onto the patellar tendon.

"It's a miracle!" Erin hugged Just Ducky after she'd taken a few steps with it on.

Just Ducky shook his head, laughing at her enthusiasm. "No, but it should help with the pain some. I assume taking a break is out of the question?"

Erin looked at me and I said, "We can do whatever you need," knowing there was no way either of us would really consider stopping long enough to heal her injury.

The next day the six of us set out walking together and by mid-day were bombarded by more hikers than we'd ever seen at once going the opposite direction.

"It's the Maryland Challenge," one of them told us. These hikers were attempting to go through Maryland on the AT from the Pennsylvania border to the West Virginia border, 42 miles, in one day. The trail in this section is mostly flat and smooth, making such big mileage feasible. Snake came up with a game where we had to greet each hiker differently ("hello," "howdy," "how's it hanging," "sup?") and if you repeated yourself, you were out. Even See Blue, who usually hiked out of our sight during the day, played along.

Kristy and Eric, two hikers we hadn't seen since outside of Damascus, caught up to us at lunch and told us they'd seen Mike and Ben in Harper's Ferry, but that they were taking the day off to meet up with Ben's family. I was happy to think that since they were just a day behind, we'd probably hike with Mike again. It bothered me that we hadn't really said goodbye after spending so much of our early days together. And I was interested to meet Ben. Pilgrim had made him sound like a great guy, had told me Ben was planning to move to Chicago with his girlfriend after the trail, so I thought we might have a lot in common. I started leaving Mike and Ben messages in the journals at each shelter we stopped at, knowing that the first thing most hikers do when they get to a shelter is to read the register. I'd tell Mike to hurry up and joke to Ben that we were going to be "best friends," eventually shortening his name to BFB- Best Friend Ben.

By late afternoon, our group had spread out, making plans to meet at a biker bar called the Dog Patch that was right off the trail. Erin and I walked together. I noticed that her gait was easy, and I hoped that the new brace really was a miracle cure. We hiked down the mountain and crossed a bridge over I-70 (a bridge every time I drive under in the years since, I honk and wave, even if no one is on it). Still with only one working Walkman between us, Erin listened to Lauryn Hill's Ex-Factor and sang along, and I listened to Erin and sang with her. We reached the turn-off for the bar and found See Blue sitting on a rock, smoking a cigarette, tears streaming down his face.

"What's wro..." I started, before realizing that he was shaking, not from grief, but laughter.

"I could hear you all the way down the hill," he managed, in between laughing fits. "Jesus Christ, you're the worst fucking singers I've ever heard. I thought someone was dying!"

Erin and I tried to look hurt. See Blue stood up, still laughing, put a lanky arm around each of us, and together we walked to the bar.

CHAPTER THIRTY

DAY 68, MARYLAND, 1134.2 MILES TO KATAHDIN

"Hiker Trash!" cat-called Soft Serve from the porch of the Dog Patch, where she sat with Just Ducky and Snake, when the three of us approached.

"Oh!" I said, taking in the row of motorcycles lining the parking lot. "So, this is like, a real biker bar."

As if on cue, four leather-clad bikers roared up behind us. As they got off their bikes, one of the bearded, bandana-ed men looked appreciatively at Erin and called out, "Hey Red!"

Erin looked at me and shrugged, "What can I say? Bikers love redheads."

"This is my kind of place," See Blue said, taking off his pack and going inside to get us a pitcher of beer. That one pitcher turned into several pitchers and a round of tequila shots turned into rounds of tequila shots. Before we stumbled the mile to the next shelter, Erin turning down offers from several bikers for a ride back to the trail, we had tried and failed to hustle some regulars at pool, called Pilgrim and Sug from a payphone in the parking lot, and danced on a picnic table with Soft Serve to Bruce Springsteen. It was a miracle that we woke the next morning hangover free, a happy side effect of the fast metabolism our bodies had developed.

The Dog Patch party was the send-off we hadn't known we needed. The next day we crossed the Mason-Dixon line, said good-bye to Just Ducky, Soft Serve, and Snake, and hiked into Pennsylvania. Even given what we'd heard about the AT in Pennsylvania (mostly that the 230 mile stretch was incredibly rocky and fairly un-scenic), I wasn't prepared for my reaction to this part of the trail. For me, hiking was almost always a struggle, but through Pennsylvania, for the first time, the trail felt like a job.

And I hated that job.

I hated the rocks that dominated the trail and in some places were more like boulder fields. Erin said it was as though, "someone turned all these rocks on their asses so the flat part is underground and we have to walk on the edges." I felt like I could never quite get my footing, figuratively and literally. My already weak ankles, a product of my many years of soccer played poorly and recklessly, turned on every slick rock. New hikers often comment that thru-hikers seem to have an innate ability to hike fast while avoiding rocks and roots in the trail. And after weeks on the trail, I'd developed some of that (even though, at my core, I'm always kind of clumsy. Every day on the trail I found a new way to bruise or bloody a different part of my body), but Pennsylvania made me feel like someone out for her first hike.

I hated the dreariness of the scenery. There wasn't much to distinguish the trail other than the rocks; no real elevation changes, no outstanding views. And even if there had been, the eleven days we spent in Pennsylvania were a blur of fog and rain. The trail through Pennsylvania was nature's equivalent of the dying steel towns that surrounded it. But it was in that state, where I made up songs as I hiked like "We Will Rock You (aka

Pennsylvania Sux)," that we met some of the kindest, most generous people we'd meet during our hike.

One evening, a few days into Pennsylvania, we came across a shelter caretaker named Jim. The whole trail is divided into many sections and generally a local trail club will take responsibility for maintaining the trail and shelters along their section of trail. In that section of Pennsylvania, the trail club had a dedicated volunteer who cleaned and made repairs on each shelter. We weren't staying at Jim's shelter that night, so we chatted with him for a few minutes and then hiked on in the rain. But early the next morning, a couple of miles into our hike, we were surprised to come across Jim waiting for us, holding a bag of what turned out to be fresh fruit, muffins, and orange juice. I looked at Erin and could see that, like me, she'd also teared up.

Jim smiled and shrugged as we thanked him for the millionth time. "You are the first thru-hikers I've met this year, and it seemed like you could use a pick me up."

After we ate, Jim offered to drive our packs up the trail to a hostel at Pine Grove Furnace State Park so that we could walk most of the day pack-free.

A guy that worked in Boiling Springs at the Appalachian Trail Conference office gave us a ride through the pouring rain to a hotel so that Erin, See Blue, and I could finally do laundry and dry out for a night. In the rundown town of Duncannon, PA (which our trail book referred to as "the jewel of the Susquehanna"), Erin and I drank beer and ate onion rings with local barflies in the middle of the day at the historic Doyle hotel. After walking on several miles of the trail that crossed a toxic waste site, with ominous signs warning "DO NOT DRINK WATER," we arrived in Palmerton, PA to find that the town provided a free hostel to hikers in the basement of their city hall (formerly the town jail). The three of us spent the night there watching hockey, drinking beers and shots provided by a hiker-friendly bartender. When we left Palmerton the next day, the woman who gave us a ride back to the trail pressed a twenty-dollar bill in Erin's hand, telling us to buy lunch on her in the next place we stopped.

One particularly awful day—more pounding rain, Erin's knee hurting so bad she could barely walk—we found ourselves standing at a deserted road crossing that we knew wasn't within 15 miles of a town.

"Let's just give it a half hour and see if we can get a hitch somewhere," I told Erin, hoping that even a futile effort would take her mind off her pain. Not only did the driver of the first car that passed us (which was also the only car that came along in the 20 minutes we waited there) stop and drive us over 12 miles down the road to a McDonalds, but a different stranger spotted us in the parking lot a few hours later and offered to take us back up to the trail.

But even with all the kindnesses we'd experienced, nothing prepared us for what we found in Port Clinton, Pennsylvania. Hiking into Port Clinton, Erin and I were both in foul moods; the rocks and rain and our cumulative months of "togetherness" taking their toll. See Blue had hiked ahead of us a couple days earlier to make sure he hit a mail drop, but was going to wait for us in Port Clinton. Earlier in the day, Erin and I had stopped at a shelter for lunch. Coming down the spur trail back to the AT, Erin, as she often did, headed the wrong way up the trail. I stood still, waiting for her to realize her mistake and turn around.

"Fuck!" Erin yelled when, after a few hundred yards, she spotted me and knew what she'd done. As she doubled back, she mumbled, "Why didn't you fucking say something?"

I didn't answer; annoyed, and for the 10 miles into town, neither of us spoke. Our squabble with each other was well forgotten by the time we ran into See Blue sitting on a bench outside of the Port Clinton outfitter, but our attitudes in general were unchanged.

"You girls okay?" See Blue asked as he led us to the pavilion in the middle of town where hikers were allowed to stay for a night. We changed into our "town clothes," which for me, meant I put on a long sleeve hiking shirt and zipped on the bottom of my pants, and for E meant black long johns that we called her "sexy pants", and were thinking about finding dinner when a big guy with a bushy brown beard and blue baseball hat bounded up the steps.

"My first thru-hikers!" He stuck his hand out, an infectious smile on his broad face. "I'm so glad you guys are here! I'm Bag o' Tricks."

We didn't know it right then, although it didn't take us long to figure out, but we'd just found our very own trail angel. Bag o' Tricks was one of those guys who was so enthusiastic and generous that a non-trail me would be convinced he had an ulterior motive. But by that point in the hike after regularly meeting people like Jim the caretaker, or any one of drivers who'd gone out of their way to ferry us in and out of towns, it seemed perfectly reasonable that there was someone who loved the Appalachian Trail and the community that had grown up around it so much that he spent his summers looking for thru-hikers that he could help while asking nothing in return.

"Come on, I'm going to take you guys to dinner," he said and started back out towards the street before we could respond. We hesitated only a minute before we followed.

That night, Bag o' Tricks loaded the three of us into his car and took us to do our grocery shopping and then to the local pub for dinner and beers, all the while regaling us with outrageous stories of the hikers he'd met over the years. It was never exactly clear to me, but I gathered that he lived nearby and over time had become part of a network of hiker support that surrounded the trail. Often the hostel operators and outfitter owners in towns on the trail were people who maybe at one time had been thru-hikers and became so enmeshed in the community that it was now a central part of their lives. And because they'd lived it, those were the people that helped each new crop of hikers, despite often being ill-prepared and under-funded, complete their hikes.

"Here's what we'll do tomorrow," he started, again, not asking, but telling, "I'll pick you up in the morning and take you to breakfast. Then I'll slack pack you to Blue Mountain summit. There's a great pizza place there and I know the owner, so you guys can camp out back. Okay? Let's get some beers."

We nodded and just looked at each other, not sure what was happening, but knowing better than to question his generosity.

"Just call me Tricks!" he boomed as he handed each of us a giant mug of cold Yuengling.

He told us that he enjoyed helping as many hikers as he could, but since we were some of the first thru-hikers he'd met, and Erin and I the first women he'd seen on the trail that season, that we were getting the royal treatment. He took a big gulp of beer and with no segue, "You guys want to hear a joke?"

Again, we nodded and gulped our own beers.

"What's the difference between a day hiker, a section hiker and a thru-hiker? A day hiker sees a fly in his beer and tells the bartender to give him a new one. A section hiker sees a fly in his beer, picks out the fly and drinks the beer anyway. A thru hiker picks the fly out of the beer, squeezes it, yells at the fly 'gimme that beer, mother fucker' puts the fly back in the beer and drinks them both."

We laughed with him, as much at his joke as at his infectious, raucous, roar of a laugh.

True to his word, the next morning Tricks was back at the pavilion, ready to take us to breakfast. Between forkfuls of pancakes and eggs, I told him about the young couple we'd surprised making out on our return to the shelter the night before. He dropped us back off at the trail with promises to meet us with our packs at the pizza place that night. About halfway through the day, though, as we walked up to a rare four-sided brick shelter, there was Tricks again, beaming when he saw us.

He said, "I thought you guys might like some snacks!" and handed us juice boxes and fruit roll-ups. We accepted them with the delight of children at the half time of a soccer game. As we ate, the caretaker of the shelter told us that he'd met Sug and Pilgrim and that they were killing themselves, hiking big miles to get to New York in time for Pilgrim's graduation and Sug's friend's wedding. We thanked the caretaker for the update, told Tricks we'd see him soon and headed back out into the rain.

I don't think I looked up once over the next 4 hours as I navigated my way over the ever-slick Pennsylvania rocks. My mind drifted. I was physically on the trail, but mentally, I was anywhere else. I'd developed techniques to divorce my mind from hiking on days when the monotony became overwhelming. A new mixtape from Erin's brother Brian would keep me occupied for days, I would listen over and over, dissecting the lyrics until the songs themselves became monotonous. I spent countless hours rewriting the awful jokes I'd told during my brief foray into stand-up comedy in Chicago or scripting my audition tape for the Real World (even though, at 25, I was already way too old to appear on the reality show). If Erin and I were hiking together, we'd develop elaborate scenarios about our made-up boyfriends (Shane and Jacob) who were also best friends, a hobby of ours since the 7th grade.

"When we go into New York City in a few weeks, Shane and Jacob are going to surprise us at the train station."

"That's so like Shane and Jacob."

"Yeah, and since we'll have no town clothes we'll go to Goodwill together."

"Oh! And each person gets to pick out the outfit for their partner."

"Is mine Shane or Jacob?"

"Whichever."

"Cool. Can we try on lots of different clothes like a movie montage?"

"Why wouldn't we?"

"And then we'll go back to the hotel room and get ready while they go get fancy appetizers and wine."

"I would eat the shit out of some cheese. And then we go dancing after dinner?"

"Of course. Shane and Jacob love to dance."

That day, though, my mind was on Trail Days, the annual AT hiker festival in Damascus, Virginia that we were going to later that week. Trail Days is held every year in Damascus and many thru-hikers, no matter where they are in their hike, find a way to get to Virginia the second or third weekend in May. Hundreds of former and current hikers, trail enthusiasts and gear vendors take over the town for a massive party celebrating the AT. Erin went when her sister and Chris had hiked the AT in '99 and said that we shouldn't miss it. Our plan was for Erin, See Blue, and I to make it through Pennsylvania to the Delaware Water Gap and somehow rent a car in time to drive back to Virginia.

I was so absorbed in the logistics of what Erin and I were calling our "AT Vacation" that it surprised me when I arrived at

Blue Mountain Summit, 28 miles from where we'd started that morning. We ate pizza with Tricks, who had arrived an hour earlier with our gear, while he told us wild stories about past Trail Days. He attended every year with a group of friends who set up a party area they called Billville.

"I can't wait to introduce you guys to Billville, they're going to love you," Tricks told me after we'd eaten two large pizzas between us and he'd helped me set up my tent in the picnic area behind the pizza parlor with the rain continuing to pour.

"I'm so glad we're going to see you again, Tricks. You've been such an angel the past two days. You have no idea how much we needed to meet you," I said when I hugged him tightly goodbye.

Later, in her bivy sack under a picnic bench with me 5 feet away in my tiny one-person tent, Erin said "You know, it was really fucking nice to have someone take care of us for a couple of days."

"Yeah, he couldn't have been more perfect."

"Well, unless he was Shane and Jacob, of course."

"Of course... which one is mine again?"

CHAPTER THIRTY-ONE

DAY 77, 944.4 MILES TO KATAHDIN

Over the next three days we covered the 50 miles from Blue Mountain Summit to Delaware Water Gap, Pennsylvania. We hiked first through a superfund site into Palmerton and then out of Palmerton to the Leroy Smith Shelter. Those days dragged. We were seventh graders with spring break on the horizon and no matter how many movies the teacher showed, we could not be distracted.

I woke up on May 14th at Leroy Smith Shelter with my stomach in knots. I'd become accustomed to the everyday body aches and with the help of ibuprofen had almost forgotten about the ever-present open sores on the heels of my feet, but I didn't have anything in my first aid kit (a Ziplock containing band-aids, gauze and duct tape) to fight the waves of nausea I felt that morning. I cursed my body. We had only 20 miles until the New Jersey border and I felt like shit. I peeked my head out of my sleeping bag and saw Erin hobbling around. The Pennsylvania rocks had taken a toll on her already injured knee. She regularly spent her mornings muttering, and occasionally yelling, at the terrain, until her knee loosened up. She then repeated the ritual toward the end of the day when her muscles grew tired.

"My stomach feels like shit," I complained.

"Take a dump, you'll feel better," See Blue said without looking up from his trail guide.

"Thanks," I muttered and stomped off towards the privy, dramatically clutching my stomach.

"NOPE!" I declared when I'd stomped back, still holding my belly, shooting daggers at Blue.

See Blue laughed and Erin patted my shoulder. I asked Erin about her knee.

"Surprise! It also feels like shit."

We tried to pump ourselves up with the reminder that this would be our last day in Pennsylvania, that in two days we'd be back in Virginia sipping beers with Roxy and Erin's brother Brian at Trail Days. But over the next few hours we struggled with what was, in Pennsylvania terms, pretty easy hiking. We were making the slow descent into the Delaware Water Gap and the hiking was mostly downhill. The sky was cloudy but the rain had held off. The rocks, though still present, were a manageable size. Within a few minutes of walking even my stomach felt mostly fine and I had to admit that my foot dragging was purely mental.

It was still before noon when I reached a road. Off to my left Erin and See Blue sat on a wall, smoking, looking at a folded up piece of paper. I plopped down next to them. I recognized the paper they were looking at as the contact information for people willing to give hikers rides that we'd picked up at the park ranger station outside of Shenandoah National Park.

"This says the owner of this motel will shuttle hikers into Delaware Water Gap," See Blue told me.

"Dude, it's cool with me. I'm fucking done," I said.

"I'm going to go ask," Erin said, leaving See Blue and I sitting on the wall.

"You're cool with this?" I asked Blue. I didn't know exactly how far we'd hiked, but we were well short of the 20 miles for the day. Getting a ride into town would mean skipping the rest of those miles.

He shrugged, "Yeah, I'm done too." I was surprised. By that time in our hike, Erin and I had stopped worrying about cutting a few miles here and there, but See Blue was a purist and as far as I knew had never missed an inch of trail. We'd never talked about it. It was a touchy subject. Even if "Hike Your Own Hike" was the accepted mantra among hikers, some people are adamant it wasn't a true thru-hike if you took any shortcuts. And this was going to be a big shortcut.

Erin came out of the motel just then and the chance to question Blue about his decision was lost. Nobody at the motel was available to shuttle us, but they'd given Erin the name of a local man who was willing. Thirty minutes later we were waving goodbye to that man and watching his pick-up truck speed away.

"Did you catch his name?" I asked Erin.

"Mike?" Erin said at the same minute See Blue answered, "Jim."

I looked at See Blue. If he felt bad about skipping those miles, it didn't show on his face, and he wasn't talking about it.

We made our way to Church of the Mountain Hostel, a Presbyterian church with two bunk rooms available for hikers. The caretaker, a woman called Reverend Karen, showed us to our rooms and then we settled in on the porch to figure out the logistics of the next few days. It was Wednesday afternoon and we didn't need to be in Damascus until Friday. Erin and I wanted to hike the next day and leave Friday morning. See Blue wanted to drive down right away; he was anxious to see

Roxy. See Blue was outnumbered, so he took to quietly pouting. Erin and I forged ahead, finding a car to rent in the neighboring town of Stroudsburg that would pick us up at the hostel, and were wrestling with the logistics of how to hike and still get back to the hostel when tiny woman with a blond pixie cut walked up to our little group and, with a serendipity that we'd almost come to expect, solved our dilemma.

The woman introduced herself as Trish. She'd thru-hiked years before and now lived nearby. Trish told us she liked to stop by the hostel to see what she could do for hikers and without hesitation, offered to drive us 18 miles up the trail the next day so that we could slack pack back to the hostel and be there Friday morning to pick up the car.

I'd talked to Cara about this phenomenon before we'd started the trail; the compulsion of former thru-hikers to come back and offer help. Cara and Chris now lived in New Hampshire and often gave rides and food to hikers. Cara explained it in terms of paying back the kindnesses she'd experienced during her thru-hike as well as a way to keep her connection to the trail alive. I didn't really understand it then, but several times the next summer I'd find myself driving to the trail from my summer internship in Washington, DC just to put a cooler of snacks and beer on the trail.

"This is so fun!" Trish said the next morning, waving goodbye as she dropped us off in the middle of the woods in New Jersey. I hadn't been paying much attention, but when I looked around and realized where I was, tears sprung to my eyes. From where we were standing, I could see part of the summer camp where I'd worked during college. I knew we'd be close—I remember hikes and bike rides during those summers on the AT—but I didn't know I'd be able to see it. I certainly hadn't expected to feel so overwhelmed being there again.

"You guys! This is it! That's the lake where I thought I saw a ghost!" I practically yelled at See Blue and Erin, pointing out memory landmarks.

They humored me for a few minutes and then set out in front of me, eager to get our last day of hiking before vacation over with. In college, I'd written a paper about the acute nostalgia I felt instantly after leaving camp each summer (both as a camper and then counselor at Camp Kern in Ohio and then later at this camp in New Jersey), about how those were experiences and feelings that I could never recapture but always yearn for, and I'd wondered if the pain of longing afterwards made the summers more or less worth it. After all, here I was, in the midst of the grand adventure of hiking the Appalachian Trail and I was so lost in this past that I was surprised when I found myself back at the hostel hours later. I'd spent the day reliving those summers at Camp Mason in my head, images popping up like a slideshow set to random. The guy I'd fallen for the first summer and then barely talked to the next summer. The camper I'd led on a mountain biking excursion, who'd flipped over her handle bars and when asked where it hurt yelled at the top of her lungs, "MY VAGIII-INNNNAAA!" The countless nights off I'd spent at the archery range doubled over from laughing with the other counselors. The weekend trip into New York City when a guy who spoke no English gave me a crooked tongue piercing. The campers who cried saying goodbye at the end of the summer; the ones who made me cry too.

"DUDE!" Erin called out from the church porch, dragging me back to the present, her pointer and middle fingers forming a big V. "VACATION!"

I returned the V sign and yelled, "VACATION!"

It took us 8 hours to drive from Delaware Water Gap, PA to Damascus, VA; a distance that had taken a month and a half to walk.

"It's kind of depressing from the outside," I muttered, as we sped past signs for towns we'd stopped in and the ridges of mountains we'd walked on.

We arrived in Damascus to a sea of people; hikers and tents and vendors had taken over, making it almost unrecognizable from the sleepy town where we'd waited out the snow storm with Sug and Pilgrim at the end of March. See Blue peeled off instantly to find Roxy, and Erin and I looked for her brother Brian and his friends, who had arrived earlier and set up camp. We were wandering around the makeshift tent village when we heard someone calling our names.

"Sweets! Not Yet!"

We turned, surprised to see Mike walking towards us, waving his arms with a big smile across his face. We ran towards him, giving him big bear hugs, a happy reunion with our long lost little brother.

I looked at the guy next to Mike. He had a mess of brown curls, a hiker's bushy beard and baggy hiking clothes from the inevitable weight loss of three months on the trail.

He stuck his hand out, "Hey, I'm Ben."

"No way!" This was the BFB (Best Friend Ben) I'd been writing to in the trail registers for the past few weeks.

"Did you guys get my messages?" I asked, looking from Ben to Mike.

"Yeah, what's weird is that those are my initials. BFB. In real life. Ben Francis Brooks," Ben smiled at me.

"Well, I guess it's fate," I said, my voice serious. "We have to become best friends."

He nodded solemnly, "Okay. I'm in."

CHAPTER THIRTY-TWO

DAY 82, VIRGINIA, TRAIL DAYS

After making loose plans to meet up with Mike and Ben later that night, Erin and I set off to find Bag o' Tricks and his Billville friends. We wandered through the maze of tents until we heard someone calling our names. I turned to find Miss Janet standing behind us, arms outstretched for hugs. We chatted excitedly, telling her about how we'd fared since leaving her house in Tennessee weeks before.

"Oh, of course I know Tricks! EVERYONE knows Tricks!" she said when we told her who we were looking for. She took us over to the Billville camp, populated mostly by people who'd done multiple thru-hikes or those like Tricks who supported thru-hikers every year. Billville was replete with a tiki bar and crowded with hikers in Hawaiian shirts drinking beer or some mysterious jungle juice-like concoction. Erin and I felt like mini-celebrities with Miss Janet and Tricks introducing us to everyone as the first thru-hikers of the season, which wasn't technically true, but we didn't bother to correct them.

It wasn't until later in the evening that I found the guys sitting around a campfire in a circle of other thru-hikers. Mike introduced me to his little brother who was hiking with him and Ben for a few days. I pulled up a camp chair next to Ben, handed him one of the beers I'd procured from the Billville gang and said, "well, if we're going to be best friends, you're going to have to tell me everything about yourself."

He laughed at my demand and started talking. We talked for hours, first in the circle and then wandering around the field of hikers. He told me that before the trail he'd been living in Madison, Wisconsin managing a Whole Foods bakery; that he'd moved there on a whim with a friend from High School (they'd put a bunch of cities in a hat and Madison was the winner) because they weren't ready to get "real jobs" and that after the trail he was hoping to go to grad school for creative writing.

I told him how I'd been living with Kevin in Florida right before the trail and in Chicago before that.

"Pilgrim told me you were moving to Chicago with your girlfriend? You're going to love it."

He laughed again and said, "Oh right. That was the plan." It turned out that after he'd met Pilgrim and Sug, he'd planned to go back to Madison to visit his girlfriend for a week. He'd found a ride from the trail to Roanoke, Virginia and then, while on a payphone outside of a greyhound bus station, they'd broken up.

"I'm sorry."

He shrugged. "It was hard, but it'd been coming for a long time. The worst part was that it then took me three days to find a ride back to the trail." Roanoke was over 60 miles from where he'd left the trail near Pearisburg.

"What did you do?"

"I found a seedy motel that had an all-you-can-eat buffet behind it. So, I ate there twice a day and watched TV."

"Sounds like paradise," I said.

"It was pretty great."

I told him about my job with Best Buddies and how after the trail I was going to law school to hopefully study disability rights. His face lit up as he told me about his older brother Ross, who had severe disabilities, about how his mom was the head of Special Education for the state of Delaware and how his dad served on the board of a disability rights non-profit and taught college courses on disability law. Even his other brother and sister-in-law were Special Ed teachers.

"It's like the family business," he joked.

"But not for you? No pressure to go into education?" I asked.

"Nah, I don't think so. My parents know I'll figure something out," he said with a self-assurance I don't think I'd ever felt.

We decided to walk around and found ourselves outside of a drum circle. People all around us bobbed their heads to the bongos. Girls danced with their eyes closed, arms flailing; apparently finding an inner rhythm I couldn't. I wanted to be open minded, but every part of me was fighting an eye roll.

"This is my first drum circle," I tentatively told Ben. I looked at him but couldn't tell from his profile whether he was into it or not. He seemed to be very laid back, and when we'd talked about music earlier, he'd told me that he liked jam bands (and had teased me when Phish was the only one I'd heard of).

"See, this is why I could never really be a hippie," he said, gesturing to a guy with dreads to his waist, so completely lost in the experience of drumming but so totally off the beat. "I can't ever not want to make fun of a drum circle and I think that is requirement number one."

I let out an exaggerated sigh of relief. "Oh, thank god. I thought I was going to have to pretend to take this seriously if we were going to continue our friendship."

Just then, Mike's brother tapped Ben on the shoulder. Obviously drunk, he held up a backpack to show us. It was a prototype of a new lightweight pack that we'd seen earlier at one of the vendor's booths.

"Look. I stole this," he said in a loud whisper, looking at us expectantly.

Ben and I exchanged a look. Ben put an arm around his shoulder and gently said, "Dude, that's not cool. You've got to take that back."

Mike's brother was deflated. He was 17 and thought everyone would laugh at the prank. Ben calmed him down, telling him we wouldn't bust him with Mike, but made him promise he'd return the backpack.

"I can't believe that just happened! What was he thinking?" I said after Mike's brother had left, head down. "I think we deserve another beer!"

I grabbed Ben's hand to lead him through the crowd as we made our way back to Billville. We found Erin hanging out with a guy named Chomp, who was engaged in a serious debate about Bill Bryson. Bill Bryson and the book about his experience on the Appalachian Trail "A Walk in the Woods" was a frequent topic of conversation among thru-hikers. I'd read and loved the book before I'd hiked, as had almost everyone we met. The argument against Bryson wasn't that the book was not entertaining or well-written, but that Bryson held himself out as having hiked the whole trail, when in reality, he'd only completed less than half of the 2,100+ miles. The other side argued that Bryson never claimed to have finished a thru-hike and that by writing about the AT had introduced the trail and its culture to a much broader audience. All of the debaters were drunk (as was I at this point) and so the debate raged with no conclusion in sight.

Erin pulled me aside and gave a stern look. "You need to watch yourself."

"What are you talking about?" I was taken aback.

"Ben. You're drunk and you're flirting with him. You were holding his hand! Does he know you have a boyfriend?"

"You're drunk!" I retorted, a comeback only ever used by the drunk. "And yeah, of course he knows about Kevin."

"Whatever," Erin rolled her eyes. "Just be careful."

"Whatever. *You* be careful."

I walked back over to Ben. I was embarrassed and angry with Erin for calling me out. She was right, I had drunk too much and though I didn't think I'd crossed the line with Ben, what if I had? I'd had such a good time hanging out with him all night and I hated feeling now that I'd done something wrong.

"I've got to go," I said to Ben abruptly.

"Okaaayyy..." he said slowly. "Everything alright?"

The words tumbled out of my mouth, "Look, Erin thinks I'm leading you on or something and I told her you know I have a boyfriend and we were just hanging out and having fun and you should know that I... I'm a good girl!"

Ben smiled, apparently amused. "Yes, you are. And tell Erin it's cool, I know."

He hugged me lightly and said, "Don't worry about it. I'll see you tomorrow.... good girl."

CHAPTER THIRTY-THREE

DAY 83, VIRGINIA, TRAIL DAYS

I opened my eyes the next morning feeling stiff; regretting my drunken decision to sleep in the cramped back seat of the rental car instead of setting up my tent. I lifted my head and immediately laid back down as the hangover hit me. I had one hand clamped my throbbing head while the other blindly rooted through my pack feeling for the ibuprofen. I found the medicine and my Nalgene and forced myself to get out of the car. Breathing in fresh air, I stretched and then trudged through the mostly quiet sea of tents and cars to the bathroom.

Erin stood at the sink washing her hands. I grunted good morning and went into an open stall.

She cleared her throat, "So. You were mad at me last night."

"No, I wasn't."

She laughed. "Yeah, you were."

I laughed, too. "Yeah, I was. Whatever, I was drunk."

"We all were."

I flushed and walked out to the sink, catching her eye in the mirror. A memory from the night before flashed.

"Oh god. Did I tell Ben I was a good girl?"

Erin's eyes widen. "Did you? Holy shit, that's hilarious!"

"Fuck. That's so embarrassing," I hung my head and caught the time on my watch. I brightened, "Oh! We need to get to our hair appointments!"

We made our way together, tension from the night before forgotten, back to the campsite. Weeks earlier, we'd arranged with See Blue's girlfriend, Roxy, to cut and color our hair at Trail Days. And so, in the middle of the field, with supplies she'd brought from home, Roxy went to work.

"We're like real women again!" Erin told Roxy as we both admired our new looks in the mirror. Erin ended up with long layers and I got a shoulder length bob with pink and blonde streaks.

Around lunch we wandered down to the main street and found Mike and Ben sitting on a picnic bench watching a blue-grass band.

"Free hot dogs!" Mike yelled as they scooted over to make room for us. We grabbed handfuls of free food and talked excitedly about everything that had happened since the last time we'd seen Mike. Mike said he'd hiked with Nasty and Shaman, until he'd run out of money.

"And then I got to Damascus and spent a couple of days doing odd jobs for the guy who owns the diner until I had enough money to get back on the trail," Mike told us. Neither Erin nor I were surprised; when we'd hiked with him, Mike had always been almost broke, needing one of us to front him until his parents sent more money.

"So, when did you guys start hiking together?" Erin asked, starting on her second hot dog. I was devouring my second bun loaded with ketchup, relish and mustard—a treat I'd started eating in college when my friends would visit the aptly named Hot Dog Lady after a night at the bars.

Ben told us that earlier in his hike he'd found an ID on the trail and had carried it with him for weeks.

"I was in town around a bunch of hikers one night and I pulled it out to ask if anyone knew this guy and Mike was one of the hikers I'd asked. I didn't even recognize him."

Mike said, "I was like, I AM that guy!"

"And then your eyes met and you knew it was true love," teased Erin.

"Totally." Ben smiled.

I watched Ben easily joke with Erin and decided that if things between us had felt flirty the night before, it was because he was just a friendly, flirty guy. Over the next hour our group grew and shrank as a few people Ben or Mike had met along the trail came over to catch up and then wandered off. See Blue and Roxy sat and talked for awhile and Brian and his friends stopped by on their way to check out the gear and craft fair.

We all exploded into cheers when faces familiar to all of us, Turbo and Lawn Ornament, walked over together. Turbo, who Erin and I had last seen at Miss Janet's in Tennessee made me laugh so hard I cried when he told us how he'd hitched hiked down to Damascus.

"So, what's it... I got a ride with this trucker who took me all the way here," he said, hands flying, eyes big, "because he thought I was Jesus. And I didn't say I was, but I didn't say no, you know."

Soon after they'd arrived, the hiker parade started. We'd all decided not to participate in the yearly spectacle of thru-hikers from past years who dress up in crazy outfits and parade down the main street. The hikers from the current year always brought up the rear and drew the most applause from the bystanders.

"You guys are the only other hikers I know. Everyone

would think I was lying if I said I was thru-hiking this year," I'd said when Mike asked if Erin and I were going to join in.

The bulk of hikers started anywhere from late March to early May and spent their days surrounded by other hikers and their nights at crowded shelters, whereas we'd only met a handful of thru-hikers during our months on the trail. It was one of the reasons why Erin and I were so excited to see Lawn Ornament, who we'd only hiked with a few days and hadn't seen since our third night on the trail. Besides Soft Serve, she was the only other woman thru-hiker we'd met. After the parade, the three of us wandered around the craft fair looking at poorly thrown pottery and mostly crystal-based jewelry, and discussed one of the foremost concerns of women hikers; peeing.

"I hate how long it takes to pee," I'd complained. "The guys don't even have to stop what they're doing. Sometimes I'll be talking to one of them and the next thing I know, I look back and their back is turned and all I hear is a stream hitting a tree. And then the next second, they're hiking again."

"I think the best day was when Sal and I mastered the pack-on pee," Erin said, referring to our newfound ability not to have to stop and unstrap our packs every time we went to the bathroom, which ate up precious hiking minutes. In the beginning, our legs weren't strong enough to support ourselves if we tried to squat down with our heavy packs still on, a sad lesson I'd learned after I'd once tipped over backwards, shorts around my ankles, directly into my own pool of urine.

"I'm getting pretty good at not even squatting all the way," I bragged.

Lawn Ornament stopped and gave us both a serious look. "Dudes. I don't even pull my shorts down."

"WHAT?!" Erin and I gasped in unison.

"Yeah," she said, a look of pride in her eyes. "I don't wear underwear so I just pull my shorts over and pee standing up."

"How do you not splash all over yourself?" I asked, incredulous.

"I don't know, I just don't. Must have a super straight stream."

Late in the afternoon, I'd found an empty phone booth to call Kevin and my parents and was heading back to the campsite to meet up with Brian and Erin. As I walked up Main Street, I heard someone calling my name.

"Not Yet! Sally!" Ben yelled, running across the street from the local outfitter.

Without explanation, he handed me a small jar of Burt's Bees lip balm.

"What's this?" I asked, confused.

"Last night you said you'd run out, so I grabbed you some while I was shopping." He said plainly.

"Oh yeah... wow... thank you," I stammered. "How much was it?"

"Nothing. It's a gift. I'll see you later," he smiled and ran back across the street and down towards the craft fair, leaving me standing alone on the sidewalk, feeling both touched and slightly taken aback, holding a jar of lip balm.

CHAPTER THIRTY-FOUR

DAY 83, VIRGINIA, TRAIL DAYS

I slipped the jar into my pocket and walked back to our camping spot.

Erin sat on a camp chair, eating a plate of grilled vegetables.

"How's Kevin?" she asked.

"Huh?"

"Kevin. Did you talk to him?"

I reddened. I'd forgotten my phone call with Kevin. "Right! Oh, he's good. He says 'hi' and to tell you he sent a big bag of Cheetos for you in my next package."

I didn't mention the lip balm to Erin.

That evening, a big group of hikers sat around in a circle, drinking beer out of Nalgenes. I took my camera out of my bag and snapped a picture of the group, saying, "I want to have a picture of everyone in case we don't see each other again," but thinking that it was Ben who I wanted to make sure I had a picture of. Mike and Ben had made it to the Delaware Water Gap before going to Damascus, which still put them seventeen miles behind us on the trail. And because Mike's brother would be hiking with them for the next week, they would be hiking shorter days and we weren't sure when or if they would catch up with us.

The next day, Erin, See Blue, and I drove back to the Delaware Water Gap for another night at the Church of the Mountain hostel, See Blue in a serious post-Roxy-visit funk. The following morning Trish picked us up at 7am to return the rental car and drop us off on the trail. She and her dogs hiked with us for the first three miles and I was close to tears when we hugged her goodbye, knowing how lucky we were to meet such a generous, kind-hearted stranger.

It was a beautiful day; the sky blue, the lush scenery a welcome change from the rocks and rain that plagued us throughout Pennsylvania. I took a deep breath, taking in the scent of the pine and thinking how good it was to be moving forward again. We'd only been off the trail for three days, but it was our longest break and with a shock that I realized I felt a bit uncoordinated and stiff hiking. I'd lost my trail legs after such a short time, and was having to concentrate on my footing more than usual.

After an hour or so of walking in companionable silence, Erin turned her head and said, "God, it just feels good to be hiking again, doesn't it?"

Startled at the sound of her voice, I looked up and started to answer but in taking my eyes off the trail, the toe of my boot got caught on a root and I fell, face first, scraping my hands and knees and knocking the right side of my head on a large, smooth rock. I lay there for a minute, dizzy, stunned, trying to assess the damage. Erin made sure I was conscious and then hauled me upright by my backpack.

"Shit," she said, eyes wide.

"Is it bad?" I asked, reflecting her expression. I could feel the blood starting to trickle down my legs and had a dull pounding where my head hit the rock, but otherwise couldn't detect anything serious.

"No... no... just a bump, but... shit. That could have been bad," she reached into the side pocket of her pack, pulled out her Trail Guide and after a moment said, "It looks like we're going to walk through a little town in a few miles, we'll reassess there."

My knees felt tight as I hobbled along behind Erin, periodically touching the growing bump, which seemed dangerously close to my temple, slowly realizing why Erin had looked so scared earlier. I was preoccupied with thoughts of my near death (it was amazing how, after three months, my mind would latch on to any new thought, person or experience and examine it from every angle just to keep me from sinking into anxious boredom), so it seemed like it only took minutes to reach the small town and seat ourselves on the nearest barstools. The bartender handed me three small bags of ice and a cold beer and Erin and I laughed too hard about the morbid image of her dragging my lifeless body down the trail.

"I'd leave your pack though. And probably your boots. Those weigh at least three pounds."

We scarfed down deli sandwiches and ridged potato chips, and I accepted a fresh bag of ice from the bartender, which I secured to my head with a bandana. Before we made it to the shelter that night, I managed to fall two more times, both times barely catching myself so that I only impacted my knees and hands.

"Dude, what is going on with you?" Erin asked after the third fall. "It's going to get hard to muster up concern every time if you keep this up."

"Yeah man, I barely give a shit at this point."

CHAPTER THIRTY-FIVE

DAY 85, NEW JERSEY, 931.6 MILES TO KATAHDIN

The next four days passed in a deluge of rain, which, at that point, had become more the norm than the exception (we would later learn that 2003 was the wettest year to date). I scrambled over boulder fields, climbed up to beautiful wet overlooks, walked over a mile through a marsh on a wooden boardwalk and white knuckled my way across a suspension bridge. Erin and I sometimes hiked together but we hardly ever saw See Blue during the days. We'd reach the shelter at the end of the day and find Blue there; smoking, humming to himself, writing in his journal, his mood turning increasingly dark after Trail Days. One of the nights I heard a rare happy Blue voice booming from the shelter and turned the corner to see we'd caught up to Eric and Kristy again. Just like each time we'd hiked with them before, I found them to be a breath of fresh air.

On the third day, I sat at a shelter during lunchtime, waiting for Erin to arrive, talking to Eric and Kristy about their time in the Peace Corps. It was rare for me to get ahead of Erin, at first because she hiked so much faster than I did and lately because I feared she'd collapse again like she did in Shenandoah. That morning, though, I'd been feeling really strong, and she'd seemed fine, so I'd passed her early on.

I'd been preoccupied chatting, but now worried about how long I'd been there when Erin walked up. I could see from her expression that something was clearly wrong.

"This fucking pump," she said as she flung off her pack and sat heavily on the ground. She told us she'd started feeling sluggish and cranky that morning, but hadn't thought much of it because that was how we felt most mornings. Then her head started to hurt and she got crazy thirsty and somehow, through the fog, put together that her blood sugar might be going high. She increased her insulin but it didn't help. She'd stopped to pee (something that happened frequently when she went high) and finally realized her pump was actually disconnected from her body so she hadn't received insulin all day.

"I feel like I'm walking through quicksand... but I'm fine now," she assured us when she saw our concern. "I just need to sit here for awhile. Seriously. Don't worry."

"Okay," I said. But I was worried. Erin was so outwardly nonchalant about her diabetes that it was easy to forget how scary things could get, especially out here, especially if no one else around. I said a quick thank you to the universe that Erin was fine, that she was able to figure out what was happening before her symptoms got too serious, for the reminder (again!) that I should be more aware. And when we started back on the trail, even though Erin would never ask me to, I followed behind.

Our fifth day on the trail, I woke up to total darkness. I had a moment of sheer panic—had I gone blind in the night? It had to be the water I hadn't carefully purified earlier that day, or the head trauma, or an infection from one of my many open wounds, right? Then I remembered, through my sleepy haze, that I'd been cold and put my fleece hat on in the middle of the night. It was now pulled down over my eyes. I lifted the flap to let the sunlight in, crisis averted, and rolled over to see See Blue putting on his pack and Erin stretching her arms out of her sleeping bag, too. She caught my eye. "THREE MONTHS," she whispered excitedly so as not to wake the sleepy day-hiker sleeping soundly next to us and held out a fist.

"Three months!" I yell-whispered back and gave her the pound.

It was May 23rd and we'd officially been hiking for three months. We made plans with See Blue about where to stop that evening.

"There's this working friary about seven miles past Bear Mountain that is supposed to be cool," Blue told us, not bothering to whisper. He took off in a cloud of cigarette smoke and as we started to pack up our things, rain began to fall.

"Cool. Rain," Erin muttered, one of our running jokes.

"Maybe there will be mist today, too," I said.

"You're a dreamer!" Erin mock exclaimed.

We hiked the 8 miles to Bear Mountain together, Erin telling me how when she worked at a summer camp in the Bronx, they would bring the kids to Bear Mountain for day trips. Bear Mountain Park is less than an hour outside of New York City and yet most of the born and raised city kids would feel like they were in a foreign country being out in the woods.

"We took them on an overnight to a lodge upstate, and the kids were like, for real, scared of how quiet it was."

As if on cue, we caught sight of school buses parked along the road winding towards the summit of Bear Mountain and then were bombarded by the sound of what seemed like 8,000 kids running around the mountain's bald peak.

"Eh, maybe we'll skip the view," Erin said, looking at children streaming in and out of the tower that stood on the summit. Our guidebook told us that on a good day, you could see the NYC skyline from the top of the tower.

"What view?" I said, looking at the mist surrounding us.

We continued on down the mountain to a swath of parking lots and development. Other than the drive to Bear Mountain peak itself, the park hosts a museum and small zoo (which was where we saw our first, and only, bear on the trail), the Bear Mountain Inn, playing fields, a merry-go-round, a pool, skating rink, and even a post office. While the area is a respite in nature for people coming from the city, for us, after three months in the woods, all of the activity felt jarring.

Of course, the smallest sign of civilization signaled one thing to us—food—and so we made a beeline for the Inn and treated ourselves to a hot meal in the formal dining room. To his credit, the waiter barely flinched at the strong smell coming off of us and our gear. After lunch we hit the post office, where I picked up packages from my mom (a funny card and book), my dad (a packages of band aids and a $20 bill), and Kevin (snacks, fuel, a sweet letter, and socks he told me were from his mom), and then found a bank of payphones. Erin was busy trying to track down the phone number for her friend Chris G, who was teaching at a school in Harlem. We had decided we wanted to take the train into New York City for a day (it was part of our master plan to give Mike and Ben time to catch up to us), and we were hoping to stay the night with Chris. I talked to my mom and then called Kevin.

"Hey darlin', you caught me at a bad time. I gotta run out the door to the jobsite," Kevin told me. He'd taken a job with a big construction firm after graduation and in less than a year was already moving up.

"It's okay, I just wanted to hear your voice and say thank you for the package. Your mom was right, I need new socks," I told him, feeling a little sad and a little relieved. We'd been having a lot of short conversations lately, but I'd also been milling around Bear Mountain for a few hours at this point and I was ready to get back on the trail.

As I hung up, I looked over to see Erin shaking her head.

"No luck?" I asked.

"Nope. I got his number but he wasn't home. But my brother checked my email for me and there was one from Sug. He and Pilgrim aren't far in front of us. We might catch them because he is getting off to go to a wedding and Pilgrim went home for his graduation."

"Dude. That would be awesome if we caught them and then Mike and Ben caught us and then we all hiked together forever!" I said, my words jumbling together in an excited rush.

"There you go again, ya dreamer."

CHAPTER THIRTY-SIX

DAY 89, 781.6 MILES TO KATAHDIN

The night at Graymoor Friary, despite its promise, was not "cool." Although it was a working friary, we never saw a Friar and the accommodation for hikers was just a picnic pavilion with a concrete slab floor. Add to that two obnoxious section-hikers (the old, white, male variety who loved explaining long distance hiking to two young women three months into a long distance hike) and a cold, pouring rain all night and I woke up in an unusually foul mood. I was up and packed before everyone else, itching to get out of there. Erin also woke up in a bad mood. Sleeping on the cold concrete meant her knee was stiff. I tried to be patient, as she moved slowly through her morning routine, clearly struggling. My impatience must have shown through—my face has never hidden a feeling—because Blue, in one of his signature bursts of kindness and sensitivity, told me to go ahead, that he'd hang back with Erin.

I took off quickly, the frustration of the morning fueling my speed. After a few miles, the anger was gone and I realized that I was enjoying hiking. The terrain wasn't taxing and it felt good to push myself to hike faster than I had before. My body was strong, I realized suddenly, and that was not something I'd felt in a long time. Before I knew it, I was only a mile from the shelter. I waited for Erin and Blue, sitting on the ground leaning against a wooden fence post, and just before they arrived, the sun peaked out of the clouds. We cheered the sun and each other and walked the rest of the way to the shelter together, Erin swearing she felt better. At the shelter, our good moods improved when we noticed a note that said there was a road a few tenths of a mile away and a pizza place that would deliver if you could find a way to call.

"I have a cell phone. Would that be helpful?" a guy sitting in the shelter, who I'd barely noticed before, chimed in. I turned and reassessed him.

"Who are you? Our guardian angel?" I asked, ordering up two large pies.

Over pizza, we hatched a plan. We'd all hike sixteen miles that next morning from the shelter to the Pawling train station. From there, Erin and I would head into the city and Blue would take the train to Connecticut to his grandma's house. We would all meet up a few days later at a shelter in CT.

We woke up super early, and as we packed up, I said to no one in particular, "Here's my wish—we somehow find a ride to the train so that we don't have to hike all the way to Pawling this morning. That way, even if we don't have a place to stay, we can spend the day in the city."

"You guys could probably stay at my place." It was the hiker with the cell phone again. We'd learned the night before that he lived in NYC, but was out for a few days of backpacking. "My girlfriend could let you in."

"Who *are* you?" I asked again.

The four of us hiked together four miles down the trail to the Mountain Top Market and ate gas station breakfast burritos while Erin tried one last time to reach her friend Chris G. While she was on the phone, I saw a flyer for a local cab company hanging on a cork board with a bunch of other advertisements. I snatched the flyer off the board and ran outside to tell Erin that my wish had come true and bumped into her running in to tell me that she had talked to Chris and we could stay the night with him.

Within 30 minutes, we were paying our cab driver and buying tickets for the train to Penn Station. E and I both had strong attachments to New York City. Erin, from her time living and working with her sister in the Bronx for a summer, and me, from the frequent weekend trips I spent exploring Manhattan during my two years as summer camp counselor in the Delaware Water Gap. As we rode South, we talked excitedly about the time I'd taken the bus from camp to visit her and several people had mistaken us for "real New Yorkers." If anyone thought twice about two dirty backpackers riding the train into the city, they didn't show it.

"You guys don't even stand-out," Chris G laughed, as he ushered us into a subway car headed up to Harlem. He told us about his work as a teacher and warned us that while he had plenty of room for us to stay, he also lived in a community with the priests who ran the school.

"Hey, as long as they don't make us sleep on cement, we're cool with the brothers," Erin said.

We dropped off our bags, took long showers, put on our cleanest clothes and took the train downtown. Chris and I teased Erin about her "town pants," the black leggings that were now sagging in the butt from her weight loss and constant wear.

"At least my pants don't zip into shorts," Erin fired back, pointing to my equally sagging, and very ugly, convertible hiking pants.

We walked around Times Square, were quickly overwhelmed, and ducked into an Irish Bar.

As we ordered our second beer, Erin blurted out, "So, dude. I think that guy Ben likes you."

"What are you talking about?" I stammered, taken aback. I was already flushed from the beers or I would have certainly reddened at her statement. I secretly liked thinking someone like Ben might like me, but I definitely didn't want anyone else to know that (even Erin, who I shared everything with).

"I don't know, I just got that vibe," she said, looking at me knowingly.

"Dude. Whatever. He's just flirty. He knows I'm with Kevin, so whatever," I said more dismissively than I felt.

Chris chimed in. "You said whatever twice."

"Yep, that totally means you like him," Erin piled on.

"WHAT... EVER," I mock-huffed. The conversation moved on but I blushed as I finished my beer and pulled the lip balm Ben had given me out of my pocket.

After the beers, Erin and I both confessed that what we really wanted was not a night out in the city, but a comfortable couch and a home cooked meal.

"I thought it would be fun to be here, but I just want to get back to the woods," I told Erin as we lay in bed that night, "but, like, after we get to sleep in these beds."

We got to Grand Central the next morning and found we had two hours until our train left. We passed the time eating (of course) and trying on clothes in Banana Republic.

"Oh my god, I'm a girl again!" Erin squealed from her dressing room.

"Oh my god, I'm a size 8!" I squealed back from mine.

CHAPTER THIRTY-SEVEN

DAY 92, 765.6 MILES TO KATAHDIN

We spent the end of May hiking through Connecticut and into Massachusetts. The weather was still mostly rainy, but we were also getting more and more peeks of sun throughout the days. The terrain was beautiful but very rocky, with all the ups and downs reminding me of the early days in North Carolina. At the end of the day, my body would be sore. Especially through Virginia, but in New York and New Jersey, too, hiking had stopped tiring me out. The fifty-one miles of trail through Connecticut was proving challenging, and that actually felt good. The hiking here was more technical—there were boulders to climb over, steep ascents and rocky descents, and what seemed like endless brooks to ford.

One morning, Erin and I were hiking along in silence. I had my head down watching for rocks (one thing that remained unchanged over the course of the hike was my clumsiness), when I almost ran into the back of Erin, who had stopped short. I looked up and saw why. In front of us was a raging river, with no bridge for crossing. The water directly in front of us was calf deep, but was moving very fast over a very slick and rocky bottom. About fifteen feet downstream was a small waterfall and there the water was much deeper and the rocks became boulders, making any slip in the shallower part potentially quite dangerous.

"Is there supposed to be a river crossing today?" Erin asked, as we both stood staring at the impossible puzzle in front of us.

I checked the guidebook and saw it listed this water as "Guinea Brook."

"They got a loose definition of brook," I said. "You think they want us to cross on that tree? There's no way. I mean, you fall off that and you could die."

To our right, about ten feet above the boulders and rushing deep water, was a fallen tree, stretching from one side of the "brook" to the other. This was not a log bridge flattened out by a trail crew. There was no safe way to walk upright over it.

Just as I was thinking, *"There is no way in hell,"* Erin announced, "I'm going to try it."

I watched in horror as Erin climbed, pack still on her back, up the base of the tree and straddled the log. She inched her way out over the water, repeating a frantic, "fuck, dude, fuck, dude." She slowly made her way across, while I stood on the ground, heart in my throat, fists clinched, joining in her "fuck, dude" chant. About halfway across, she started feeling a little more confident and sped her progress. I began to breathe normally too, when suddenly, her pack shifted, throwing her weight off balance and causing her to lurch sideways to the right. Instinctively, Erin's thighs tightened around the log, she lowered her torso, and her left hand flung out. As her body tipped perilously, her fingers found a branch stub to grasp. Pulling on the branch, she righted herself slowly and sat there for a minute, calming her rapid breathing.

"Fuck. DUDE," she said, and started inching again. When she'd teetered, my body had unconsciously collapsed into a ball and as Erin finally made it safely to the other bank and off the tree, I unwrapped my arms from around my knees and stood up, shaking out the tension.

"Well, there's no fucking way I'm doing that," I called across.

"Why not? Piece of cake," Erin's laugh was full of nervous energy.

I decided fording the shallower part was my only option. I took off my boots and socks and strapped them to the back of my pack. Crossing in boots might be safer, but my feet were still torn up from blisters, and walking in soaked boots for the next few days sounded almost worse than falling off the log. I walked as far upstream from the waterfall as I could, and slid down the bank. I plunged both feet in and sharply inhaled—the water was freezing and the current was strong. I used my hiking poles to find firm holds and tentatively made my way across. With only a few tense moments in between, I found myself at the other side. I threw my poles up onto the bank and just as I was pulling myself up onto the shore, I heard a splash. I turned quickly and saw that my boots and socks had slipped from my pack and were now caught, underwater, on a rock about three feet away. I said all the cuss words I knew, retrieved the now soaked boots and finally hauled myself up the bank.

"Jesus. It's not even 9am," Erin said as I sat down beside her.

Later that same day, we found See Blue at our designated meeting spot. He'd hiked in pizza and candy to the shelter for us. We cheered. Both for our pal and for the food. He told us about visiting his grandma and we told him about New York City. Erin and I talked over each other, describing our harrowing river crossing earlier that morning, an incident we were already describing as funny, rather than scary. I watched Blue's face turn dark.

"I don't like that you girls were alone," he said gruffly.

"What are you talking about? We're always alone out here," I said, sincerely confused.

"Yeah, but I would have come back to look for you."

Erin and I exchanged a look, not sure what had triggered this sudden bout of concern.

"We know, Blue," Erin said gently. "You're the best big brother."

The next day, May 29th, the three of us hiked the last bit of Connecticut, the trail running right through the picturesque town of Salisbury, and up Connecticut's Bear Mountain, which sits on the border with Massachusetts. We were getting a sense of New England—beautiful scenery, but also plenty of road crossings, which meant plenty of opportunities to go into town and eat.

"I definitely prefer this Bear Mountain," I said, as we sat, three across, on the rocky peak, eating lunch. "You guys! It's almost summer." For once, the sky was clear and we had an unbelievable view of the now lush green mountains and valley below. I looked at my two friends, happy that our little trio was together.

That night, we lay in our sleeping bags at the shelter, watching the last of the sunlight fade away, when we heard a commotion outside.

"Sweet n' Low? Not Yet?" A familiar voice called out our trail names.

Erin jumped out of her bunk, and peered around the corner.

"Nango! And Ben!" she exclaimed, hugging them one after the other. "I can't believe you guys are here!"

What followed was, as I wrote in my journal afterwards, "the craziest day ever."

CHAPTER THIRTY-EIGHT

DAY 96, MASSACHUSETTS, 675.4 MILES TO KATAHDIN

"What took you so long? We'd written you guys off!" I said, as way of a greeting.

Mike and Ben had only been 17 miles behind us after Trail Days. We'd tried to give them the chance to make up the mileage by doing shorter days and going into the city. Just earlier that night, Erin and I had decided that they probably weren't ever going to catch us, so we should start doing bigger miles again.

Mike and Ben had both gaped at me, exasperated.

"What are you talking about? We've been hiking 30 mile-days to catch up," Ben told me.

"We hiked 36 miles yesterday!" Mike looked at Ben, "This is the thanks we get?"

"Aww, come on, I'm happy you're here," I put my arm around Mike. If See Blue was our big brother, Mike was definitely the little brother. "But seriously... we've been hiking soooo slooowwww."

We decided that this reunion deserved a celebration in the form of massive amounts of food, so the next day we hiked a quick 8 miles to the road and got a hitch in a car with flames painted on its sides into Great Barrington, MA.

"Your flames match my flames!" Erin tried to joke with the driver, pointing to the matching flames on the arms of her sunglasses. She'd found them at a shelter in Pennsylvania and had been wearing them whenever it was sunny enough to warrant sunglasses. We'd taken to referring to them just as "the flames." You knew it was a good day when the flames were out.

"Yeah," the driver grunted, the only word he said during the 3-mile drive.

"Cool guy," Ben said plainly, as we stood on the curb outside of a Friendly's waving goodbye.

"I felt a connection," Erin agreed. "Maybe I'll take him to Cara's wedding."

Cara's wedding was coming up quickly and our plan was to get off the trail, wherever we were, on June 4th to spend a couple of days with her before the big event on June 7th. I was excited for the time off, and also because Kevin was flying from Florida on the 5th and staying for the weekend. Cara and Chris were getting married at a summer camp on Lake Winnipesaukee in New Hampshire. It was going to be a pretty casual weekend, with all the guests staying in the camper cabins, and since they had met hiking the AT, Cara told us to invite other thru-hikers to the festivities if we wanted. We'd already put out the offer to See Blue, Mike, and Ben (and a cute red-bearded hiker that we'd met one night at a shelter who understandably declined), and although Blue had agreed, the other two were non-committal. Four days off the trail was a lot, so we understood their hesitance, but we all knew that if they didn't come, these next few days would be the last we saw of them.

That day, though, we were just excited to all be together.

After we gorged on ice cream, we stood around the parking lot, not quite ready to get back on the trail.

"I saw a bowling alley just up the road. We could have a game and a beer before we get back on the trail," Ben suggested quietly.

I looked at Erin, who shrugged her agreement. At the beginning of the trail, Erin and I had been so rigid about making a plan and sticking with it. We'd been so worried about finishing "on time" that we were unwilling to take detours or unplanned stops. That was how we'd lost Mike in Virginia; he'd wanted to take a day off and that wasn't in our plans. Now, while we still had the drive to finish (well, Erin had the drive, and I was happy to be driven), those detours seemed increasingly necessary to keep us motivated.

The bowling alley was a perfect distraction. We took our time, bowling, drinking pitchers of beer, laughing at how bad Erin and I were, laughing at how weirdly good Ben and See Blue were.

"I love how we're acting like we have nowhere to be," I said to Ben, as we watched See Blue bowl another strike.

"I mean, we don't, really," he replied.

"Don't say that, I'll never leave," I told him, half serious.

But by the time we'd finished our game and our beer, we were all ready to go. We found an easy hitch back to the trailhead and right away, Erin and I fell behind the group. Erin was moving particularly slow and just as my frustration started to build, I noticed that her shoulders were shaking.

"Ernie? What's up?" I asked, using her childhood nickname.

She turned and I saw tears streaming down her face.

"My fucking knee," she said. She was angry and hurting. After weeks of minimal interference from the injury, the pain was back full force.

"We can stop right here, you know. If we lose those guys, we lose them. We have nowhere to be, really," I told her, echoing Ben's words from earlier.

"Thank you for saying that. But no, I think it just needs to warm up a little," she said firmly, as I figured, and hoped, she would. She fumbled around her pack for a few seconds, pulled out a bottle of Ibuprofen, took a handful, and started walking. No one was tougher than Erin.

We walked slowly at first and then a bit faster as the pain reliever kicked in. We'd hit a stride, and had even started laughing about a hiker with a bowling injury, when we came upon See Blue sitting on a stone wall, smoking.

"What? Did you hurt yourself bowling, too?" I said flippantly.

"Girls..." he started. His already scratchy voice broke, and I realized that he was holding back tears. "I'm going home."

"Blue, what? No. What do you mean?" Erin had her pack off in a second and was sitting on the wall beside him, arm on his shoulder. He told us, now openly sobbing, that he'd been thinking about it for days, that he hadn't been happy since he'd left Roxy after Trail Days and he just felt like his hike was over. We tried to talk him out of it, pointing out how close we were to the end.

"You've already gone 1500 miles, what's 700 more?" I was smiling, but tears were now streaming down my face, too. "What are we going to do without our big brother? What if Erin falls in a brook?"

"You girls are going to be fine. I feel like I can leave now, knowing that you'll be with Mike and Ben."

"You think they'd be any help if something happened?! They're idiots, too!" Erin cried, forgiving his paternalism, because, well, it was See Blue and we loved him.

But no matter what we said, it was clear that Blue was leaving. He'd always said that he didn't care if he made it to the end, that he'd know when his hike was done. Fifteen hundred miles was enough for him, he told us.

"Now, get out of here, you two, before I change my mind. I don't want you to lose those other idiots because you stood around here crying over me." We each hugged him one last time, told him we loved him, and that we wouldn't forget him, and then continued down the trail.

We hiked in silence, both shocked by what had just happened. I couldn't understand how Blue could think of quitting when we were so close to the end. I tried to put myself in his shoes, but I just couldn't. I had a boyfriend who I missed, too, but we'd been out here working towards something and I needed to finish that before I went back to my life at home. All I thought about, every day, was moving forward, taking one step closer to Maine, achieving this goal. If I left the trail now, I'd feel like the whole thing was for nothing.

I was just starting to say that to Erin when I got distracted by a hiker coming down the trail towards us.

"Doesn't that kinda look like..." I started.

"PILGRIM!" Erin finished.

CHAPTER THIRTY-NINE

DAY 97, MASSACHUSETTS, 653.7 MILES TO KATAHDIN

"How is this still even the same day?" Erin wondered aloud as we sat around a campfire with Mike, Ben, and Pilgrim early that evening. After an explosively loud initial reunion, we'd finally settled down to eat. I laughed at Erin's phrase, but I knew exactly what she meant. Still fresh from finding Mike and Ben the night before, we'd gone into town, bowled, Erin had hurt her knee, we'd lost See Blue, ran into Pilgrim, hiked 20 miles, and it was somehow still daylight.

"Brie?" Ben offered, and I started laughing.

"Why not? This day is so weird," I said, taking a small bit of this fancy, new (to me) cheese. Ben had hiked in a package of hard salami and a wheel of brie, which he'd heated over the fire so that it was warm and gooey, and was now offering them around like a fancy waiter.

"How'd you know where to find us?" Mike asked Pilgrim.

"I didn't. I didn't even know you guys were with Sweets and Not Yet."

After we'd said goodbye to Pilgrim and Sug in Harper's Ferry, they'd continued hiking North until Pilgrim had left the trail to go home for his college graduation from SUNY Gene-seo. Sug had kept hiking, and would be getting off the trail soon to go to a wedding the same weekend as we'd be going to Cara and Chris's wedding. Pilgrim got back on the trail the day before and saw a note Erin and I had written in the last shelter log, so knew he must be close. Unbeknownst to him, he'd passed us while we were in town, so when he got to the shelter he thought we'd be at, he'd turned around in hopes of finding Erin and I. Somehow, he'd missed Mike and Ben completely.

"If we hadn't been saying goodbye to Blue, you would have missed all of us," I said in wonder. "God! What a weird day!"

"I still can't believe See Blue is gone. I was so excited to see him again," Pilgrim lamented.

Mike raised his slice of salami, "To Blue."

"TO BLUE!" we repeated.

We stayed up late filling each other in on what had happened in the others' absence, everyone so genuinely in awe of the crazy set of circumstances that had brought us all back together again. Pilgrim had last seen Ben on a chance encounter in Blacksburg, Virginia, and Mike when he'd decided to stay behind at the hostel in Tennessee. It had been over 500 miles since Erin and I had last hiked with Pilgrim. And now here we all were, in the same shelter on the same day. We were missing See Blue and still needed Sug, but knew that if we were with Pilgrim, he'd be able to find us when he got back on the trail. I don't know who, but someone brought up the idea of trying to finish the rest of the trail together, and we all jumped on it. It was as if we'd all been thinking it (I'd actu-ally wished it out loud days earlier), but we were all so ingrained with the notion of "hike-your-own-hike" that no one had wanted to impose their schedule on anyone else. In the beginning, we never would have dreamed of changing our end date, but now we were all comparing notes and mileage and the days Erin and I needed to take off for the wedding—the boys were now thinking they may come after all—and trying to find a way to make it work for all of us. It felt good to finally admit that these friendships were important enough not to leave to chance reunions on the trail.

I had a happy glow, and a newfound love for brie cheese, as I rolled my sleeping bag out and pulled on the new warm socks that Kevin's mom had sent me. Ben sat down beside me.

"I brought this for you," he said, handing me the Kurt Vonnegut book, Sirens of Titan. I must have looked confused because he added, "You told me you only read crap books and so I thought I'd bring you something that wasn't crap. This isn't my favorite Vonnegut, but it's the one I found."

"I like reading crap," I said, taking the book from him and examining the cover, "but I guess I can give this 'literature' a try."

I felt Erin's gaze watching the exchange, but I didn't look at her.

"Shit, does this thing have aliens in it? Ugh," I said dramatically after I read the cover.

Ben laughed and then said simply, "Only read it if you want."

I rolled my eyes, but put the book in my bag anyway.

CHAPTER FORTY

DAY 98, MASSACHUSETTS, 653.7 MILES TO KATAHDIN

I f meeting up with Mike and Ben necessitated ice cream and bowling, then the chance encounter with Pilgrim and loss of See Blue required a full-on town party. Luckily, we would be walking close to Lee, MA the following day and they happened to have bars and hotels, the only two things that mattered. The 18-mile hike between the shelter and road into Lee flew. At one point during the hike, Erin took a huge tumble. I gasped, as I involuntarily did every time someone fell, stumbled, or stepped too close to a ledge. After a stunned silence, Erin jumped back up, yelled, "LEE, MASS!" and kept hiking. Such was the power of a hot shower and meal—it could make your legs move faster and injuries miraculously stop hurting.

Once in town, we all crowded into a small room at the Super 8, and proceeded to take turns making phone calls and showering. I called my dad to wish him and my stepmom happy birthday, and Kevin to relay all the craziness of the past two days and confirm his plans for coming to Cara and Chris's wedding.

"Whoa, it's only 5 days from now!" I told him.

"Yeah, but Sal..." he started.

"But what?" I asked, watching Erin emerge from the bathroom in her town clothes and throw her wet towel in my direction, mouthing "You're up."

"Ah... nothing, I'm excited to see you."

"Yeah, me too," I told him, quickly getting off the phone before someone else stole my turn in the shower.

"I think it's going to rain tomorrow," I heard Ben say from his position stretched out on the floor in front of the TV as I headed into the bathroom. He'd tuned into the Weather Channel, and had finally caught the local forecast.

"We should probably take a zero day tomorrow. It looks really bad," Pilgrim chimed in from one of the beds.

"Storm of the century, I'd say," Ben quipped back.

The rest of us just kind of laughed because if we took a day off every time it rained, we'd still be in Georgia. While town stops were frequent, full days off were very rare for us. The last, and only, unplanned zero day Erin and I took was exactly two months earlier when we'd woken up to snow in Damascus.

Because we'd showered first, Erin and I now lay side-by-side on a bed and watched as Ben helped Mike blow-dry his mohawk into place. He'd had another hiker cut it a few weeks earlier. I listened, contentedly, as Pilgrim narrated the undertaking. Suddenly, Erin elbowed me.

"Stop it!" she said sharply. I'd started to move back the covers and she put out a hand to prevent me from burrowing underneath. "Dude, I know you. I know if you get under those covers you're not leaving this hotel room. So, sit up and get your mother fucking game face on."

"But what if I just closed my eyes for like 5 minutes?"

"That's what you've said at every sleepover we've had since we were in seventh grade and I'm not falling for it this time."

Erin had history on her side. I was notorious for falling asleep at the beginning of a movie, leaving her to watch the whole thing by herself, or sneaking off during parties to "rest my eyes," leaving Erin to wonder where I'd gone.

"Fine," I said, sitting up straight, and shooting her my meanest look, "but let's get out of here."

Erin hustled everyone out the door and we walked to the nearest bar that didn't card (Mike was not yet 21) and set to the task of getting really and truly drunk. Our mission was a rousing success and we shut the bar down, but not before Erin had commandeered the jukebox and bullied the guys into a dance party, we'd played a million rounds of very bad pool, Pilgrim and I'd almost been kicked out for swapping shirts in the middle of the bar (we thought it'd be funny to see him wearing my tank top and thought nothing of me undressing to my very unsexy sports bra in public), and making friends with and then consoling a very drunk, crying middle-aged woman named Robin whose boyfriend had just broken up with her.

We all stumbled back to the hotel, Erin trying to relieve her drunkenness by telling herself out loud, "1, 2, 3... SOBER" over and over.

"How's that working?" Mike asked.

"How's your dumb mohawk working?" Erin slurred.

The seed Ben had planted earlier about the "storm of the century" was now fully blossoming in my mind, thinking how wonderful it would be to sleep in (and sleep off this inevitable hangover). I linked my arm through Ben's and told him conspiratorially, "Let's make this zero day happen."

He laughed and we fell into an easy conversation. While the others wandered off--Erin and Mike to watch our newest obsession, "Doggy Fizzle Televizzle," an improbably hilarious MTV show starring Snoop Dogg, and Pilgrim to find snacks— Ben and I sat on a transformer outside of the hotel. At one point, he asked me what Kevin was like, and I tried to picture him.

"I don't know, he's really nice, and fun, and just, like, a real dude," I said, and then laughed, trying to imagine Kevin and Ben hanging out. "You'd probably hate him."

"What? No. If you like him, I'm sure he's great."

"What about you? What was your girlfriend like?" I asked, referring to the woman he'd been supposed to move to Chicago with before they broke up over the phone earlier in his hike.

"She's nice, she was just in a bad place in her life. It wouldn't have worked out," he paused and laughed. "You'd DEFINITELY hate her."

"So, what are you looking for? Like, what's your kind of girl?" I asked, emboldened by a bucket of beers.

Ben looked out, thinking for a minute and then said, very matter-of-factly, "You. You're my kind of girl."

I sat still, suddenly at a loss for words. Ben playfully punched my shoulder, and said, "Not like, 'you' you. Don't be weird. But someone like you."

"So, like someone who is gorgeous and brilliant?"

"I meant more someone who is a total shithead."

"You obviously have excellent taste," I said, hoping we were back on safe ground.

Soon after, Pilgrim found us, having struck out on finding anything open for snacks, and Ben told us he was going to go to bed.

"Do you want to go in, too?" Pilgrim asked.

I was feeling unsettled after talking to Ben, not uncomfortable, but unsure about what to make of his comment.

"Nah," I said, "let's go on a snack adventure. I refuse to believe there is nowhere open."

Pilgrim and I wandered the streets of Lee for another hour,

laughing together like little kids, finally finding a big 24-hour gas station on the edge of town.

"So much flair!" Pilgrim marveled. He'd been collecting trail flair in every state—small items he'd incorporate into his gear, like a NASCAR radio in Tennessee, a trucker hat from Georgia, and gas station aviator sunglasses in Virginia.

I laid out a plan where we'd each pick out one piece of flair for the other but we both had to promise to keep it in our packs until the end of the trail. We searched the aisles, picking up and discarding items, until we finally approached the register together, Pilgrim picking out a giant pair of fuzzy dice for me, and me finding a hideous bobble head dog for him.

We burst back into the hotel room with our newfound flair and gas station snacks to find the TV on, but Mike, Ben, and Erin fast asleep.

"Oh shit, it's 4:30am!" I whispered.

"Shit!" Pilgrim groaned.

"1, 2, 3... shut up and go to sleep," Erin mumbled, her face in the pillow.

CHAPTER FORTY-ONE

DAY 99, MASSACHUSETTS, 637.5 MILES TO KATAHDIN

The next morning was a slog for everyone. Mike seemed the most anxious to get back out on the trail, but the rest of us were dragging our feet (Pilgrim literally refusing to get out of bed). The "storm of the century" I'd hoped for as an excuse to take a zero day hadn't developed, which didn't stop me from looking out at the gray, but dry, skies and announcing repeatedly that it looked like rain to me. We dallied so long, watching more Snoop Dogg and catching the end of Shawshank Redemption for the second day in a row, that Erin had to call the front desk to ask for a late check out.

Finally, as the late check out time approached, and we still hadn't come to a consensus, Ben said, "Alright, I'm making the call. I'm hungover and we're not hiking today." He picked up the phone, asked for another night, and lay back down on the ground.

Mike looked annoyed but didn't protest, while I think Pilgrim, Erin, and I were all relieved that we didn't have to make the choice not to hike. Half of the day already gone, we wasted the rest of it eating, doing laundry, bowling (again), watching TV, and eating (again). I watched Ben throughout the day to see if I could detect any weirdness after our conversation the night before, but he seemed normal, not ignoring me, but not paying me more attention than anyone else. I decided to chalk it up to drunkenness all around and forget it, but every so often him saying, "you're my kind of girl" would pop in my head, and I'd get a tiny jolt of something that was equal parts awkwardness and excitement.

We left Lee late the next morning and hiked, sun shining, mocking my storm predictions, 19 miles into Dalton, MA. The hiking was boring but easy, and when we were finished, I realized I hadn't noticed one thing about the trail that day, other than the warmth of the sun. The day off the trail had left everyone renewed, and we all walked together, chatting about music that came on Pilgrim's NASCAR radio, but Erin seemed a little quiet. She'd talked to Cara that morning, who told her that a few of her friends were around and going to get tattoos and drinks the next day as sort of a mini bachelorette party. Erin confessed she was feeling guilty and sad to be missing out on pre-wedding preparation. It was June 2nd and we weren't supposed to get off the trail for two more days.

Besides Erin, the rest of us were excited when we arrived that afternoon on Tom Levardi's doorstep. Tom Levardi was a trail legend who had been hosting hikers for over 15 years. We knew from the trail books that if we stopped at Tom's, he'd have some sort of treat. Sure enough, within ten minutes of our arrival, we were all seated on his porch, eating ice cream sundaes. After our Snoop Dog marathon of the past two days, we'd started speaking in his signature "fo shizzle" language, and the boys were busy renaming each other, so Ben became Benizzle and Pilgrim, Pilgrizzle (which became Grizzle and then eventually, the Griz). Erin leaned over and touched my arm.

"I think I need to get off the trail earlier than we planned. I can't miss Cara's bachelorette party. I just really think I need to be there," she looked close to tears. "You can come up later, but I need to go, like, today. I'm going to call and see if Chris can come get me."

I looked at the boys, knowing this would be another chance for us to lose each other, but also knowing that I'd get nowhere without Erin.

"Dude. No, if you're going, I'm going," I told her, resolutely.

Mike, Ben, and Pilgrim were understanding, they'd seen how sad Erin had been that morning after talking to Cara. Pilgrim assured Erin that if someone could pick them up in a few days, they'd still come to the wedding, and Ben told us that we'd worked this hard to all find each other, so we could figure it out how to do it again after the wedding. Mike gave us both a hug and told us that we couldn't shake him that easily a second time.

Erin looked so happy and relieved when she got off the phone. "Chris is coming to pick us up! It's like 3 hours away but he was just like, 'yep, I'm on my way.' He didn't tell Cara, it's going to be a surprise."

"Holy shit, she's going to fucking die!" I said, getting caught in the excitement.

When we got to their apartment in Dover, New Hampshire later that night, seeing Cara's reaction (she did, totally, fucking die) made any misgivings about being off the trail for so long disappear. Cara was so touched and happy to have her little sister there to help with preparations and celebrate her wedding, that I wondered why we hadn't planned for this in the first place.

* * *

The days leading up to the wedding felt surreal. Erin and I had each mailed a box of wedding and town clothes to Cara before the trail and so not only were we not hiking, but we were walking around town looking like normal women. I felt like I was playing dress-up instead of back to my regular self; so much had changed since I'd last worn those clothes. I was at least 25 pounds lighter, making everything fit differently, yes, but mostly I felt like a different person than the one who'd packed this box. That person had been isolated, and anxious, and unsure of the future, and now I felt strong, happy, and confident. I couldn't put my finger on when the change had happened, and I wondered if Kevin would see it when he arrived.

The first full day we were there, Cara, her friend Amy, Chris's sister Michelle, Erin, and I went to a tattoo parlor and everyone, except me, got tattoos of the wild woman petroglyph that Erin and Cara's mom often used in her artwork. At the beginning of our hike, Cathy had mailed Erin and I each a drawing of the stick figure woman with wild hair, describing it as a "wild woman: \noun: sister, mother, daughter, granddaughter, married, single, natural, living, instinctual, endangered, friendly, untamed, playful, fierce, inquisitive, artistic, intellectual, spirited, nurturing, unconquerable, universal."

I loved this symbol, but I already had two horrible impulsive tattoos and promised myself I would only do it again with A LOT of forethought (I'd get the wild woman tattooed above my tribal sun and Chinese dragon lower back tattoos five years later). Afterwards we all went for drinks and Cara asked Erin and I how we were feeling.

"I remember how hard it was to get in and out of that trail bubble. You start to not feel normal anywhere but in the woods. It'll be like that for a long time," she told us. I knew she still felt this way after her hike thru-hike four years ago.

"It's nice to be with people who understand," I told her. "And honestly, it's nice to be surrounded by women for a change. We're hiking with really good dudes, but they're still dudes."

"Uhhh, yeah, I definitely remember that, too," she laughed. "So, I remember you guys talking about Mike from the beginning, and I know Pilgrim from Perrysburg but I'm excited to meet Ben, Erin says he's cool. And cute."

I felt that tiny spark and "you're my kind of girl," popped in my head. I hadn't told Erin, or anyone, about that night in Lee, and I wondered what Erin had told Cara about Ben.

"Yeah, I'm hoping Kevin will go pick them all up on Friday," I told her, hoping to change the conversation. "So, what's left to do tomorrow?"

CHAPTER FORTY-TWO

DAY 101, NEW HAMPSHIRE, CARA'S WEDDING

On the 4th, we worked on wedding favors and packing up decorations, and Cara took Erin and I to a local thrift store where we picked out ridiculous wedding outfits for the boys. Weeks ago, Erin and I had talked about what a fantasy date would be and one thing we'd come up with is going with our dates to a thrift store, where we'd pick out ridiculous clothes for each other that we'd then have to spend the day in. This was our one-sided way of living that fantasy. I'd talked to Kevin, who'd agreed to go with me to pick Mike, Ben, and Pilgrim up in his rental car on the 6th, and to the boys, who'd stuck around Tom Levardi's house after Mike had collapsed face down in his cereal bowl from what we later learned was Lyme's disease (although at the time we joked that it was SARS, the flu-like disease that had sent the country into a face-mask wearing panic). They were going to hike out of Dalton on June 5th and we'd pick them up in North Adams, MA, near the Vermont border, the following day.

On the 5th, we packed up Cara's Subaru and drove up to a small summer camp near Lake Winnipesaukee where the wedding would be held. After unloading the decorations into the dining hall, Cara told Erin and I that she had a surprise for us, that the three of us were going into town to get pedicures. Erin and I looked at each other and I started crying.

"It's. Just. So. Awesome," I managed when we all had our feet soaking in bubbly water, feeling so honored to be included and so grateful for the pampering. The woman doing my toenails pretended not to be horrified that I was missing one nail completely, and that three others were black.

"Yeah, I haven't been touched this much in months," Erin said. "Is it weird to fall in love with your pedicurist?"

We arrived back at camp and I heard someone call out my real name, not my trail name. I turned and saw Kevin striding over. I let out a breath that I hadn't known I'd been holding, and ran over to greet him.

We hugged for a long time, and then kissed, and then he finally said, "Hey darlin', let's go somewhere and talk."

I took him to the porch of the cabin that I'd reserved for just him and I, and after a little small talk about his trip, we sat side by side in silence.

He finally spoke, and said, with a cracking voice, "I think we should break up."

I was so shocked that I wasn't sure what to say. I immediately said, "What? Why?" even though in my head, a little voice said, "He's right."

"It's too hard, your being gone. We hardly talk, and when we do, you're distracted, or I'm distracted, or you're talking about people and places I don't know. I know this is temporary, but what's going to happen when you're done? You're going to move to Ohio to go to law school, and I just quit my job and move there?" His words tumbled out of this mouth quickly, making it hard for me to follow.

"Is that what you want? To break up?" I asked, thinking

how easy it would be if he said yes and that was it, but then also thinking about how long we'd been together, and how much we'd been through, and how, after the trail, we were supposed to get engaged, and also, what the fuck, I'd only applied to law schools in Ohio because he'd wanted to be closer to his family in Indiana.

"No," he said quietly, "I just hate how things are right now."

Oh, I thought, *he doesn't want to break up, he just wanted to get my attention.* I felt bad for him in that moment, because I could see the toll that my being away was taking on him, but I also felt resentment building for saying something that he didn't mean, for blindsiding me with it, and for making me feel guilty, once again, for leaving to hike the trail.

"Okay," I said, measuring my words. "I get that."

"Well... what do you want?" He asked, eventually. Silent tears streamed down both of our faces.

I took a deep breath, and looked at him. I wasn't sure what I wanted. It honestly hadn't occurred to me to think about it; our relationship had always felt so inevitable and comfortable. I'd viewed it as something permanent, and I'd felt grateful for that for a long time. We'd been together for over two years, had made it through a year of living long distance, and months of living together. I was a part of his family, and before I'd left for the trail, we'd talked about getting engaged at the end of it. But now, something had shifted and we were no longer solid, and I knew it was because of me.

I answered, "I... I just want us to have fun this weekend. This is one of my dearest friend's weddings and you're here and I love you and I just want us to have fun. Let's think about the future later, okay?"

"Okay," he answered, holding my hand in his, "We can do that."

And we did. For the rest of that day, as we helped set up for the weekend's events, we fell back into our comfortable rhythm. Kevin was nice and helpful and hardworking and it made me happy to see how easily he got along with everyone. I could see that he was really trying and it made me want to try, too.

"He's so nice," Cara said, as we watched him haul yet another cooler of beer to the barn where the reception would be held.

"Yeah, he really is," I said, and gave him a little wolf whistle and a wink as he passed by.

CHAPTER FORTY-THREE

DAY 103, NEW HAMPSHIRE, CARA'S WEDDING

The tension returned, full-force, the next morning on our drive down to North Adams to pick up the boys.

"What's wrong?" I asked, for the third time.

"I just don't understand why we're spending one of the three days we have together in a car to pick up a bunch of dudes who don't even know Cara and Chris," he said.

"You said you didn't mind," I retorted.

"You didn't really give me the option," he spat back.

Of course, the disagreement wasn't over the drive. We were both avoiding talking about our relationship, but it was right below the surface. And it didn't help that we were making this effort to pick up three guys that I'd been spending so much time with, at a time when my boyfriend and I felt so much distance from each other.

"I'm sorry," I said, again, covering his hand with mine. "I appreciate you doing this."

He gave my hand a little squeeze, and drawled, "You better."

We met up with Pilgrim, Ben, and Mike at the outfitters in

North Adams, where I was picking up a new pair of hiking shoes. The LL Bean boots that Kevin had bought me to start the trail had finally worn through. They'd lasted me over 1500 miles, but had also left me with horrible blisters that I still dealt with every day. Instead of boots, my new shoes were trail runners, and just walking around the store, I already felt lighter and faster. As I waited at the register, I heard Pilgrim call out, "Not Yet, look who's here!" and turned to see Lucky and Sparrow, the couple we'd last seen at Mountain Moma's outside of the Smoky Mountains.

"What are you guys doing here?" I said as I embraced them both, amazed again by the magic of the trail, that always seemed to lead people back around to each other. They told us they were hiking random sections, skipping around a bit. As we caught up, I noticed Kevin, standing off to the side, holding my shoe box, looking defeated.

Back in the car, the boys made a real effort to get to know Kevin, and to my surprise and embarrassment, Kevin, who just the night before had been so kind and easy going, was reserved to the point of being rude. They told us stories about Tom Levardi (who they'd dubbed Tom Levardi the One Man Party) catching Mike as he passed out from SARS, and of the town fair where they'd won a goldfish and a Justin Timberlake poster. Kevin barely reacted. Pilgrim, who'd met Kevin when he'd visited me in Tennessee, asked questions about his work and family and Kevin gave one or two word responses. Eventually, they stopped trying to include Kevin and lapsed into trail talk.

After what seemed like an eternity, we made it back to camp. The boys jumped out of the car, shooting me sympathetic looks, and ran to find Erin.

I turned on Kevin, "What the fuck was that? Why were you rude to my friends?"

"Why would he know your birthday?" Kevin demanded.

"What?" I asked, genuinely confused.

"Why would Steve, or Pilgrim, or whatever his name is, know your birthday?" he asked again.

I realized Kevin was talking about a random conversation we'd had after he'd gone silent in the car, where Pilgrim had guessed my email password because he knew my birthday and middle name.

Frustrated, my voice rose, "Because we're friends! Because we've spent 24 hours a day together for months and there's only so much to talk about! Why the fuck does it matter?"

"You like him. I know you do. I saw how you guys were in the car. Is something going on?" I could see he was close to tears again.

"You're so off base," I told him, trying to soften my voice. "We're friends."

"Really?" he asked, his eyes pleading for me to say yes.

"Yes, really," I hugged him tight. I could feel how tense he was. "We should get a beer, right?"

"Oh god yes," he said, still holding on to me. "Sally... I'm sorry."

"Me, too," I whispered into his shoulder.

* * *

The next time I saw the boys was at the welcome cookout later that night. They'd showered and were busy talking to Erin's 85 year-old grandma, who was carrying a handle of gin and a pack of Virginia Slims. Erin came up and hugged me, which I knew meant that the boys had told her about the disastrous car ride.

"What's up with Grandma Clark?" I asked.

"Dude, she brought her own gin. She said she couldn't trust that Cara would have some here and she obviously couldn't go a few hours without. The dudes are calling her the Don," she laughed, and then, when Kevin left to find us drinks, in a low voice asked, "You guys, okay?"

"For this minute, I think?" I told her, not sure what was the truth.

"If you want to talk..." Erin started.

"Maybe later. You have enough going on," I told her. "In fact, I think you're up."

Erin's brother, Brian, was frantically motioning her over. She gave me another quick squeeze and walked away. Five minutes later, everyone was laughing as Erin and Brian gave a touching, hilarious toast that ended with them singing Sea of Love, complete with choreographed hand motions.

* * *

Kevin and I were busy the next morning, helping set up chairs for the outdoor ceremony and putting up decorations in the barn, and then getting ready ourselves. While Kevin showered, I walked over to the cabin where the other hikers were staying. A chorus of, "Not Yet!" came as I opened the cabin door, and I was greeted by Mike, Ben, and Pilgrim dressed in the thrift store clothes we'd bought a few days earlier. We'd picked out a bunch of options, and I wasn't sure what they'd choose, or if they'd even wear them at all. But here they were, looking so perfect and ridiculous that I had to stop and catch my breath from laughing before I could speak.

"You guys," I gasped. "You guys look amazing."

Mike wore black pants with suspenders and a pinstripe blazer over a red mesh tank top, that somehow perfectly complimented his mohawk and Pilgrim's aviator sunglasses. Pilgrim had chosen a 70's floral button down, purple pants, a cream blazer and a Panama hat. Ben had slicked back his long curly hair and wore dark sunglasses, a matching peach blazer and button down, and brown polyester pants.

"Did Erin help you?" I asked.

"What!? I'm insulted. This was all us," Ben told me, and I felt such a deep gratitude that we'd found friends who were willing to embarrass themselves in front of strangers just to play along with our silly ideas.

"Be honest, is Cara going to be mad that we are basically dressed as clowns at her wedding?" Pilgrim asked, and I was grateful again, now for his sensitivity.

"Yeah, we don't want to be a distraction," Mike added.

"Are you kidding? Cara helped us pick this stuff out. You guys are going to be a hit."

*   *   *

A hit was an understatement. Other than the bride and groom, the boys were the life of the party. They danced with all the old ladies, took pictures with almost every guest, and just generally injected fun into an already joyful event.

Early in the evening, Chris grabbed Erin and I from the dance floor, where we'd been stationed since the bluegrass band had started to play, saying, "We're going to take an AT hiker picture."

Outside, we found the boys, but also Cara, Chris, and the crew that they had hiked the AT with, including a man who'd acted as their wedding officiant. It struck me that even though we didn't all know each other, even though we were hiking years apart, we were all connected, and all part of the same community.

Kevin was there, too, standing off to the side, watching. We'd been so busy that day that we hadn't had the chance to talk about things. Earlier, as Cara walked down the aisle, radiant in her simple white gown, carrying a wildflower bouquet, Kevin had squeezed my hand and I'd leaned into him. I'd looked at him then, my eyes filled with happy tears, and tried to picture the two of us in Cara and Chris's place, but the picture wouldn't come into focus. He'd looked down at me, too, and I thought he might be trying to see the same thing.

As the night wore on, I could feel Kevin's patience with me wearing thin. It was understandable, our two-and-a-half-year relationship was faltering and all I wanted to do was hang out with my friends. I resented that he couldn't just be happy and nice. I was avoiding being alone with him because I didn't want to hash through everything, and he started to catch on. He grew shorter and more sarcastic with me, making jokes at my expense in front of other people. By the time we sat around the campfire at the post-reception sing-along, we were barely speaking. Pilgrim came and sat down next to us and asked if either of us needed a drink.

"I think she's fine, dude," Kevin answered for me.

"Oh shit, Not Yet, did you lose your voice?" Pilgrim said with a wide smile, raising his eyebrows at me.

"I guess so," I said, giving him a little shrug.

"I'm going to bed," Kevin announced suddenly, getting up. He looked down at me, "Are you coming?"

"In a minute, I'm going to say goodnight to Cara," I said. I noticed Ben and Erin sitting together across the circle, Ben strumming a guitar, both watching the whole exchange.

"Of course," Kevin muttered, and walked away.

We watched him walk for a few beats and then Pilgrim spoke, "Wow, I'm sorry, I hope I didn't make that worse."

I shook my head, and then grinned at Pilgrim, "He thinks something is going on between us."

Pilgrim let out a short burst of laughter, which made me laugh, which set us both off for a full minute.

I finally said my goodbyes, assuring everyone that I was fine, and made my way to the cabin. Kevin was sitting on the porch, waiting for me.

"I'm sorry," he said.

"Yeah, me too," I said.

We stayed up late, talking in circles, neither of us quite saying what we wanted, not quite willing to end things for good, until we both fell asleep.

The next morning, we lay side-by-side on two bunk bed mattresses we'd placed on the floor, quiet, holding hands, until he had to leave to get to the airport. I walked him to his car, he got in the driver's seat and then looked up at me. "This isn't going to work, you know."

"Yeah, I know," I said. I couldn't tell if he was trying to get my attention again, or if he really meant it. Either way, I felt tired and done. "Do you want me to call you?"

"I don't know. Maybe not," he put the keys in the ignition and started the car. "I've got to go."

I leaned down and kissed him goodbye and then shut his car door.

As he drove away, I felt a wave of relief wash over me. There were still things to figure out, after all, we'd been building a life together—we had a cat and an apartment and friends and family to tell—but that goodbye felt like THE goodbye, and I found that in the moment I wasn't sad. It was like I was closing the door on a different person's life, one that I had fond, but distant memories of, but that wasn't mine anymore.

Erin ran over, "Dude, what happened?"

"I think we broke up?" I said, not sure if that was exactly right, but sure that it was what had happened for me. Her eyes went wide with surprise, but I smiled, "I'm good. I am actually really good."

We chatted happily as we walked over, hand in hand, to

where the boys were playing basketball, Erin telling me about her failed quest to make out with one of the guys in the blue-grass band the night before. Everyone paused as we approached, so I blurted out, "Well, that sucked and now I'm ready to play ball." Ben nodded, and passed me the basketball.

We spent the rest of the day at camp, playing any sport we could find and canoeing (Pilgrim making everyone laugh when he emerged from the cabin wearing only my bikini bottoms). After I told Ben I'd always wanted to learn to play the guitar, we sat together on his bunk bed while he tried to teach me how to play a few chords, even writing down the finger placements so I could practice. Finally, we joined everyone left at camp around a campfire, where we ate s'mores and sang songs while people played guitars, banjos, and mandolins. I looked around, feeling warm and content, and realized that I hadn't thought about Kevin all day.

I said as much to Erin, "Is that awful?"

"Can I be honest with you? You know I love Kevin, but you guys are different people. And I think you've known that for a long time. You just got the space to move on out here," Erin answered.

"Do you think I've changed that much?" I asked.

"No, I think you're just finally being 100% yourself and not apologizing for it."

"Dude, fuck, that was deep," I joked. Then sincerely, "Thank you for that. He is a good guy, you know. And we were together for a long time."

Erin nodded, "I know. But that doesn't mean you have to marry him."

CHAPTER FORTY-FOUR

DAY 106, MASSACHUSETTS, 609.8 MILES TO KATAHDIN

By the time we got back on the trail, we hadn't hiked in five full days. We'd said goodbye to the boys that morning. They were 20 miles ahead of us on the trail, but they promised to hike slowly to let us catch up. As Erin and I got back into Cara's car, she asked, "Okay, so Dalton? Or somewhere else?"

We knew that she was asking whether we wanted to get back on the trail where we'd gotten off, or if we wanted to skip some miles to put us closer to our friends. While our goal was always to stick to the trail, Erin and I were okay with the occasional blue blaze if one of us was feeling bad or injured or just plain "done." Mike, Ben, and Pilgrim were pretty strict about hitting every white blaze, and as far as I knew, hadn't missed a mile of the trail. Cara was proposing dropping us off ten trail miles ahead of where we'd left the trail, which was far beyond anything we'd done before. It felt like a heavy decision.

Erin looked at me, "I'm game, but I'll do whatever you want."

I thought about how we'd all just vowed to finish the trail together, how these guys felt like our family and the prospect of hiking without them made the trail seem dull and depressing, how 20 miles didn't seem like much but would be really hard to make up, especially as the trail was going to get infinitely harder as we approached Vermont and New Hampshire, and then that tiny jolt and *'you're my kind of girl'* popped in my head.

"Okay, let's do it."

The fog was thick in the mountains, which made the hiking slow, and we didn't arrive at the Wilbur Clearing Lean-to, a few miles beyond the peak of Mt. Greylock, until after dark. We quietly pulled off our packs and were trying to get dinner out without disturbing the other hikers, some already in their sleeping bags.

From the dark shelter we heard, "Sweets! Not Yet!" and saw Turbo peak his head out.

"Turbo!" we both yell-whispered.

"So, what's it, like, what are you guys doing here? How did I get ahead? Are you going backwards? Am I going back-wards?" Turbo asked, and we laughed at his familiar word jumble.

"Oh my god, you guys are Sweet n' Low and Not Yet?" an unfamiliar female voice called from inside the lean-to. "We've been, like, following your shelter entries for weeks, it's like meeting celebrities."

The girl introduced herself as Peaches and her friend as Crumble (although Erin and I could never remember that, so we just referred to them as Peaches and Cream). They were section hiking the second half of the AT and had met up with Turbo a few weeks earlier. It became apparent that Turbo had a huge crush on Peaches, and he had been walking at their pace in hopes of hooking up. A few of the other hikers in shelter introduced themselves—one was Fiver, another was maybe Fixie—all thru-hikers that we'd never met because we'd kept so far ahead of the pack before getting off the trail for the wedding.

As we hiked together the next day, I whined to Erin, "I don't want to meet new people, I don't want to hike with Peaches and Cream. I'm sure they're fine but... I don't want to."

"Yeah," Erin agreed, "No new people. Unless he's hot."

Despite my childish rant, I had nothing against any of the other thru-hikers, but after three and a half months, the trail had become more than just the physical rock, roots, trees, and mountains; the trail was our people and our rhythm. Being around a new group, who had their own inside jokes and rhythms, felt like we were intruding on someone else's hike.

In an attempt to outpace the new pack and catch up with the boys, we'd decided to hike thirty-two miles to where we thought Pilgrim, Mike, and Ben might be stopping for the night. When we started out that morning, we were seven miles from the Vermont border and we were both excited to be back on familiar ground. The Long Trail and AT run together for about 100 miles, before the Long Trail continues North to the Canadian border and the AT turns East for New Hampshire. When we'd hiked these same miles two years earlier with Cara, I'd been so out of my depth, physically and mentally, and I thought it'd be a good gauge of how strong I was now.

"Oh my god! Remember this bridge?" Erin exclaimed, as we came upon a suspension bridge right after crossing into Vermont.

"Yes, do you remember how scared I was? I waited until everyone was on the other side and then I ran across?"

"You want to run across this time too, don't you?"

"YOU KNOW I DO!"

We were so busy reliving our Long Trail memories, that we'd hiked over 24 miles by 3pm. We walked up to a shelter to take a break and have a snack before pressing on for the last 8 miles of the day, but instead of an empty shelter we found Mike, Ben, and Pilgrim there, packs off, done for the day.

"Dudes!" Erin yelled.

"Dudes!" Pilgrim echoed.

"How are you here?" Erin asked.

"How are YOU here?" Pilgrim echoed.

It turned out that they'd been held up because "SARS-Boy" as Mike was now dubbed, had fallen on the trail earlier, so they'd decided to quit for the day. He assured us that he was fine, but he didn't really look fine.

"That tick did us a favor, you on death's door is the only way we'll be able to keep up with you. Plus, Erin used to be a nurse's aide so she can take care of you," I told Mike.

"Unless you need me to wipe your ass, I'm not going to be much help," Erin told him.

CHAPTER FORTY-FIVE

DAY 108, VERMONT, 576 MILES TO KATAHDIN

Mike seemed fine the next morning, so we left early and were instantly rewarded with gorgeous mountain views from Little Pond Lookout.

"Remember when we saw all those camp kids who hated their counselors up on this peak?" I asked Erin, reminiscing again about our Long Trail hike.

"Not really," Erin answered, irritated.

"Uh, okay," I mumbled.

An hour later, Erin turned off the trail onto a side trail accidentally. I pointed it out to her and she snapped at me again. We walked for another 20 minutes and saw a shelter up ahead, where the boys had stopped for a break. I was just suggesting that we take a break, too, when Erin stopped in the middle of the trail.

"Dude," I said, "you okay?"

"Shit," she said, squinting her eyes to look at me, "I think I'm high. Can you check my pump? I can't see very well."

I raised up her sweaty shirt and found the end of her insulin pump tubing disconnected from the site on her hip. She pulled out her glucose meter, lancet, and test strips, and despite having tested her blood sugar a million times, she was struggling to make it all work. She finally got the blood on the test strip and the test strip in the meter and we both waited, anxious for the glucometer to beep and give us her blood sugar number.

"What does it say?" she asked when it registered, and I knew if she couldn't see well enough to read it, it was really bad. The screen just read "HIGH."

"What does that mean?" I asked.

"Oh fuck," she answered. "Dude. Fuck."

"HIGH" meant that her blood sugar was above 500. Once blood sugar gets that high, there is not much you can do other than start insulin and wait out the symptoms. If we'd been in a town, a blood sugar above 500 would have prompted an ER visit for IV fluids. Blood sugar above 600 can lead to coma or death.

I walked Erin over to the shelter and she laid down. "Ummm... I don't think I can hike anymore today. You guys can go ahead."

The guys all looked at me, worried, and I shrugged my shoulders but returned their worried looks.

"Sweets," Ben said, "we're with you. If you need to stay at this shelter, we're going to stay at this shelter."

"It's not even lunch time," Erin moaned, her arm covering her eyes, her speech slow. "It's too early to stop."

Pilgrim pulled the Justin Timberlake poster they'd won at the Dalton town fair out of his bag, ripped a piece of duct tape off the outside of his Nalgene bottle and hung the poster in the shelter.

"Timbo says we stay, Sweets," Pilgrim told her.

"I think he's looking at me," I said.

Eyes still closed, Erin mumbled, "No, he's definitely looking at me."

We passed the time playing cards and listening to NASCAR radio. Hikers walked through, including the crew we'd met the few nights earlier, and admired our set up. Turbo hung out a bit, excited to catch up with the boys, and then ran down the trail after Peaches. Gradually, Erin was able to sit up, and said the fog was clearing a little. After lunch, Ben sat on a log at the fire circle set away from the shelter, reading a book. I walked over and sat down next to him.

"Thanks for sticking around," I said.

"You were right," Ben said, "I did hate your boyfriend."

"Ahhh, I feel bad. I'm sorry he was being a shit to you guys, but you caught him in a bad situation. He's usually very nice," I said, feeling a little defensive.

"If you say so. Look, I didn't care that he wasn't nice to me, but I hated how he was treating you," Ben said, quietly.

"Oh."

"So... did you guys break up?" Ben asked, his knee accidentally brushing up against mine.

"I think so," I said, keeping my leg in place, acutely feeling the points where we were touching.

"But you're not totally sure," he said, moving his leg away, in a movement that was reflexive but felt like a rejection.

"Well, *I'm* sure... there just wasn't an official pronouncement." I put my hand between us.

He glanced at my hand and kept his in his lap. He gave me a wry smile. "Well, I don't think it's cool to make-out with girls with boyfriends, so we probably shouldn't make-out until it's official."

My heart sped up, but I nodded gravely, "Yeah, definitely not...but just to clarify, you think we're going to make-out?"

"Oh yeah, for sure. I just want to make sure you know that you can't be all over me until you're really single." His tone was joking, but I knew he meant it.

I felt bold. I looked him in the eye. "And you wanted me to know that because you think if I was 'really single,' I'd just make-out with you here, in front everyone."

He laughed, holding my stare. "Yep."

"Ummm, that lust you're sensing is for Timbo and only for Timbo." I got up and walked over to the cabin, where we'd taped up the Justin Timberlake poster, touched it fondly and gave Ben a pointed look before I sat down with the rest of our friends.

I thought he might follow me, had definitely wanted him to follow me, but Ben sat by himself on the log for a long time, reading his book, and that only made me like him more.

CHAPTER FORTY-SIX

DAY 109, VERMONT, 567.5 MILES TO KATAHDIN

The next day we planned to get up early and hike 27 miles to Spruce Peak shelter a few miles outside of Manchester Center, VT, so that we could go in for a quick resupply the following day. Sixteen miles later, we were ready to stop for lunch at the summit of Stratton Mountain. The morning was hard hiking; we'd started by immediately climbing up Glastonbury Mountain, dropped 1400 feet of elevation to a small stream, and then back up 1500 feet to Stratton. As Erin and I approached the fire tower that stands on the peak, I could tell, just from the way Pilgrim and Ben were looking at us, they'd come up with some scheme they were going to try to pitch us. Sure enough, before we could even get our packs off, Pilgrim was explaining how Ben had mentioned that Manchester Center was only three miles from where we'd planned to stop anyway, and the trail was almost entirely downhill from Stratton, and how we'd been in the woods for a solid 4 days, and so shouldn't we just press on into town tonight?

"Erin and Mike both almost died in the past two days, don't

you guys deserve a drink?" Ben added, making the hard sell. "Besides, there's free camping in town."

"Ohhh, and that really good Mexican place we went with Cara and Chris when we hiked the LT." I was sold, but then I was never one to pass up a chance to go into town. Erin and Mike agreed, too, Pilgrim and Ben's enthusiasm too infectious to deny.

"We'll do a walk and talk!" Pilgrim promised, which was what we called those rare times when we all walked together, instead of alone at our individual pace.

We arrived at the Manchester Center road crossing around 7pm, just as the light was beginning to fade, but easily caught a hitch into town. Manchester Center is a combination of high-brow outlets and cozy Vermont mountain community, and the residents are used to smelly hikers wandering among the Kate Spade and Coach shoppers. We'd decided to head straight to the Mexican restaurant, since we didn't want to put up tents or leave our gear in a public field until we were ready to sleep.

We started off with margaritas and chips, which, after a 30-mile day, went very quickly. Another round of margaritas came with dinner and then a shot and another margarita when we'd migrated from the patio to the restaurant bar. I was definitely well on my way to drunk as I sat next to Pilgrim at one end of the bar, Erin deep in conversation with Ben at the other. Mike was chatting with the bartender, a pretty young woman with long, wavy hair, and a peasant blouse.

I'd just finished telling Pilgrim what had happened with Kevin at the wedding, and he asked me if I was going to call him.

"I don't think so. He didn't seem like he wanted me to. And honestly, I'm not sure what I'd say at this point," I told him.

"You seem happier," he said.

"I am," I said. "Do you remember, like, months ago, when

you asked me why I thought I was going to marry him and I told you because we'd been together for a long time and our friends were getting engaged and it just seemed like the right time and you told me that was the stupidest reason you'd ever heard for someone getting engaged?"

"No."

I laughed, "Well, it was the first time I'd actually considered the question. I mean, I could have just gotten engaged because it was the thing I felt obligated to do without ever stopping to ask myself if this was what I wanted. And it's not. Can I say something without it being weird?"

Before he answered, I blurted, "Meeting you made me realize that there are guys out there that are into more than just sports and beer."

"I like sports and beer."

"Yeah, but you also like art and books and have interests and opinions. You know what I mean!"

"No, I do," he answered, and I knew he understood.

I finished my drink, and thought for a minute. "I just think that after being around so many frat dudes at Purdue and then in Chicago my world got so narrow, and I didn't even consider that there were other kinds of people out there, that maybe I was a different kind of person. It's just good to feel like my life isn't set, which is what it fucking felt like."

"In conclusion," I said grandly, suddenly embarrassed by my confession, "Thank you. For being my friend and making me think. We should have another drink."

I ordered another round, switching to beer as I realized that I don't really like tequila.

"What do you think those two are talking about?" I asked, motioning to Erin and Ben.

"You, I'm sure," Pilgrim said, talking to me like I was being dumb. "You know he likes you, right?"

"I guess," I muttered, my cheeks flaming. "Did he tell you that?"

"Yeah, and he's really great."

"I know he is," I said.

Mike interrupted then, too excited to notice we'd been in the middle of something serious, "Guys, I found us a place to stay tonight."

"Like, a place other than a field?" I asked hopefully.

"Uh, yeah, dude, like the bartender's house. She said if we meet her here when the bar closes, we can all crash there. We can leave our packs behind the bar for now if we want."

"Whoa, SARS Boy, I thought you were just trying to hook up, but this is so much better!" I patted Mike on the back.

We spread the news to Erin and Ben, who, like us, were excited about the possibility of not sleeping outside, and we decided to walk to another bar in town, with cheaper drinks, where Mike could drink, for the next hour until the bartender, who we now knew as Ginny, got off work. Mike, Erin, and Pilgrim fell in line, leaving Ben and I to walk together.

"So," Ben asked, "What were you and the Griz talking about?"

Alcohol had dulled my filters, so I answered honestly. "You. He told me you were a really good guy. What were you and Erin talking about?"

"You. She said you were a really good girl, but I knew that because you told me that the first night we met," he teased.

"Ha. Ha. Hmmmm... it kinda feels like our friends are setting us up. What should we do about it?" I said boldly.

"We should probably listen to them."

He stopped walking, so I stopped walking. Our friends kept going, oblivious that we were no longer behind them.

"Okay," he said, taking a step closer to me, "I'm going to kiss you."

"Finally."

And then we proceeded to make-out for two hours. At the time, it felt romantic and sexy and exciting. I couldn't believe this was my life and my luck. How was I in Vermont, kissing this hot, smart, funny, kind person who somehow thought I was those things, too?

That's how it felt. But in reality, we were two drunk, dirty hikers, doing a lot of sloppy tongue kissing while standing in the middle of a street. This became clear when, after a very long time, a car honked its horn at us to move and the driver, our waiter from the restaurant, yelled out the window, "You two need to get out of the street and go home."

"Okay, thanks man," Ben managed. He looked at me and raised his eyebrows and we both burst out laughing.

"Oh hey, wait!" I called after the waiter, "Do you know where Ginny the bartender lives?"

When we found our way to Ginny's house, it was after 3am. We stopped on the front porch to kiss one last time.

"Awww, look at you two." It was Ginny the bartender, closing the door behind her. "Your friends are all inside, asleep. I'm going to go across the street to the neighbors. Just come get me if my kid wakes up, okay? Here, this is for you."

I looked down at my hand and saw she had handed me a glass pipe filled with weed. "Wait... your kid?" I stammered, confused, but she was already across the street.

Ben and I looked at each other and bust out laughing again and decided it was time to go to bed. I set the pipe on the stairs so that she would see it when she got back, and laid down next to Erin on the pullout bed. She turned over and whispered, "oh my god, did you kiss Ben?" and I whispered back, too excited to be cool, "YEEESSSS! What did you guys do?"

She squeezed my hand and then said, "It's a long story. Oh, so, dude, Ginny is going to drive me to Bennington in the morning so I can pick up my insulin from the post office, will you come with me? I think she's crazy."

I whispered back, "She went across the street and left her kid here!"

Erin lifted her head, "Wait... there's a kid here?"

CHAPTER FORTY-SEVEN

DAY 110, VERMONT, 537.5 MILES TO KATAHDIN

The next morning, both bleary-eyed from lack of sleep and too much alcohol, Erin and I climbed into Ginny's pickup truck. Erin had mailed an insulin resupply to Bennington, which was about 30 minutes South by car. Our schedule had been all thrown off by the wedding and the day Erin's blood sugar had spiked, so we hadn't made it into town to make the mail drop as we'd planned.

As we buckled our seatbelts, Erin said, "Ginny, this is so nice of you. I really, really appreciate it."

Ginny smiled at Erin and then turned to me and hissed, "I can't believe you."

"Me? What? Why?" I said, unsure what I'd done.

"You left that pipe on the stairs where my landlord could have found it," she said, swerving a little as she turned to face me.

"I'm sorry?" I apologized. Even through my pounding headache I was pretty sure I hadn't done anything wrong, but I also didn't want to jeopardize Erin's ride. "We didn't use it, and I thought you might want it when you came back."

"Well, I didn't come back. It was just really irresponsible," she huffed and I thought of how before we left that morning, I'd asked if she was sure she was okay leaving her sleeping child (who turned out to be an adorable five-year-old girl) in the care of three sleeping male strangers and she'd looked at me like I was being ridiculous. I'd woken up Ben and told him we were leaving, "Good luck babysitting, I guess?"

We returned a little over an hour later to find Ben and Pilgrim watching cartoons with a little girl while Mike slept on the couch. True to Ginny's word, she did indeed seem fine. We woke Mike and said our goodbyes and thank yous, dragging ourselves to the nearest diner for a greasy breakfast and coffee.

On the way out the door Mike turned to Ben, "Uh, why was there a kid in there?"

Ben patted him on the back, "Did you not know you were babysitting that whole time?"

* * *

At the diner, everyone cheered as the waitress arrived with our coffees and waters. I passed around the Ibuprofen. As soon as we put in our orders, Pilgrim got right to it.

"So, you two..." he motioned his fork from me to Ben, "is this a thing?"

Ben and I looked at each other and both shrugged.

"Yeah?" I said. Ben nodded. It wasn't like we could hide anything from them anyway. And it did feel like a thing. I wasn't sure if it was a big thing, but it didn't feel like a random drunken kiss. We told them about getting kicked out of the street at 3am, and Ginny leaving her kid to go party with her neighbors all night. They told us that when they'd gone back to the restaurant to find Ginny, the cook had let them go to the back to make late night food.

"Oh my god! Pilgrim was laying on the counter, eating his sandwich like the cookie monster; nom nom nom nom," Erin snorted.

"Shit, it was so good."

By the time our food arrived, everyone except Mike was having a hard time keeping their heads up. Mike hadn't been served at the Mexican restaurant, and so wasn't as hungover as the rest of us. He kept asking when we thought we'd get back on the trail and growing increasingly frustrated when we wouldn't give him a definite answer. He'd been antsy since before the wedding. Despite his SARs/Lymes disease he was obviously itching to hike big days.

"Look, dude, first I'm gonna finish this waffle, and then I'm going to go to the grocery, and then, I'm probably going to sit on a bench and pray my head stops pounding, and then I'll think about hiking, okay?" I finally snapped at him.

"I can't sit around all day," he said, standing up and putting on his pack. "I'll just meet you at Killington."

We watched him go, by now used to his occasional petulance, and went back to eating.

* * *

Mike was right to go, because we did indeed sit around all day. We ate and then sat around. We went to the grocery and then sat around. We made phone calls and then sat around some more. We sat around so long and had such a hard time getting a hitch that by the time we got back on the trail we only had a few hours of daylight left. Our initial plan had been to hike ten miles to Peru Peak shelter, but it was a hard 4-mile climb to the top of Bromley Mountain and we were completely enveloped in fog. When we'd hiked the Long Trail, the peak of Bromley had been covered in wildflowers, so many wildflowers that it could have been the setting of a dryer sheet commercial—picture a woman running through the field of lavender, overcome by the scent of her freshly dried cotton dress. Bromley covered in wildflowers remains one of my most vivid memories of that hike. This day, we couldn't see more than six inches in front of our faces. Once at the top, we discovered the Bromley warming hut was open. In the winter, the warming hut is for skiers who've taken the lift up to the peak, and in the summer it's left open for thru-hikers.

"I think we should just stay here," Ben declared when Erin and I arrived. He and Pilgrim had obviously already agreed to this plan. "This weather is shit."

"What about Mike?" I asked. When Mike took off, he'd said he would meet up with us again near Killington Mountain, which is where we planned to pick Sug up after his long hiatus off the trail. I worried that we would now be late for that meeting, and Mike would take off again.

"He'll either wait for us, or he won't," he answered, shrugging. While I was annoyed when Mike couldn't just go along with the group, Ben and Pilgrim were understanding. "Mike needs a few nights to himself."

Erin and I both nodded our agreement.

"This is just like Clingman's Dome," Erin said to me. "He'll come back around."

"Yeah, but why does he have to be such a baby about it?" I rolled my eyes.

We spent the rest of our evening in the hut, playing cards, dancing to NASCAR radio, initiating Ben into AT Gym. I was relieved by how very normal everything seemed, but I was also surprised. I'd spent the evening before making out with Ben in the middle of the street and while no one was pretending it didn't happen, no one was making a big deal out of it either.

Part of me wanted to yell out, "So, this is the thing we're all going to decide to be mature about?! We're all going to high-five at every fart but me making out with Ben is what we're going to be cool with?"

The only weirdness came that night when we all set out our sleeping bags. Erin and I always slept next to each other, and not just on the trail, but ever since our first sleepover in seventh grade. But tonight, Ben and I maneuvered so that we were side-by-side. Erin hesitated a second and then laid her bag next to Pilgrim. I felt guilty, but was grateful that she hadn't said anything.

As it grew dark and our chatter tapered off, Ben and I held hands in the dark. He leaned over and softly kissed me.

"Gross! No kissing!" Pilgrim yelled.

"*You* stop kissing!" I yelled back, blushing furiously in the dark.

"Yeah! Gross!" Ben chimed in. He gave my hand a quick squeeze.

CHAPTER FORTY-EIGHT

DAY 111, 533.8 MILES TO KATAHDIN

We had almost 60 miles and two days until our scheduled meet-up with Sug. Poor Sug had now been off the trail for eight days waiting for us to catch up to the spot just before Killington Mountain where he'd left the trail to go to a wedding. He'd only planned to be off for the two days of the wedding, but because the rest of us had collectively taken so many zero or low mileage days, first for Cara's wedding, and then around towns, Sug had been cooling his heels in his hometown outside of Rochester for more than a week. Being the nice guy he was, he always just said, "okay, just let me know when to meet you," every time Pilgrim called to let him know we'd be delayed another day, but we knew he had to be frustrated. Pilgrim had left the trail for just a few days to go to his college graduation, but said that the trail felt different after. Even just going to Cara and Chris's wedding and experiencing the small slice of real life there had been jarring for me.

The trail was a powerful bubble where the only things that mattered were miles and friends and food, but every time you stepped outside of it, reentering the bubble, or maybe more accurately, re-creating the facade of the bubble, became harder. The mental game of long distance hiking is tricky, the biggest reason people don't finish a thru-hike is not for physical ailments, but because they couldn't reconcile the often aching loneliness with a lack of privacy, or the monotony of doing the same thing every day while rarely sleeping in the same place two nights in a row. You need a tunnel vision to Katahdin to convince yourself that it's a good idea to keep putting one foot in front of the other. I felt like I had two lives, trail life and real life, and every brush with something outside of the trail—small things like a call to the financial aid office to figure out how I was going to pay for law school or Erin learning that her 100% perfect guy had started dating a mutual friend; or big things like watching the news in town and learning that while we were hiking, our country had gone to war—made it harder to separate the two. At least for me, separate was necessary. I couldn't imagine how Sug was going to feel after eight days at home.

As unappealing as hiking two thirty-mile days in a row sounded (and honestly, kinda impossible to me, since Erin and I had only ever hiked one 30+ miler) we knew we couldn't ask Sug to wait any longer. We set off from Bromley in good spirits. Early on, though, Erin took a tumble and her knee started bothering her, so we were moving slower than usual. For Erin, the time off for the wedding was a good mental break, but it was a hard break physically. Despite her fierce determination that it not be, her knee was more frequently a factor, something she had to consider and manage and think about every day. In a way, it was more frustrating to her than dealing with her diabetes; she knew how to manage the diabetes when something went wrong, but her knee wasn't something she could troubleshoot. An hour passed and she fell again, this time into a patch of stinging nettle. Stinging nettle is a plant that grows all over Vermont, and when you rub against it, the tiny hollow hairs on the leaves can inject histamine and other chemicals and causes your skin to itch like hell for about seven minutes (which is why it's also known as the Seven Minute Itch).

But despite the rough start, Erin was in a good mood. She joked about her falls and reminded me of the song we'd made up on the Long Trail called the "Long Trail Blues" and the line "Life can be a bitch, with the Seven Minute Itch."

No, even with the left side of her body inflamed from the nettle, her knee a constant pain, her unpredictable blood sugar, Erin was upbeat. It was me who was silently stewing.

While Erin was finding hiking harder, I was getting faster and stronger, and those were two things I'd never been in my life. I'd been involved in sports since I was 5 and my parents signed me up for t-ball, soccer, and basketball, all the way through my high school years and even playing college intramural leagues, but I was always slower and bigger than the other girls. I'd been "okay" at lots of activities, but I'd never been really good at anything, and lately, I'd been feeling like I was really good at hiking. Where I'd struggled so much at the beginning of the trail, now I had no problem keeping up with even the fastest guys. I loved the feeling of bounding up a mountain (okay, maybe not bounding), instead of stopping every 100 yards because I was out of breath, of keeping up a conversation while zipping past other hikers, of miles passing without notice. But because I also wanted to stick behind Erin in case something went haywire with her diabetes, or now her knee, I wasn't often getting the chance to go as fast as I'd like.

Like that day, more and more often I was finding myself frustrated by Erin's pace. I wouldn't say anything to Erin, after all, she was injured and it's not like she'd asked me to walk behind her (in fact, I'm sure she'd have loved me to get off her heels). If I had brought it up, she'd have told me to go ahead;

but I couldn't. Every time I passed her, I pictured her passed out on the trail in Shenandoah, the rest of us too far ahead to help. If I was being honest with myself, even though I could go faster, I hadn't really felt a need to hike ahead of Erin before now.

Because now, there was Ben.

Even though I wasn't admitting it, my sudden frustration with Erin was unsurprisingly coinciding with my new feelings.

We'd had a late start that morning out of Bromley and with our slow pace, by the time we reached Minerva Hinchey shelter, three miles short of our thirty-mile goal, we were running seriously low on daylight. Erin and I found Ben and Pilgrim waiting for us, their stuff unpacked all around them.

"What are you doing, dudes?" Erin asked. "We have three more miles to hike."

"It's getting dark; I think we should stop here," Ben told her.

"Get yer headlamps out, nerds. Let's do some night hiking." I demanded. I was exhausted, but I knew hiking less miles today only meant hiking more miles tomorrow.

"Night hiking is dumb," Pilgrim told us, as Ben took my hiking poles out of my hand and leaned them against the shelter. "We'll just get up early tomorrow."

"Well as long as you have a plan," Erin sat on the edge of the shelter, skeptical, but obviously ready to stop. Erin turned stern, "But we have to get Sug tomorrow."

Pilgrim gave her his best used car salesman smile. "Dude... we're getting Sug tomorrow."

- - - -

Pilgrim was the first person to poke his head out of the sleeping bag that morning.

"Shit," he said, which was the word the rest of us woke up to.

Uncharacteristically, we'd all slept in. I'd never been a morning person, but on the trail, you went to sleep when the sun went down and woke up when the sun came up. Most mornings we were hiking by 7am. And that day, because we were supposed to cover 33 miles, I had set my watch alarm for 5:30am to make extra sure we would have enough time. Or, I *thought* I had set it for 5:30am, because now, when I blinked to look at the watch through my bleary eyes I saw that it was almost 8am and the alarm had never sounded.

"Shiiiiiit," I echoed and bolted out of my sleeping bag, frantically trying to pack up my stuff so we could get on the trail. I'd just returned from peeing and saw Pilgrim, Ben, and Erin sitting on the edge of the shelter, looking at the guidebook, their stuff still strewn around.

"What are you doing? We gotta go," I asked, incredulous.

"They have a plan," Erin told me, with a shrug.

"Well, as long as you have a plan," I said, dripping sarcasm. "You guys, we *have* to get Sug. No more making him wait."

Ben reached for my hand, and I felt a little spark from the touch.

"We're getting Sug," he said, and I decided to believe him.

Their plan was far from foolproof, but true to their word, at the end of the day, we not only had Sug, but we'd found Mike, too.

Pilgrim laid out the scheme and we finally left the shelter that morning. First, we would do a "walk and talk" three miles down the trail to the road crossing at VT 103, where we'd walk a half mile up the road to the Whistle Stop Cafe. Then, Pilgrim would call Sug's girlfriend, Jen, hopefully before they were set to leave their hotel and have her bring Sug to the Cafe instead of our agreed meet-up point more than 30 miles up the trail.

"And then we'll just ask Jen to slack us over Killington and we'll only do 20 miles instead of 33 and all have the best day ever," Pilgrim concluded. He looked pointedly at me, "There are no holes in this plan."

"Yep. No holes," Ben repeated.

"I see none," Erin chorused.

They all looked at me.

"No holes!" I answered, certain that we would be walking 33 miles in the dark that evening because there is no way we'd catch Jen and Sug before they left.

But as soon as we got to the Whistle Stop, Pilgrim first called Sug and then Jen's parents, and somehow got the number to the hotel where Jen and Sug had stayed the night before. He gave us a thumbs up and a few minutes later and came over to where we sat on the Cafe's wide deck. "It's done, they're on their way."

"What? That's amazing!" I said, surprised.

"It's almost like you didn't have faith in the plan," Ben teased.

I put on my most innocent face, "Me? No. I totally believed. I'm talking about this menu. Amazing!"

"Uh huh."

An hour later, we had just finished breakfast when Jen and Sug arrived. Our reunion was boisterous, everyone talking, trying to make up for the days and weeks we'd been apart. Erin and I drew in Jen, so happy to meet Sug's person, and always grateful for more estrogen. She fit right in, she was comfortable and sarcastic, and there was an incredible ease between she and Sug that I envied. I wondered, as she sat joking with us at the table, if after having him home for so long, she resented him leaving again. But if she felt that, she didn't show it. She seemed excited to talk about the trail and for Sug to be back. I thought about how different it was from my phone calls and visits with Kevin, where even when he was being supportive, I always left feeling vaguely guilty for not being there.

The two of them ordered their food, and the rest of us, deciding it would be rude for them to dine alone, ordered milkshakes for breakfast dessert. I'd forgotten how infectious Sug's broad smile and easy laugh were. I watched the way he leaned his head toward whoever was talking, intently listening, patient and engaged. It felt right to have him back, and I realized, sitting there, that if everyone in our motley crew had a role to play, Sug was the heart.

"Dude, do you think you lost your trail legs while you were home?" Erin asked Sug. We always joked that after even a day off the trail, we'd lose our "trail legs," our ability to seamlessly navigate the rocks and roots and climbs.

"Let's see the calves!" I demanded. Sug's amazingly muscled calves were one of our favorite topics of conversation. He obligingly lifted up his legs, revealing that they were most definitely intact.

"You guys," Jen told us, "he's been hiking nine miles from his house to mine every morning just to keep in shape."

"Shit dude, I'm sorry we kept you waiting for so long." Erin put an arm around his shoulders. I think we were both feeling bad for every additional day we made him sit at home, walking the streets to keep in shape, so that we could take a short day, or spend longer at the wedding, or just because we didn't feel like hiking.

Sug laughed and smiled at Erin. "It was worth it to have everyone back together."

After over an hour, we reluctantly agreed it was time to go, because even though we weren't going the full 33 miles that day, we still had twenty miles to hike. We loaded our packs into Jen's trunk, apologizing for the smell, gave her quick hugs, and left her and Sug to say their goodbyes. Jen was going to drop our packs near where we were stopping for the night, giving us the day to walk free of the 30-plus pound weights we carried with us at all times. As much as I hated to admit it, as Pilgrim had predicted, this was feeling like the best day ever.

We all started out walking together, still full of questions for Sug and stories about our misadventures. Eventually we spread out, Erin with Sug and Pilgrim, and Ben and I walking together. I marveled at how different walking this stretch of trail was this time from when I'd done it on our Long Trail hike. Killington mountain was the big peak of the day and on the Long Trail that climb had seemed so epic and impossible. I remembered crying on the way down, just needing the day to be over. But this day, walking with Ben, with no pack and with months of hard-won trail experience behind me, the hiking was easy and I was surprised when we reached the top.

On the way down the mountain, I followed Ben's fluid steps, finding myself fixating on his hands. I liked them. A lot. Unlike the rest of us, Ben didn't use hiking poles and so seeing his hands swinging back and forth as he walked was a novelty.

"What are your feelings about holding hands while hiking?" I asked Ben.

"I'm pretty sure I'm against it, but we can give it a shot," he responded, turning to look at me with a grin.

He reached back to grab my hand and pull me up next to him. We walked hand-in-hand next to each other for about 10 seconds.

"Yeah, I'm against it," he said, rubbing his sweaty palms on his shorts.

"Right. Holding hands and hiking is a definite no," I agreed. "But what about kissing on the trail?"

"I could give that a shot," he answered, leaning his head down to meet mine. After what felt like a full minute, he pulled away and smiled at me. "Should we run the rest of the way?"

"YES!"

Ben took off and I ran after him, both of us giggling as we sped down the trail. I felt light and happy, lucky to be where I was and to be with this person.

- - -

Later that night we all sat around the campfire—Ben and I, Erin, Sug, Pilgrim, and Mike, who, true to his word, had waited for us at the bottom of Killington.

"So..." I turned to Sug, "Kevin and I broke up."

"Oh really? Are you okay?" he asked, sincere, but obviously not surprised by this news.

"Erin told you."

"IT'S NOT A SECRET!" Erin protested.

"I know, I know, it's fine," I told her. I looked at Sug. "But, like Ben and I are kinda... uhhhh..."

Sug looked at me expectantly.

"JUST DON'T BE WEIRD ABOUT IT, OKAY?!"

Sug laughed, "I won't if you won't."

CHAPTER FORTY-NINE

DAY 113, VERMONT, 487 MILES TO KATAHDIN

Over the next two days we made our way out of Vermont and into New Hampshire. We hiked in different formations throughout the days, sometimes all together, singing along to Pilgrim's NASCAR radio, sometimes in small groups—Ben and Pilgrim discussing literature I'd never heard of, Sug with Erin and I, talking about the food we'd eat if we had unlimited time, Mike sprinting ahead of all of us—and sometimes by ourselves.

On the 17th, we hiked a hard 26-mile day into Hanover, New Hampshire, the home of Dartmouth University, and, notably for Appalachian Trail hikers, the home of Bill Bryson who wrote the most popular Appalachian Trail book, *A Walk In The Woods*.

Erin and I had taken a leisurely lunch on a couple of boulders with sandwiches from a deli in the last small town in Vermont.

"You'd think I'd learn not to get mayonnaise from a store that has questionable refrigeration," I mused, "but I crave it."

"Yeah, it's worth it," Erin said as she bit into her egg salad on a hoagie roll. She chewed and then asked, "So, do you think you should talk to Kevin?"

Her question punched me in the gut. I'd gotten so caught up in the newness of Ben that I hadn't wanted to think about Kevin and where things stood with him.

"Ugh," I sagged. "Yeah, I do. I just don't want to."

"Just do it, dude. I know you. You're going to feel anxious and guilty about Ben until you talk to Kevin," she said, telling me what I already knew.

"I know, it's just he said he didn't want me to call..."

"Yeah, but you know he didn't mean it. And if you're starting something with Ben, you need to really end things with Kevin."

I let out a long groan. I wasn't sure what was going on with Ben, but it wasn't nothing. "You're right. I'll call him tonight."

Erin and I arrived in town last and the boys were excited because they'd found us a free place to stay for the night.

"It's the basement of a fraternity house!" Mike told us as we walked over.

"Have any of you ever been to a fraternity house?" I asked, looking at five heads shaking no. I'd been in a sorority in college and had spent my fair share of time in fraternities, and the prospect of sleeping in a frat basement sounded pretty sketchy.

"We asked everywhere and this was the only place open," Mike answered, looking a little less excited, "and it's free."

"It'll be great!" Erin told him.

It wasn't. The basement was just that—a concrete slab with no furniture next to a room where the frat brothers played beer pong all night long. There was a little bathroom with no shower, so we all took turns washing ourselves from the sink and decided to head to a bar. I spotted a payphone at the entrance and told everyone to go ahead. I called Kevin, half hoping he wouldn't be there. He answered on the second ring.

"Hey, it's me," I said.

"I thought it might be," he answered, weary. "How are you, darlin'? Where are you?"

"Kevin," I stopped him. "We need to talk."

And he started to cry. And then I started to cry. I told him that I loved him, but that it was over, that I'd been thinking about this since before I saw him at the wedding, that I felt myself changing and I didn't think we were in the same place anymore. I didn't tell him about Ben, because the truth was that I'd come to this before I'd met Ben. I'd been thinking about it since Pilgrim asked me early in our hike, "Why do you want to marry this guy?" and the only answer I could give was "We've been together three years."

Kevin asked me to not make this final, saying that things would be different once I was off the trail and back home.

"But I don't want things to be different," I told him quietly.

Eventually we ran out of things to say, and I was just sitting on the phone, crying and listening to him cry.

"Kevin? I think we should get off the phone."

"I can't hang up; this feels like the last time I'll talk to you."

"You have my car and my cat- I'm going to talk to you again!" I said, hoping he could joke with me. He was silent.

"Okay," I said quietly. "I love you, I'm sorry. I'm hanging up."

He didn't say anything, so I hung up. I saw Erin hovering at a safe distance, and as soon as I caught sight of her, I burst into hard tears. It was the first time I'd really cried about Kevin. I'd had so long to get used to the idea of us not being together, that I almost forgot that it was a real person, a person I'd loved and shared a life with for so long, a person whose family I'd spent holidays and vacations with, a good, genuine, kind person, who I was going to be hurting.

"Fuck. That was hard," I wiped my eyes on my already dirty shirt, and looked at Erin, "Can I get a giant beer now?"

"YEESSSS!"

* * *

The next morning, I woke up cuddled next to Ben on the cold cement floor and immediately regretted opening my eyes. My head was killing me and my mouth tasted like dirt. I looked over at Pilgrim, who sat in his sleeping bag across the room.

"Did we... steal liquor from the frat bros?" I asked him, trying to piece together the very drunken night.

"Yeah, you and I went on a pretty covert secret mission," he confirmed. "Dude. Do you remember the end of the night?"

I searched my blank mind, "No..."

"You were so drunk that you were talking in what you obviously thought were sentences, but made absolutely no sense. You were like talking to a baby. It was awesome."

"Oh, was it? Was it awesome?" I asked sarcastically.

"Yeah," Ben poked his head out of his sleeping bag, "it was pretty awesome."

My head didn't feel awesome, and I didn't feel awesome about how drunk I'd been, but thankfully, everyone else just let it go. We spent the first half of our morning doing all the things we'd normally do in town before we hiked out—we did laundry, resupplied at the grocery, made phone calls, and ate a big breakfast. We were back at the frat, talking about but not making moves towards actually leaving, when Lucky and Sparrow walked in. Their arrival tipped the scale. Mike, Pilgrim, Ben, and I had run into them in Massachusetts and knew they were skipping around to different sections, but Sug hadn't seen them since they'd hiked the first few weeks together in Tennessee.

"Alright," Ben declared, "today is a zero day. The decision is made and so there will be no more worrying about it or talking about it. We are just going to enjoy our zero day."

Mike looked annoyed, but went along with it, and even suggested we all go bowling. After bowling, where I miraculously bowled three strikes in a row to win, Ben asked if I wanted to go on a date that night.

"Like a real date?" I asked.

"Yeah, now that you're officially single, I think we should go on a date."

I agreed, but later, when Erin asked what I wanted to do that evening, I suggested she come, too. For some reason it was hard for me to just tell her that I wanted to spend time alone with Ben. So, Erin, Ben, and I went to Hanover's Thai restaurant together.

About halfway into dinner, Erin looked from me to Ben and blurted out, "Oh my god, I'm on your fucking date."

"What? No!" I stammered.

Ben laughed, "Yeah, dude, I was wondering when you would figure it out."

Erin laughed, too, and I was relieved. "Well, I'm definitely not going to the fucking movie with you."

"Thank god," Ben said.

CHAPTER FIFTY

DAY 115, NEW HAMPSHIRE, 441.9 MILES TO KATAHDIN

Hiking in New Hampshire was significant because it was our second to last state. But also, I'd been hearing about the White Mountains of New Hampshire since before we started our hike; it was supposed to be the most beautiful and rugged section of the trail. It took us two days to hike 43 miles from Hanover to the Hikers Welcome Hotel in Glencliff, New Hampshire, six miles shy of Mt. Moosilauke and the official start of the Whites. We took it easy the morning of June 21st, in no rush to start the day. Everyone told us that the Whites were a different beast, that even thru-hikers like us who were easily doing 20-30 miles a day should plan on doing much less over the Whites' steep, exposed climbs. The Whites are also managed by the Appalachian Mountain Club, and because of the popularity and fragility of the area, they had very strict rules about where hikers could camp and very limited options for shelter, meaning we'd have to plan our mileage strategically. That day we'd only planned to do 8 miles, up and over Moosilauke to ease ourselves in and to avoid hiking 17 miles to the next shelter.

Lucky and Sparrow had hiked with us from Hanover, and with Mike and Sug, there were now eight of us hiking in a pack. The extra numbers made us a boisterous group, so much different from the quiet days in Pennsylvania when it was just Erin, See Blue, and me. That morning Lucky had informed us that June 21st was naked hiking day, "so all you motherfuckers best be ready to get naked." Lucky had hiked thru-hiked the AT before, the same year as Cara and Chris, which was why he didn't care about skipping around now. Cara had told us that she'd actually met Lucky when she was hiking, that she'd remembered him being there the day she'd fractured her foot in North Carolina.

I had no intention of hiking naked, but Lucky was charismatic and had the boys persuaded, so to prepare them, we found a sharpie and Erin drew tattoos on their arms and chests. Mike borrowed clippers from the hostel owner and had Pilgrim freshen up his mohawk. At the last minute, Pilgrim decided he needed a change and ended up with a mohawk of his own. With his aviator sunglasses, Ben told Pilgrim he looked like the thru-hiker version of De Niro in Taxi Driver, a reference that was lost on me. Pilgrim had taken to wearing the red mesh tank top that was part of the wedding garb we'd bought at the thrift store before Cara's wedding and the whole effect was pretty hilarious.

Within a half mile, we were crossing a series of bog bridges when I heard a snap. I looked up to see Erin holding a broken hiking pole.

"Fuck," she said, but kept walking. Two minutes later, there was another snap and another, "fuck!"

She turned and looked at me, two useless hiking poles in her hands, tears springing to her eyes. I realized how much she was probably relying on her poles to ease the weight off her knee. We'd bought those poles before we'd hiked the Long

Trail, both opting for children's poles because they were cheaper. They weren't made for adults, or for the miles we'd put on them, so it was no wonder they'd broken.

"Here," I said, "use mine."

"Dude, are you sure?" she asked.

"Yeah, Ben doesn't use them, I can figure it out!" I answered, actually kind of looking forward to the new challenge.

It hadn't taken us long after that to reach the top of Mt. Moosilauke; Sparrow, Erin, and I laughing at the horrified looks on the faces of day hikers passing us going the other way. They'd obviously met our naked counterparts, unaware when they'd set out for a nice Saturday afternoon hike that it was Naked Hiking Day. The approach to the summit was the first time on the trail we'd climbed above the alpine zone. Trees gave way to shrubs, which gave way to rocks and alpine tundra. An alpine climate happens in mountains with high enough elevation and cold enough weather that trees and much other plant life are unable to grow. In bad weather, hiking above tree line can be dangerous, but on this clear, warm day, the rocky, broad peak of Moosilauke gave us a 360 degree view of the jagged ridges of the Whites ahead of us, and of the comparatively rolling green mountains of Vermont behind us.

That night in the shelter Lucky divided us into teams of two to play competitive crossword puzzles, Erin and I losing by a mile.

"Yeah, that probably wasn't fair to put you guys on a team, you basically share a brain," Ben remarked.

"No, we don't!" Erin and I said in unison, and then with a look at each other, "Yeah, we do."

Erin and I had been a team since we were 12, and out here had become even more in sync. We'd learned to anticipate when the other needed support, or to be left alone. In the beginning when all I'd wanted to do was quit, Erin had gently pushed and championed me, not giving me the out I thought I'd wanted. And I hoped that I'd been as perceptive and helpful about the pain she was in with her knee. We'd been together 24 hours a day for four months and while there had been a few tense moments here and there, we'd never fought. But now, things were shifting. Where Erin and I had been together at the center of the trail experience, no matter who else we'd been hiking with, my time and focus now were more often turning to Ben. I didn't know how she felt, other than happy for me, but I felt vaguely guilty.

We woke up on the 22nd to rain, making the steep mile-long hike down the mountain to the road crossing a slog, the water on the rocky trail bordering on dangerous. Erin winced with almost every step. About halfway down we found a note pinned to a tree.

"Erin/Sweet n' Low," it read, "It's 6pm on June 21st, I was hoping to catch you guys tonight, but it's getting dark. I'll be in the parking lot at the road crossing for another hour! I have beers! Love, Cara."

It seemed Cara was back from her honeymoon in Peru, and had been just a half mile away from us the night before, waiting in the parking lot while we sat doing crossword puzzles in the shelter. The thought of her sister being so close and now gone tore something apart in Erin, and she cried the rest of the way down. We found the guys waiting for us at the road crossing and explained what had happened.

Sug gently asked Erin what she wanted to do.

"I just want to see Cara," she said, tearing up again. "I feel like I got punched in the gut. She was right here."

"Look, we're a few miles from a town, why don't we hitch in and you can call her? Maybe she can meet us for breakfast or lunch?" Sug suggested.

Pilgrim agreed, "Yeah, who doesn't want breakfast?"

"You guys are sure?" Erin asked, looking relieved. "I don't want to hold the whole group up."

Lucky and Sparrow were getting off the trail in a few days, so decided to hike ahead, and we once again said goodbyes. It took awhile to get rides for the six of us, but Erin eventually did find a payphone to call Cara. Cara was staying at her in-laws about an hour away, and jumped in the car as soon as Erin called.

Erin looked apprehensive as she hung up the phone. She gave me a nod and I broke away from our circle of friends, who were trying to decide on where to eat.

"So..." she started slowly, "I think I want to go back with Cara tonight."

"Okaaaay..." I said.

She looked sad. "But there isn't a way for everyone to come."

"Oh!" I said, a little surprised. "Oh. You should go. I know you want to see Cara and hear about the honeymoon."

"Like... go by myself?" she asked.

"Yeah, we'll figure it out."

Hurriedly, she qualified, "Well, if you guys want to keep hiking, I'll just have her drop me at the next road crossing to meet you or whatever."

I couldn't tell whether she had wanted me to come too or was relieved that I had suggested she go alone. All I knew was that she needed to go.

She told the group her plan and Pilgrim immediately said, "Nah, Sweets, we'll just take the day here. Why would we not wait for you?"

We walked around town for a little bit and then waited with Erin for Cara to arrive. Just as they were packing up to go, Mike stopped them.

"Cara," he asked sheepishly, "Do you think you could give me a ride back to the trailhead?"

He told us that he really wanted to finish the trail by his 21st birthday and that there was no way we would make it at our current pace. He wasn't wrong. With Erin's knee and our frequent stops and starts, there was just no way we could push it as much as he wanted to.

"I'll wait for you guys at the end and summit Katahdin with you, too," he promised as he got in the car. As we waved good-bye, I was sure this was the last time we'd see him.

"And then there were four. Anyone else want to leave?" I asked Ben, Sug, and Pilgrim as we watched the car drive away.

There wasn't much to the town, and we'd done laundry and grocery shopped a few days earlier, so after we ate, we got a room at a motel that looked like it was from the set of a Western.

"Do you guys want to get your own room?" Pilgrim had asked me on our way to the motel.

"No! I'm not made of money!" I'd joked, assuring him that Ben and I could share a room with him and Sug just as we had every other night. "I'd be lonely without you guys. Who else is going to listen to us try to quietly kiss in the dark?"

The thought of "getting a room" with Ben made me nervous. Since the night we'd kissed in the middle of the road in Manchester Center, there'd been a lot more kissing and holding hands (not while hiking, of course) and a little bit of making out. I really liked Ben, like, *really*, liked him. From the first night, being together had felt fun and easy and exciting, but also right and settled. But I knew we only had another month together, at most, and I was not sure how much deeper in I wanted to let myself get.

CHAPTER FIFTY-ONE

DAY 120, NEW HAMPSHIRE, 389 MILES TO KATAHDIN

Cara picked us up the next morning with a much happier Erin, and dropped us all back off at Kinsman Notch. Cara told us she'd try to catch us again over the next few days, but would definitely meet up with us on the other side of the Whites in Gorham, NH.

As we hugged, she smiled at me, "Erin told me about Kevin. So... Ben, huh?"

"Yeah...." I blushed.

"He seems like a really good person," she said. "And he's totally hot. I'm happy for you two."

"Yeah..." I said, my heart rose as I looked to where Ben stood, playing stick baseball with Pilgrim. "He's kinda great."

* * *

Hiking out of Kinsman Notch, we were instantly confronted with the challenge of the Whites. The trail rose in steep boulders that were unrelenting. There were no switchbacks to make the climb easier, and in many sections, we were less hiking and more climbing hand over foot. Even the quickest hikers had to slow down to navigate the rocky trail.

Cara had given Erin her old hiking poles, and almost immediately one and then both of them broke, brittle from sitting unused.

"Oh my god, it's like you've suddenly gained a super strength, but you don't yet know how to handle your newfound powers. Did you get bit by a spider?" I asked as I handed Erin my poles once again.

Erin and I quickly fell behind the boys—Erin slowed by her knee pain, and me, feeling unsteady without the aid of my hiking poles—but I was happy for the time alone together. We carefully made our way up and over the big rocks, climbing our way up 2000 feet to Mt. Wolf, down 1000 feet through 20 ft. slick rock walls and rock jumbles to a stream, and then up another 2000 feet of steep, worn rock stairs to the North and South Kinsman peaks. She told me about Cara's honeymoon, and I told her that she'd missed nothing other than watching a bunch of TV in a musty motel. We ate lunch sitting next to the big cairn marking the top of South Kinsman peak.

Looking out at the vista, Erin sighed, "Whoa. Look at this fucking view."

"Dude," I said in agreement.

In the afternoon, we hiked the few miles to Lonesome Lake Hut, which was the first of the AMC's hiker huts reached by northbound hikers. There are eight huts in the Whites, modeled after the hut system in the Alps, which are spaced every six to eight miles along the AT. Most have bunk rooms and dining rooms. In the summer, they each employ a staff of caretakers that serve breakfast and dinner to their guests. While the huts would have been luxurious accommodations for thru-hikers like us, in the summer they were mostly booked months in advance. Even if they hadn't been booked, at $68/hiker a night, were well out of our meager budgets. The problem for us was that the huts, along with a few fee campsites, were the only legal places to stay overnight in the Whites.

I'd found a list of stealth campsites at the Glencliff hostel and had made note of them in our mileage book.

"You rebel," Erin teased, but knowing that breaking the rules was not normally in my DNA.

"Fuck the AMC. They shouldn't make it so hard for thru-hikers to hike this part of the trail. What else is it fucking here for?" I ranted. This was not a unique complaint, many thru-hikers complained about the AMC, calling it the Appalachian Money Club. We'd been hiking for four months, through beautiful, mostly wonderfully maintained trails and shelters, all free and cared for by volunteers. Now in the Whites, the most scenic part of our journey, the trail was worn and dangerous, everything cost money we didn't have, and we felt unwelcome and unwanted on the trail that had become our home.

An unfamiliar male voice cut into my diatribe, "Hey! Are you Sweet Something and Not Low?"

We looked up to see a young guy coming towards us.

"Close enough," I said.

"Uh, so, your friend was looking for you, you know the one..." He stuck his pointer fingers and thumbs up in a shooting gesture.

"Double fart guns?" Erin asked.

"Wha? No... this guy!" He turned his fingers so that the fart guns were pointed towards each other.

"Oh! Pilgrim!" I exclaimed, realizing he was mimicking the image of Adam and God's fingers from the Sistine Chapel that Pilgrim had tattooed across his ribcage.

"YEAH!! Pilgrim!" The stranger looked relieved. "He said if I saw two lady thru-hikers, I should tell them that your friends were all swimming in the lake but would meet you at the hut."

We got to the hut and didn't see Ben, Sug or Pilgrim, but did see a familiar figure standing at a sink at the far end of a row of picnic tables, washing dishes.

"TURBO!" Erin yelled.

His eyes lit up when he saw us, "Dudes! I've been waiting for you guys! So, what's it... where's everyone else?"

As if on cue, Pilgrim, Sug and Ben walked in, and another trail reunion ensued. Peaches and Cream had left the trail for a few days and Turbo had decided he was going to wait and hike with us. He'd been doing kitchen work at the hut for food. Depending on their occupancy, the hut caretakers would occasionally allow one or two thru-hikers to stay or eat in exchange for work.

"Yeah, so, no, they, like, said I could eat whatever if I did these dishes, but all that's here is a bowl of peas. But whatever, I'm going to eat them." He dug a giant serving spoon into a bowl of green peas and took a huge bite. Ben recoiled in disgust. I'd come to learn that even though he'd run an organic bakery in his pre-trail life, Ben had the eating habits of a picky 8-year-old. He ate maybe three vegetables (broccoli, cooked carrots, and plain lettuce), almost no fruits, and rejected all condiments except ketchup. He ate the same ramen or macaroni with tuna every night on the trail.

By then it was early evening, so we hung outside the hut and made our dinners and then hiked a few miles down the trail, looking for the stealth camping site I'd marked in my guidebook.

"I vote we just throw down on the trail," Pilgrim said, when it became apparent that we'd either passed the spot or it had never existed. "It's already dark, no one is going to police the trail this time of night."

"And if they do, we'll just be like, whoops, we all just accidentally fell at the same time, and move on," Erin agreed, already dropping her pack on the ground. Even though we'd only done 15 miles that day, I was exhausted.

It was a clear night, so we decided to just sleep under the stars. None of us was carrying a tent anymore, anyway. A few weeks back, Erin and I had traded in the one-person tents we'd each been carrying for a two-person bug bivy, which was basically a mosquito net that went over our bodies, and a light tarp that we could prop up with our hiking poles and stake to the ground to fashion a tent. Sug, Pilgrim, and Ben had also given up their tents in a quest to lighten their packs. Turbo had picked up a lightweight hiking hammock, but could never figure out how to make it work. Before the Whites, we had always found shelters to stay in, so the tents had seemed unnecessary.

We lay head to foot in a line down the trail. Our voices bounced off the trees and rocks.

"Goodnight Ma."

"Goodnight Pa."

"Goodnight John Boy."

"I hope it doesn't rain."

"Why would you say that?"

"Damnit, Pilgrim, did you fart?"

"One, two, three, stop talking."

* * *

The following afternoon, I sat with Erin and Sug on the rocky summit of Mt. Lafayette.

"I feel like I'm going to cry," I told them.

"Why? Are you okay?" Sug asked, concerned.

"Yeah, it's just... it's just so fucking beautiful."

Erin looked like she was going to burst, but managed to choke out, "Totally, dude," before she and Sug dissolved in huge waves of laughter.

"I was serious!" I protested.

Erin wiped tears from her eyes, "Oh I know you were serious. That's why it's so funny."

She paused and then said thoughtfully, "But I know what you mean. This is unreal."

It was June 24th. The day before had marked four months on the trail. In that time, I'd become inured to the scenery. I still appreciated a great overlook, but at the end of the day if someone had asked me about what I'd seen that day, I'd have been hard pressed to come up with a solid answer. At some point, I just stopped noticing my surroundings. I wrote vivid, specific descriptions of climbs and trees and clearings in my early journal entries, but now, if I wrote in my journal at all, it was about the people I was surrounded by and our off-trail shenanigans.

This view from atop the 5,260 foot Mount Lafayette, a knife's edge spine of mountain ridge in either direction, showing us exactly where we'd come from and exactly where we were going, had shaken me from my malaise. The sheer openness of the view, of its rocky summits jutting out of the earth and snaking northward, was unlike anything I'd seen or felt on the trail. Looking out, I was awed. Awed by the beauty, and awed by our accomplishment. We'd started our day by hiking down to Franconia Notch at 1,450 feet, and over the course of six miles, had climbed almost 4,000 feet.

"Can you take our picture?" Sug asked one of the many hikers lingering at the summit. I handed over my disposable camera. We were hiking in the era way before smartphones, when digital cameras were just becoming ubiquitous, but held too few pictures and were too expensive to take on a hiking trip. I had started the trail taking pictures with an old camera, but it soon became too cumbersome to carry batteries and film, so I switched to buying disposables when I needed them.

Erin, Sug, and I leaned in as a stranger captured our tired faces, happy to be sitting together on top of the world.

* * *

From our perch on the south peak of Lafayette, we followed the exposed ridge over its North peak and then climbed down another 2,000 feet and four miles to the Garfield Ridge Campsite.

"Was today really only 13 miles?" I asked, arms and legs splayed like a starfish across the shelter floor, my pack still sitting where I'd thrown it off when I'd first arrived. Before the Whites, we'd have finished 13 miles before lunch, and would have considered 13 miles practically a zero day.

"Yeah," Ben answered, and something in his tone made me sit up and look at him.

"What's up?" I asked.

"Huh? Nothing. I was just saying, yeah, it was 13 miles," he answered, his face giving away nothing.

He never said, but I suspected that he was feeling frustrated by our pace, and wished we were hiking longer days. I understood, but I was actually appreciating the lighter hiking load. Hiking without poles was proving to be more strenuous physically and mentally; I was using muscles to balance and climb, and thinking about my footing more than ever before. But I also just liked being able to take time to enjoy my unique surroundings, I liked not feeling rushed to move on from a stunning view, or to cut a fun lunch with the whole crew short. I was keenly aware how close we were to finishing, and while we all spent hours dreaming about life after the trail (The food we'd eat! The mindless TV we'd watch!), life after the trail also meant life without Pilgrim, Sug, and Turbo; without Erin, and without Ben. I wasn't ready to let go.

CHAPTER FIFTY-TWO

DAY 122, NEW HAMPSHIRE, 362.4 MILES TO KATAHDIN

We left the campsite the next morning in good spirits. We'd heard horror stories about hiking in crappy weather through the Whites, and I could imagine how scary it might be to hike above tree line in a rain or snow storm, but we'd had nothing but blue skies and sunshine. People had been telling us that our hiking season was the rainiest on record, and I believed it. The dry, blue skies that stayed with us above tree line in the Whites made this section feel even more alien from the rest of our soggy trail experience.

We spent the morning hiking all together, me teasing Ben about the book I'd seen him take with him to the privy.

He shrugged, unfazed by my taunts, "What? Haven't you ever read on the toilet?"

"But it's not a toilet!" I exclaimed, "You're literally sitting on a mountain of other people's poop, and you're over there reading Moby Dick like you're on an EZ Boy."

"I'm not reading Moby Dick."

"That's not the point!" I said, exasperated.

He was walking in front of me, and now he turned his head

and focused on me. His big green eyes twinkled with amusement.

"So, what, you don't poop?"

"Dude, you know I poop." And he did, we were all intimately aware of each other's bathroom habits. "But I'm not fucking lingering in the privy with a book like an old man reading a paper on the shitter."

"I'm not lingering, I'm just not in a rush. It takes the time it takes. Besides, your sense of smell is mind over matter; I don't think about it, so I don't smell it."

"Okay weirdo," I shot back, resorting to middle school retorts, but enjoying the sparring.

Turbo piped up, "What do you do, Not Yet? Hold your breath the whole time you're in there like you're underwater or something?"

"YES!!"

* * *

We reached Ethan Pond Campsite around 4pm after a day of alternately hiking up and over the Twin mountains and then lounging at two AMC huts; Galehead and Zealand Falls. As AT hikers, we still had to pay to stay in the campsites in the Whites, a fact that incensed me. I was complaining about this to Erin and Sug when we noticed the other three guys waiting for us at the turn off to Ethan Pond.

Pilgrim waved a piece of paper, "Cara left us a note!"

Erin's face grew still and I could see her steeling herself for disappointment, "If we missed her again..."

"No! She's at Crawford Notch, she said she'll wait there until 6pm!" Pilgrim reassured her. "It's 3 miles away and all downhill. Can you make it, Sweets?"

Relief washed over Erin. "Yes! What are we still doing here?"

We started toward Crawford Notch, a road crossing at 1,200 feet between two big peaks—the North and South Twins at almost 5,000 feet to the South and Mt. Washington, the second tallest mountain on the trail at 6,288 feet. We hiked as a group, going as fast as we could on the steep, rocky, descent.

There was a lull in the chatter when Sug started to sing, "Blue jean baby, LA lady..."

Erin chimed in, pointing to her headphones, apparently tuned to the same station, "Seamstress for the baaand."

In cinematic unison, all six of us joined in, belting as we walked, "BUT OH HOW IT FEELS SO REAL, LYING HERE..."

"Wait, has it always been, 'lay me down in sheets of linen?'" I broke in during the chorus. "I thought it was 'Lady darlin' she's so blended.'"

"Whatsit, I thought it was 'Lay me drowning she's of Lennon,'" Turbo said.

"WHAT THE FUCK DOES THAT EVEN MEAN?" Erin laughed.

"How should I know? I didn't make it up!" Turbo answered, incredulous.

We started talking about misheard lyrics, Erin telling us that when she was little, she thought the Beach Boys song "Little Douce Coupe" was "Little Loose Tooth." Sug brought us all back to the song with the second, "But oh how it feels so real..."

I could feel myself getting nostalgic for the moment while it was still happening, knowing that I could never recreate this precise feeling of happiness and warmth.

That warmness grew until I almost burst into tears of joy

when I finally glimpsed the gravel parking lot through the trees and there was Cara, standing next to her car.

"CAW CAW!" Erin crowed.

"BASTIAN!" I called.

Cara's head turned towards the trees, a smile breaking across her face, "WHOOP WHOOP!"

We'd developed our call system when the three of us had hiked the Long Trail together, a way to locate everyone in the woods if we couldn't see each other. Mine was a reference to the Never ending Story, a movie Erin and I watched on repeat in the seventh grade, when the princess yells out, "BASTIAN! CALL... MY... NAME!"

By the time we'd descended the stone steps into the parking lot, Cara's trunk was open, revealing a cooler full of Long Trail Ales on ice. Cara handed out the beers, cheers-ed us all, and looked at her Subaru. "It'll be a squeeze, but if you guys want to pack in, there's a restaurant down the road."

She barely had the words out and we were stashing our packs behind a grouping of trees and piling into the car—Erin and I in the front, Ben, Pilgrim, and Sug in the backseat and Turbo curled up in the tiny hatchback's trunk. At the restaurant, we ate disgusting amounts of food that barely filled us up and then ordered dessert to celebrate Turbo's birthday.

"How are you 23?" Pilgrim demanded of Turbo. "I'm 23 and you just seem...so much younger than me."

Turbo did seem younger than Pilgrim, younger than all of us, in a rascally little brother kind of way. He'd graduated from college and had been bumbling around before the trail, trying to figure out his life. At twenty-five, two years out from college and with professional work experience under my belt, I felt like an adult. I thought about my friends at home, many married or engaged, all several years into their careers, some with new houses and kids on the way. That trajectory—college, job, marriage, house, kids before 30—had seemed inevitable for me too just a few months ago. Now my future was murky. Out here in the woods, surrounded by this ragtag group of wanderers, the murkiness didn't bother me, it seemed natural, but I was headed back to the real world soon.

* * *

We piled back into Cara's car after dinner and started down the road winding through the mountains, on our way back to the parking lot where we'd left our packs earlier that night. The soundtrack to "O Brother Where Art Thou" was on and as "You Are My Sunshine" started Sug yelled, "TURN IT UP, THIS IS MY JAM."

Cara obliged and we all joined in, singing the lyrics at the top of our lungs.

"Again!" someone demanded from the back as the song faded out, and we started the song again from the top. We repeated this ridiculousness until we were back in the parking lot, where everyone stayed crammed in the car until "You Are My Sunshine" was over one last time.

"So, I guess we should just sleep in the parking lot?" Ben asked, after we'd said our goodbyes and thanks to Cara and collected our bags from their hiding spot. Cara had offered to drive us to a hotel for the night, but we were all ready to tackle the beast that stood in front of us—Mt. Washington.

CHAPTER FIFTY-THREE

DAY 123, NEW HAMPSHIRE, 345 MILES TO KATAHDIN

M t. Washington is the highest peak in the Northeast at 6,288 ft. It's notorious not just for its height but for the erratic and often dangerous weather conditions that can occur at the peak, often with no warning. It holds the record for the highest measured wind speed in the Northern Hemisphere at 231 miles per hour. The summit has hurricane-force wind gusts more than 100 days every year. Over 150 people have died on Mt. Washington since 1849, due to sudden changes in weather, bad equipment, and poor planning.

Every other car I saw in New Hampshire had a bumper sticker that read, "I climbed Mt. Washington." If it was a brag for a car to get up there, I knew it was going to be a feat for us.

We did indeed sleep in the gravel parking lot that night and woke up the next morning with a plan to hike 11.1 miles to the Lake of the Clouds hut that lay just 1.5 miles and 1260 feet from the Mt. Washington summit.

Lying in my sleeping bag that morning, I stared at the trail as it snaked steeply into the woods across the street. Our sprint down the mountain last night meant that it would be a slow slog up out of the notch that day. Everyone else was making some motions towards starting the day except for Turbo, who somehow remained asleep despite the hubbub; sleeping bag pulled tight up to his chin, hat down over his eyes, and handkerchief tied around his neck. I took a deep breath and counted to ten in an effort to force myself to sit up. When that didn't work, I counted to ten again, this time groaning loudly as I rose.

My body ached from the night on the gravel, and the initial 2700 foot climb up Mt. Webster didn't give me any time to warm up to the day. At several points along the trudge up the mountain, the trees cleared and I was able to catch my breath while looking behind me to the notch below. It was immensely satisfying to watch the parking lot and road become specks in the distance, the cars become hot wheels, and the people tiny ants.

Around five miles into the day, we reached Mt. Jackson, at over 4000 feet. The last two tenths of a mile were steep boulders and rocks that made hiking upright impossible. I scrambled up, finding handholds and nooks in the rocks to lodge my feet in, to propel my body up and over. Erin had to stow her hiking poles, the boulders rendering them useless.

The famously fickle weather of the Whites continued to hold off and as we stood on the summit; I could see the ridgeline stretching in front of us. Hiking above tree line, a rarity South of New Hampshire, was a surreal experience. The day was a rollercoaster. We hiked from Mt. Jackson down to Mizpah Spring hut for lunch, then up 500 feet to Mt. Pierce, down below 4000 feet to a notch, before starting the climb to the Mount Washington Summit. We reached Lake of the Clouds, which stood at just over 5000 feet elevation, in the early evening.

"So.... who wants to go ask about work-for-stay?" I said as we approached the hut. Because of the weather on top of Mt.

Washington, we knew we needed to give ourselves plenty of time to get up and over the summit. We were too late in the day to tackle it that afternoon, so our only option was to stay at Lake of the Clouds hut. And that meant doing work at the hut in exchange for space to sleep.

Everyone simultaneously kicked at the dirt for a long beat, until, as we all knew she would, Erin said, "FINE," and walked off towards the hut. Erin was always the one we volunteered to ask for rides, negotiate places to stay, or talk a motel owner into letting six of us stay in a room without charging us. She didn't have the anxiety around talking to strangers that I did and people naturally liked her easy laugh. Plus, she's impatient, so the rest of us knew that if we just stalled long enough, she would just "do it her own damn self."

Pilgrim, Sug, Turbo, Ben, and I milled around outside for a few minutes when Erin returned, telling us with a shrug, "Well. We can stay, but they don't have any bunks left. If we help with serving dinner and cleaning up, they said we can sleep on the dining tables after everyone goes to bed. But... they also said we need to stay out of the way and get up and leave before breakfast."

"Fuck that," Pilgrim and I retorted in chorus. The idea that we would have to serve pampered hikers their meals and scurry around hoping not to disturb anyone just so that we could sleep on their floors made me furious. Especially when we would gladly just camp outside if it wasn't forbidden by the AMC. It wasn't paying for the huts that I objected to, we couldn't pay if we wanted to—these huts were reserved almost a year in advance—it was that we were basically denied access to this part of the trail in favor of wealthy weekend adventurers. And for now, at least, the trail was our home, so it felt like being kicked out of our own house.

"We don't really have another choice, do we?" Ben pointed

out, evenly. More and more, Ben was becoming our collective voice of reason. I gave him a withering eye-roll, but I liked that he was calm and reasonable without being condescending.

And, of course, he was right, even if camping outside of the huts and designated campgrounds was allowed in the Whites, sleeping outside when none of us were carrying tents anymore wasn't a great idea in an area known for its unpredictable weather.

Pilgrim and I continued to grumble, but eventually gave into our fate and headed into the hut. The rest of the night only solidified our skepticism. There was a weird dynamic between our group and the hut workers, who were all around our age. At other huts we'd stopped at, we'd had fun talking to the people working at the huts. We generally had a lot in common, all of us were recent college grads choosing to escape to the mountains for a season. But we were resentful at being treated less-than the other guests and in return, the Lake of the Clouds crew treated us like adversaries rather than allies.

We finished a long evening of chopping vegetables and cleaning dishes and were exiled to wait outside until the paying guests had cleared out of the dining area.

Ben and I lay side by side on the lawn outside of the hut, holding hands. I'd briefly leaned my head on his chest, but as he lifted his arm to drape around me, I was quickly reminded that neither of us had showered in days. We talked quietly about the book he'd given me, that I'd finished the night before. I confessed that I'd liked my first Vonnegut more than I thought I would.

"Get a room, you two," called out Turbo.

I looked back to see Sug, Pilgrim, Erin, and Turbo all sitting about 10 feet away. They'd obviously been talking about us.

"Yeah, but even if we got a room, you weirdos would still be there," I called back.

I looked at Ben and said in a low voice, "Are we being annoying?"

Ben shrugged, "Maybe... but I don't think they really care. I mean, I don't care. Do you care?"

"No! Well, I don't know. No," I answered tentatively. In truth, I didn't really care what the guys thought about Ben and I being "couple-y" but I did care what Erin thought. I was spending more and more time with Ben—during the day while we were hiking and at night. And that was time I'd normally spend with Erin. I didn't want her to think I was abandoning her for a guy, even though I worried that was exactly what I was doing.

One of the young hut workers stuck his head out of the front door, "you guys can come in if you want."

We'd been told that we could sleep in the dining area, but that we couldn't move the heavy wooden tables and benches. That left us the option of throwing our sleeping bags down on the dusty floor in between the tables or sleeping on top of the tables. I chose a spot on the ground, while Erin settled on the table above me.

"Dude, this is like when we used to sleep on your trundle beds!" Erin said, peering down at me.

"Am I going to wake up to you staring at me like you used to?" At every sleepover, Erin would wake up before me and stare until I finally roused myself out of a sound sleep.

"You're probably going to wake Not Yet up when you roll off the table on top of her in the middle of the night," said Pilgrim, struggling in his sleeping bag to find a comfortable position.

* * *

No one rolled off a table that night, but none of us slept much either. Worried we'd be scolded for not getting up before the paying guests were ready for breakfast, we were all up and out of the hut before sunrise.

Erin was antsy to get going, knowing that her knee would slow her down on the big climb, so while the rest of us finished our breakfasts, she took off towards Mt. Washington.

"See ya at the top!" I called.

I watched her tiny figure disappear up the rocky incline and wondered if I should have gone with her.

The morning was clear and fairly warm, and I wondered how many hikers were lucky enough to get to Mt. Washington on a clear day.

Pilgrim left next and then Turbo and Sug, following the trail while the sun rose in the sky. Ben and I were last, starting maybe 15 minutes after Erin, figuring we'd catch her on our way to the summit. We were already above tree line, so the trail was marked by sign posts, rock cairns and the occasional white blaze painted on a boulder.

It took less than an hour for us to reach the top, and as the summit came into view we saw Pilgrim, Turbo, and Sug waiting for us, looking confused as they spotted us.

Pilgrim asked, "Where's Sweets?"

"She's not here?" I responded, feeling a little panicky, "How could we have missed her?"

I flashed back to Shenandoah, when Erin had passed out on the trail. It was why I always tried to stay behind her these days. But if she had fallen or passed out, we should have come across her on our way up.

"There were a few spur trails, do you think she maybe got lost on her way up?" Turbo wondered aloud. And as soon as he said it, we all knew that was exactly what happened.

Just as we were organizing ourselves to go search for her, I heard the telltale click-clack of hiking poles on rock, followed by a peek of Erin's red hair rising up a trail I hadn't noticed before off to our left.

"Erin!" I yelled, running towards her.

"What the fuck, dude?" she asked, now the one who was confused. "How did you guys all get here before me? And why the fuck did that take so lo... dude, I fucking went the wrong way, didn't I?"

"Sweets, I'm constantly in awe of your ability to use the words dude and fuck in any sentence," Pilgrim mused.

"It is pretty amazing," I agreed.

We made our way across the summit to the weather observatory that sat on top of Mt. Washington. The building was open now, and later in the year would have a snack bar for hikers and tourists who rode the train or drove to the top of the mountain to claim their "This Car Climbed Mt. Washington" bumper sticker.

The sun was still out but wind had picked up and the temperature had dropped about 10 degrees, so I was grateful to be indoors for a few minutes.

We spread out, Erin to the bathroom and I headed for the pay phone. After I tried without luck to get ahold of my mom and then dad, I thought about who to call. It felt weird not to call Kevin, but instead I decided to call two of my best friends, Hadley and Bethany. They were both in the middle of planning their weddings, weddings that I was excited to be a part of, and I was long overdue to hear what was happening in their lives. They'd also spent a lot of time over the years with Kevin, and I felt like I needed to tell them that we'd broken up.

It turns out, they'd already guessed. I caught Hadley at her Cincinnati, Ohio apartment. We spent a few minutes catching up and I took a deep breath and said, "Hads, I have news."

"You and Kevin broke up, didn't you?" She interrupted.

"Yeah. Wait, how did you know?" I said, taken back.

"I called it!" she sounded triumphant. "You're totally dating one of those guys, aren't you?"

"Wait, what? I mean yeah, but how do you know there are guys?"

"Oh my god, I told Bethany! I knew as soon as I saw pictures of you and Erin with those guys posted on your website that was what happened!" In addition to our emails and mail drop updates, Erin's brother had been posting a few pictures we'd sent him from the trail on a Geocities site that he had set up for us called "HikerGirlz." Apparently, Brian had included one of us with all of the dudes from Cara and Chris's wedding.

"You don't have to sound so excited," I mumbled.

"Oh, sorry, are you upset?" She tried to sound sincere, but I still detected amusement in her voice.

"Well... no."

"I can't believe I nailed it! You have a mountain man! I knew you were going to come home with a mountain man!" Hadley demanded I tell her everything about Ben, and I found myself grinning as I gave her the rundown.

We'd just left Mt. Washington and were headed down the peak when we heard a rumbling. Erin and I lagged behind the boys but could see them, the size of action figures, down the trail. We saw them stop as they, too, heard the loud sound.

"Oh shit," Erin said, realization spreading across her face, "it's the train!"

The Cog Railway runs from Marshfield Base station six miles up to the top of Mt. Washington. When it started running in 1869, it was the world's first mountain railway and still remains the second steepest track in the world. P.T. Barnum called it "the second greatest show on earth." It ran entirely as a steam engine until 2008, when they introduced diesel engine trains. Many hikers resent the train for its noise and air pollution, and for people getting to go to the top of the mountain with so little personal effort. For whatever reason, whether it's animus or just a nod to the Cog Railway's nickname "railway to the moon" there's a long-held tradition of thru-hikers mooning the Cog Railway as it passes by.

Erin and I yelled together, pointing wildly at the smoke billowing above the next peak, "TRAIN!"

As the train rounded the mountain on its final ascent up to the top of Mt. Washington on the morning of June 27, 2003, passengers of the Cog Railway were greeted with four bare thru-hiker butts.

* * *

"You're not like a lot of girls I know," Ben said to me a little later that day as we walked together. More and more, we'd been lagging back from the group for small parts of the day to have time to walk just the two of us.

I cocked an eyebrow. "What do you mean?"

He hesitated and then said, "Well, you're not overly-emotional, but you're also not like one of those women who prides herself on being a guy's girl."

The part of me that loved that he saw me as special and different wrestled with the baby feminist who knew it was dangerous to be held up as an exception to "most women."

He laughed at my skeptical expression and said, "I'm obviously not saying this right."

He took on a mocking stereotypical "bro voice" and said, "You're like... all the cool parts of a girl without the dumb parts."

"Oh dude, you obviously don't know me that well," I laughed. "I've got *allll* the dumb parts. My move is just to bottle up all those emotions and then break down or shut down when it gets too much."

"I'd like to see that," Ben quipped. "Sounds super healthy."

As if he'd conjured it, just a few miles later, I was walking by myself. I looked up and saw Madison Hut, our afternoon lunch destination. Distracted from the trail for one second, my foot caught on a rock and I pitched forward, landing on my hands and knees on the rocky path. As I struggled to stand, my pack slid up my back, knocking the back of my head and forcing me back down onto my bloodied limbs. I froze in that position for what seemed like a full minute and then with a rush, I burst into tears. Not quiet tears, but big, wracking, unstoppable sobs. It wasn't the pain, but the indignity of the fall, coupled with the already long day—the poor sleep at Lake of the Clouds, the stress of telling my friends about Kevin, the rocky trail requiring complete concentration, probably even the rush of happy but confusing feelings for Ben—broke something open.

I finally unfastened my pack, roughly casting it to the side and sat on the ground, hugging my knees and still crying.

I was finally startled out of my state by a voice, "Sally?"

"Shit," I looked up to see Ben, standing over me, looking very concerned.

"Are you hurt?"

"No..." my voice quavered, "I'm just tired of these fucking rocks."

"The rocks are making you cry," he said, not judgmental, but also not buying my explanation.

"YES," I said emphatically. "They're fucking rocky and stupid."

"Okay," he said, picking up my pack and helping me up.

"So... everyone saw that?" I asked, finally getting a good

look at the Hut and noticing Erin, Turbo, Sug, and Pilgrim all standing outside, watching us.

He barely suppressed a smile, "Ahhh... yeah."

"Cool," I took a deep breath and stood up straight. "Well dude, welcome to my dumb parts."

* * *

It was decided that we should hike down to Pinkham Notch and try to get a room at the lodge there for the night. No one was saying it was because of my meltdown, but I knew it was because of my meltdown and I felt grateful. I was exhausted. It was another 7.8 miles, up to Mt. Madison at 5366 feet and down to the notch at 2050 feet elevation. Erin and I found a blue blaze trail that looked like it would cut about a mile and a half off the hike and talked the boys into taking it. Turbo and Sug were pretty indifferent to shortcuts, but Pilgrim and Ben were pretty staunchly against deviating in any way from the official trail. But between my crying and Erin's flaring knee pain, they surprisingly relented.

About halfway down the blue blazed trail, we realized we had made a mistake. The trail became super steep and then devolved into almost completely vertical sheer rock drops of between 6-10 feet. I felt the tears welling back up. I was scared of heights, and I felt guilty for forcing the guys down this path that now seemed dangerous to navigate.

"I think we have to go back," I said, looking at the steep climb back up and thinking about the added miles. "I don't know what else to do."

For the second time that day, I felt paralyzed. It was Sug who took action.

"I'm not hiking back up that trail," he said firmly. "We're going to get down."

Sug had us take off our backs and slide them down the rocks. Then we formed a chain- lowering each other down to safety. After a half mile of drops, the trail finally leveled back out.

"No more blue blazes," Pilgrim said, and I saw a small nod from Ben. Erin squeezed my hand and I let go of the tension I'd been holding on to.

The rest of the trail was an easy descent and we made it to Pinkham Notch by 5pm. Sug, Turbo, and I sat on the porch of the visitor's center while Erin went in to see about getting a room in the Joe Dodge Lodge, both owned and operated by the AMC.

She reappeared ten minutes later looking annoyed. "No rooms. No matter how I tried to sweet talk the front desk guy, he kept telling me they were full."

"This fucking day," I said. "What do we do? I can't hike anymore today."

Like the rest of the AMC territory, camping was not permitted anywhere that was not a designated campsite and the next one of those was over five miles away.

"Maybe one of these families will feel sorry for us and let us stay in their room," Turbo offered, watching a fresh-smelling family of four emerge from the visitor's center and walk across the parking lot to their room.

"Yeah right," Sug retorted. "Nobody is going to invite four bearded men and two women who smell like garbage to stay in a room with their precious children."

"Speaking of four bearded men, where are Pilgrim and Ben?" Erin asked, looking around. Ben and Pilgrim had wandered off when we'd first arrived, and I realized I hadn't seen them since.

Just as we were starting to worry, they came sauntering over, bags of McDonalds in their hands.

"What the..." Turbo started, "What's it? Where did that come from?"

"Some guy offered us a ride to McDonalds! We thought it'd be a fun surprise!" Pilgrim grinned.

"Finally, something good in this shitty day," I said, grabbing fries from the bags Ben was handing around. We all ate in silence for awhile, savoring the greasy food that tasted all the better because it meant that we wouldn't have to cook our dinner and clean our pots.

Erin broke the silence, "Dude...do you guys remember when I got FUCKING lost this morning?"

"That was THIS morning? Jesus." I said.

CHAPTER FIFTY-FOUR

DAY 124, NEW HAMPSHIRE, 319 MILES TO KATAHDIN

When it had become clear that no room was going to magically appear for us, we'd ended up walking about five minutes back up the way we'd come and sleeping right on the trail. We reasoned that no one was going to make us move in the middle of the night. We woke early the next morning, both to avoid detection and because we were all excited about our last big day before we were out of the Whites. As a reward, we were going to meet Cara and Chris and spend two nights in Gorham, New Hampshire.

Only 21 miles of trail stood between us and town.

* * *

We started off strong, excited by the impending time off but also giddy that we were so close to crossing off another state and finally walking into Maine. As we climbed all together the 2000 ft. out of the notch to Wildcat Mountain, Erin tripped on a rock, swearing as she stumbled to regain her balance, "Fuck dude. Fucking mother fucking boulder. Dude!"

"Sweets, your trail name really should have been Dude Fuck," Ben laughed.

Pilgrim turned back, saying, "And then after med school, you'll be Dr. Dude Fuck. People will be all, excuse me, Dude Fuck? And you'll be like, 'That's DOCTOR Dude Fuck. Show a little respect.'"

"Oh my god!" I was delighted with this idea. "It really could work for any patient situation. If it's bad news, you could be all 'dude, you're fuuuuucked....'"

Erin laughed, "Or if it's good news, I'll just be like 'fuck dude... YOU'RE GOING TO LIVE!'"

"Oooohh, I like the pause for dramatic effect," I said.

"Dude. Fucking thank you."

One of my favorite things about Erin is that she is always up for a joke, even if she's the one being teased. We all agreed, Dr. Dude Fuck was the perfect name for her. And it stuck. Four years later, when she did graduate from med school, we chipped in to get her an official name plate that read Dr. Dude Fuck.

* * *

The day flew by, it was by far our longest day in the Whites, but also the easiest hiking we'd had in awhile. Before we knew it, we were sitting in the parking lot, drinking cold Long Trail Ales out of the back of Cara and Chris's Subaru.

Chris told us all about the Moose study he was doing that summer as a student at the University of New Hampshire. A few days a week he would stay at a little cabin in the woods with other students and they would track the moose in the area.

We finished our beers and the two dropped us off at the Barn Hostel right on the edge of the small, picturesque town of Gorham. They were going to spend the night at the moose lodge and pick us up in the morning so we could slack pack the 16 remaining miles of New Hampshire and stay in town a second night.

The hostel was a small barn attached to a beautiful historic Victorian bed & breakfast. Inside we found a small kitchen and seating area with tatty old couches and an ancient TV set. Photos of hikers lined the walls and a sign hung from the rafters that said, "If no one is here when you arrive, bunk space is up in the loft. Toilet & shower inside on right. Be back soon... Doc." We ventured upstairs and found a large loft with mattresses.

There were a few packs on beds, indicating there were hikers already here. I vaguely wondered if it was someone we knew. We'd already hiked ahead of the pack that had caught up with us after the wedding and from the registers, we knew there were only a few other hikers that were still ahead of us. It wasn't that we hiked so much further in a day than other hikers, it was that, compared to most thru-hikers, we rarely took days completely off. Even on occasions like this, where we were going to stay in town for two nights, we would arrange to slack pack, so that we were still clocking mileage and moving forward.

Erin and I wandered down to a stream that ran through the town while the boys took turns showering and making phone calls. We waded in the water, cooling our tired feet and watching some young kids splashing nearby with their mother. As we walked back to the Barn we heard a voice calling out from the loft, "YOOOOOOOOOO!!!"

Hanging out of the top floor window was Nasty, who we hadn't seen since we'd left him, Mike, and Shaman at Kincora hostel in Tennessee.

"Ho-lee shit," I murmured to Erin as I smiled and waved back to him. "How did he catch up to us?"

He came down to greet us as we entered the Barn, hugging

us like long lost friends. I'd liked Nasty when we'd hiked with him, but I didn't have the impression that he was going to ever become a thru-hiker motivated by miles and forward momentum. It turns out he actually hadn't caught up with us. He told us that he'd gotten off the trail for a bit, because, "You know, I met a guy who was going to go rafting, and I thought, brah, I'd be down for some rafting." Then he'd heard about some work in New Hampshire and had made his way up to Gorham.

Nasty kept us entertained with stories when we all went out to dinner at a big Italian place and then when we went to the bar down the street.

"He's funnier than I remember," Erin said to me at one point in the evening.

"Totally..." I agreed, eyebrows raised in a question.

"WHATEVER," she said, elbowing me. "You don't get to judge. You came out here with a boyfriend and you still found a new boyfriend. I haven't kissed a dude in months."

"No judgment," I told her, unable to keep the laughter from my voice.

"You suck," she said with faux anger. "Why don't you go make out with Ben?"

* * *

Later that night, back in the Barn, I was doing just that. We'd hung out on the downstairs couches while everyone else headed upstairs to bed. It'd been quiet for awhile and things were getting...intense, when we heard a creak on the stairs. We pulled apart like teenagers whose parents caught them in the basement. A sleepy Pilgrim walked by to go use the bathroom. On his way back he whispered to us, "By the way, Sweets is up there making out with Nasty. Goodnight you guys!"

Ben looked at me and we both started laughing. When we

stopped, he said in a low voice, "I think we need to get a hotel room tomorrow night. Like, just for us. Unless you don't want to..."

"No, no. I want to." I assured him, snuggling up on his chest and closing my eyes. I lay there for a few minutes, listening to his heart beat, and said, "Soooo.... you won't be offended if I go sleep on that other couch, will you? This is so uncomfortable."

"Oh, thank god. I'd just resigned myself to no sleep."

* * *

Early the next morning, after we gorged ourselves on a big diner breakfast in town, Cara drove us back to the trail. Our plan was to do the 16 miles to the New Hampshire/Maine border. It was 9am and Cara said she'd pick us up around 2pm and then we'd hang out the rest of the afternoon with her and Chris. Turbo decided to stay in town because a girl he'd been hiking with earlier, Peaches, was supposed to be getting in that day.

"Where's your stuff?" Cara asked as we piled out of her car.

"What stuff?" Sug asked.

Cara looked at all of us stuffing our water bottles and Clif bars into our makeshift daypacks. "Like, did any of you bring rain gear and long sleeve shirts? You're going to be up above tree line for a little bit at least and it can get cold, super fast."

She looked at our blank stares and seemed to resign herself to our stupidity. "Okay, have fun!"

This part of the trail was relatively mild compared to the Whites we'd just finished and so we sped through the miles, staying together to do a "walk and talk." We were all so pumped to be so close to Maine, a destination that at times had seemed almost fictional, finally in sight.

"Damn," Erin said, rolling her head from side to side. "My neck hurts."

Without turning around or missing a step, Ben said, "That's what happens when you spend all night making out."

"Awww, dude, how did you know?" Erin asked, her freckled face reddening. She looked from face to face. "Fuck, do you all know?"

"Sweets, we were like 5 feet away from you," Sug blurted, "You weren't being quiet."

"Oh maaaan. I'm sorry guys. I thought everyone was asleep!" She stopped and looked at me and Ben. "Wait, did you guys hear us all the way downstairs?"

Ben nodded his head yes, and her eyes widened before I took pity on her and told her no.

We walked a little way down the trail when Pilgrim said, "Sweets, I have a question. When you guys get married are you going to be Dr. Dude Fuck Nasty?"

Erin laughed, "I can't believe I made out with a person named Nasty. I don't even know his real name. It could very well be Nasty."

We'd gone about 13 miles when we heard a crack of thunder and saw lightning flash through the trees. And just to prove Cara's point, the skies opened up and started to pour. We knew from our trail book that the last part of the day was going to be up and over the exposed summit of Mt. Success.

Erin looked at the trail map. "I think there's a side trail down to a logging road just up ahead. Let's take that and then maybe we can walk up the logging trail to the spot where we're supposed to meet Cara."

By the time we'd made it to the logging road, the storm had passed. As we decided what to do, the boys played rock baseball. One of them would throw a rock up in the air and then hit it with a stick. Another would call the ball—single, double, out, foul, etc. The game mystified Erin and me, but was one of their favorite time wasters.

Erin and I pored over the trail map, trying to figure out if it actually connected to the spot where we'd need to be in an hour. It didn't, but we thought we'd figured out a way to get there through a series of side trails.

As we were getting ready to move out, we heard car tires crunching on gravel.

"No way!" I exclaimed as Cara pulled into view in Chris's pick-up truck.

Erin ran to hug her sister, "How the hell did you find us?"

When the rain started, Cara, always exceedingly thoughtful and perceptive, knew that we might cut down the mountain. She'd been with Chris at his moose cabin. They'd looked at the map and figured if we had tried to get out of the rain, this was the spot we'd go to. She said she was just going to come check here first before going to our original meeting spot.

"You're amazing," Ben said, voicing the awe and gratitude for us all.

The boys all piled in the back while Erin and I slid into the cab with Cara.

As we drove back into town, I leaned over to Cara. I said in a low voice, "Can I ask you a huge embarrassing favor? Do you think you could drop Ben and I off at a motel later... like, instead of the Barn?"

She smiled knowingly and said, "Of course. Don't forget, I was you once. I remember never having any privacy with Chris."

"I know, it's just, I've known you since I was 12 and now I'm asking you to drop me off for a sex date."

"YOU'RE GOING TO HAVE A SEX DATE?" Erin busted in.

I put my head in my hands. "Shhhhhhhhhh! You know I hate talking about this stuff."

Erin whispered, "Seriously, you're going to have a sex date?"

"I think so...." I said, now losing confidence, "Do you think I shouldn't?"

"No, of course you should!" Erin said seriously, "I can't believe I finally just made out with a guy and now you're going on a sex date."

Later, Ben and I gathered our things from the Barn and Cara drove us down Gorham's Main Street to a cute, hilariously named motel—the "Top Notch"—that Ben had found in the phone book.

I'd felt awkward saying goodbye to our friends who obviously knew why we were leaving. As we walked up to the reception, hand in hand, I said to Ben, "It's not every day all your friends know exactly where and when you're going to have sex. It's like we're virgins on our wedding night. At least they didn't throw rice."

"Wait. We're going to have sex?" Ben joked.

"Oh, *we're* not having sex. I was just telling you so you knew that I was going to go have sex with some hot stranger."

CHAPTER FIFTY-FIVE

DAY 126, MAINE, 281.4 MILES TO KATAHDIN

"So..." Erin asked the next morning after Cara had once again dropped us back off at the trail, wishing us luck with the day's hike.

"Sooo.... what?" I asked, feigning ignorance.

"Come on dude. I don't need details but like, was it nice?"

"Yeah," I said, smiling in spite of myself. "Yeah, it was really nice."

I did tell her a few sparing details, reserved for only a best friend, and asked her how her night was. It was one of only two nights we'd spent apart in months. She told me that they'd had a few drinks, and she and Nasty had made out again. I asked her, "So, was Nasty nice?"

"Very funny. Dude, that was just a necessity after four months with no action." It turned out Erin and Nasty weren't the only ones making out in the Barn. Peaches, the woman Turbo had been hiking with before we'd met back up had come into Gorham the day before with her hiking partner, Cream. Apparently, they were also going at it in the loft.

"Poor Pilgrim and Sug!" I laughed, "Awwww, I'm going to miss Turbs."

"He said he'll catch up before we summit, but... you know..." Erin said wistfully.

As we hiked up and over the beautiful alpine peaks of Goose Eye Mountain, I looked back to see the Presidential range of the Whites looming in the South. It had been a gorgeous stretch, but I was so happy to be finished and back to a wilder and less populated part of the trail. We climbed up again to Fulling Mill Mountain, and I thought about the night before. My cheeks get hot with the memory, but I also noticed the absence of something. I didn't feel any of the usual guilt, regret, embarrassment, or uncertainty. I watched Ben striding up ahead, his mass of curly, sun-streaked, brown hair peeking over the top of this pack, and felt only happy.

* * *

We were all buzzing as we descended Fulling Mill, not just because we were excited to finally be in Maine, but we were about to go through the Mahoosuc Notch. We'd been hearing about this one mile stretch of trail since the beginning of our hike. This glacier-worn boulder field is deemed "the longest mile on the Appalachian Trail" because it takes longer to traverse than any other stretch. The notch is full of rock formations that you have to crawl through, climb over, slide down. There's no going around it, the mile-long gulch is surrounded by sheer granite walls on either side.

We reached the notch mid-morning and I knew that the mile was going to be slower for Erin and I (her with her knee and me with my fear of heights) than for the guys. We told them to go ahead and that we'd see them at the shelter later that night. As we prepared to start, we made sure to take anything hanging from our packs (our water bottles, hiking poles, sleeping pads) and cram them into our already full bags. Squeezing in and out of rock crevices could easily knock items off and down into unreachable holes. As we slowly made our way through, we saw plenty of evidence of hikers who'd lost precious items along the way.

The air was cooler in the Notch and we could hear water trickling underneath the boulders as we carefully made our way over, under, and through the rock. We talked each other through tricky parts, pointing out handholds or hidden caves. At times we had to stop and laugh at the absurdity of the precarious positions we found ourselves in. When we finally made our way to the other side, it was over an hour later. We would generally hike 3-4 miles an hour, so the Notch had definitely lived up to its nickname.

I took a pack of celebratory cigarettes out of a side pocket and handed one to Erin, saying, "I think we earned it."

"That was actually kinda fun," Erin mused, "like a giant obstacle course."

* * *

Four days later, on July 4th, Erin and I were alone together again. This time we were in the middle of the dense Maine woods, looking for a good clearing to set up our bug bivy and tarp. It was our first time using the tarp since we'd abandoned our single tents over a month ago. We had only ever used the tents once, always finding shelter or clear skies to sleep under, and couldn't justify the weight. I connected the poles that gave structure to the bug bivy, turning it into a dome that could cover both of our heads and keep the black flies and mosquitoes away, and then Erin and I covered it with a lightweight tarp that we set up with our hiking poles and a few tent stakes to keep us dry.

"Do you miss Ben?" Erin asked, looking serious. She was holding the hiking poles and tarp upright while I tried to stake out the sides.

"Dude, shut up. It's you and me, baby. We're going to Maine!" I said echoing the words she'd said when she'd passed out on the trail in Virginia. The phrase had become the rallying cry of the group.

* * *

After we'd made it through Mahoosuc Notch and up to Baldplate shelter our first day into Maine, a general unrest had seemed to spread over the group. Ben and I were somewhat immune, being in the throes of a fresh romance, but the other three were completely, as we often said, "anti." Erin was in constant and increasing pain, Sug had never recovered his enthusiasm for the trail after he spent those nine days at home, and due to his frequent "why are we even out here?" comments we joked that Pilgrim seemed to be in the middle of an existential crisis.

On July 3nd, Ben and I had been hiking together in the morning. We were happy for what seemed to be a relatively milder start to our hike. The day before had been exceptionally hard hiking, there were climbs that required metal hand and footholds dug into the sheer rock cliffs. Sug and I had questioned why everyone talked about how hard the Whites were but no one warned you about the beginning of Maine.

As Ben and I walked that morning he'd surprised me with a question. "What do you think about me moving to Cincinnati after this is over?"

I'd decided on University of Cincinnati for law school, so I knew what he was really asking was if I would be okay with him moving there to be with me.

I immediately tensed and thought of all the reasons I should say no. His question made me incredibly nervous. I was already scared about this new chapter of my life, starting law school was going to be a huge change from working and hiking and on top of it I was moving to a new city. I was already having a hard time imagining a life after the trail that was so different from the one I had envisioned with Kevin when I started.

"I don't know, Ben," I started. "You know Cincinnati is in Ohio, right? Like, what would you even do there? And like law school is going to be super busy..."

"I'll find a job, think about grad school. I don't know. But it's not like I have somewhere else I need to be." Once Ben had broken up with his girlfriend in Wisconsin earlier in the hike, his plans of moving to Chicago after the trail had been dashed. He'd been tossing around maybe moving to Wilmington, North Carolina, but he didn't have any obligations.

He stopped hiking and turned to face me, and said gently, "Look, I don't want you to answer now. But, I really like you and I feel like maybe we owe it to ourselves to see where this thing goes. And I don't know anything about Cincinnati, but you'll be there, right?"

"Right," I said. "Okay... I'll think about it."

"Good."

"Hey... I, uhhh... I really like you, too."

We walked along in silence for a few minutes when we reached a clearing on the peak of a mountain. We found Pilgrim laying on his back on a large rock, absently nibbling on a rice cake.

"You alright, Griz?" I asked.

"I'm just so fucking tired. I feel like shit... I'm all weak," he answered, not sitting up.

Erin and Sug came up the trail behind us.

"What's with him?" Sug asked.

"I FEEL LIKE SHIT," Pilgrim answered.

Erin took a look at him. "Well, maybe you should eat more than a fucking rice cake."

Pilgrim looked offended, "I like rice cakes."

"Nobody likes rice cakes. They have zero nutritional value. What are you, on a diet? What else have you eaten today?" I demanded.

He slowly sat up and smiled, "Pine nuts."

"GET THE FUCK OUT OF HERE! PINE NUTS," Erin said, shaking her head. "That's like the least fatty nut."

As we talked more, Pilgrim admitted that he thought he was "over hiking." Erin and I looked at each other with wide eyes. That was the same thing See Blue had said before he got off the trail in Massachusetts. Pilgrim, although prone to dramatic emotional swings, was also sensitive to the emotions of others, so when he saw Erin's and my worried look, he assured us, "I'm not going to quit, I just want to complain about it for a little while. We're going to Maine, right?"

Ben, who had been quiet the whole time, looked up from his trail book, "I have a plan."

Ben's plan was to hike a few more miles to a road crossing and get a hitch into a restaurant in the town of Rangely to eat at a place that had subs and pizza. When in doubt, feed the angst.

Buoyed by the break to our routine, we all hiked together down the mountain, playing a game we often did when we were together. We'd each pretend to be racecars and try to over-take each other while speed walking. One of us would narrate, "Sweets in the red car is taking the lead... Oh wait, here comes

Sug down the stretch, he's bumped out of the way by Not Yet, but it's Pilgrim that emerges in the number one spot!"

There was no point, just as there was no point to any of our games, other than to pass the time and make each other laugh.

When we'd arrived in town and ordered our lunches—we made Pilgrim order the biggest sub on the menu—Ben announced that he had another plan. There was a guest house on a lake nearby and the guidebook said the owner would come pick up hikers from Rangley.

"The last couple of days have been hard, and I think we all deserve a break. It's practically a holiday," he said, referring to the date, July 3rd.

The mood at the table made it clear he was right. The other three had already been in a funk and now I was also in internal turmoil over Ben's proposal to move to Cincinnati. He hadn't said another word about it, but I couldn't stop thinking about what to do.

Ben made the arrangements, and we all teased him for being the "hiking dad," for his knack of taking charge when everyone else was floundering.

"Somebody has to take charge of you idiots," he laughed.

It turned out Gull Pond Lodge was a perfect respite. The setting, right on the water, was beautiful and the owner, a sweet man named Bob, welcomed us in and made us feel instantly at ease. He showed us upstairs to two rooms with bunk beds and told us we were some of his first hikers of the season.

Pilgrim decided that what he needed to get him through the rest of the hike was a shake-up. "I'm going to shave."

"Shave what?" I asked, dubious.

"My hair, my beard, EVERYTHING," he answered, going off to ask Bob if he had clippers.

The rest of us sat around the table and started to talk about our plan for the rest of the hike. We had over 220 miles left to go. Ben was saying that we might need to start hiking big miles. He'd planned to meet his dad for the last part of the trail. They'd hiked the first three days together and his dad wanted to come to hike the last few days together, too. His dad was supposed to receive a big award from the ACLU on July 15th so Ben needed to be finished in time to be back in Delaware for the ceremony. He'd originally wanted to be done by July 10th, but that was seeming less likely with each day. He thought maybe he could make it to the 11th or 12th at the very latest.

"Okay, yeah, we can bust out some big miles," I said, trying to wrap my head around finishing within a week.

Erin gave a wry laugh, "I mean, I guess *you guys* can."

"What are you talking about, 'you guys?'" I asked, matching her sharp tone.

"Did you forget about my fucking knee? I can't hike 30-mile days every day. So maybe you guys should just go ahead," she said, her voice firm, but her eyes welling with tears. She stood up abruptly and walked outside.

Ben and Sug looked stunned, and I pushed my chair back and followed her out.

I found Erin sitting on the steps, staring out at the pond.

"I'm sorry," I said, sitting down. "I'm just feeling... a little torn in two directions."

"No, I'm sorry," she said. "I'm just so frustrated. I'm always in pain and I hate always feeling like I'm the one holding everyone back."

"I know..."

"But dude. I can't hike those big miles. I just can't." Her eyes started to fill up again. Mine did, too.

"I know, and it's okay. We don't have to," I told her.

"But I know you want to finish with Ben and everyone, so I think maybe you should just go and I'll finish on my own." She looked resolute now.

"Are you fucking out of your mind?" I asked. "I'm with you. I started with you and I'm finishing with you and I'm not going to make you kill yourself to get there."

"But what about Ben?" she asked.

"Ben who?" I answered, grinning. I paused and then told her, "He wants to move to Cincinnati with me... like, after the trail."

"WHAT? When did he say that?" Erin shrieked. "Wait. What did YOU say?"

I told her about my hesitation. We talked for a bit, agreeing it "was huge" but coming to no conclusion as to what I should do. Eventually we stood to go back inside.

I laughed, remembering Ben and Sug's expressions as we'd walked out. "The boys definitely think we were out here fighting."

"We should really play it up when we go back in, call each other bitches and stuff," Erin said, opening the door.

We found Ben and Sug upstairs and tried to convince them that we were truly upset with each other, but neither of them were buying it.

"Look," I said to Ben, "I know you need to finish by the 11th, but we can't do that. So, I think you guys might just need to go ahead."

"Nah," Ben answered.

"Nah?" I repeated, looking at Erin and Sug to make sure I'd heard right.

"Yeah. Nah. I called my dad while you guys were out there 'fighting' and told him I couldn't be done by the 11th and he said he didn't care if he missed his awards, that he'd wait." He said it like it was no big deal, like of course he wasn't going to finish without us. He looked at Erin, "Sorry, Dude Fuck, you're stuck with me until the end."

I was so relieved and went to hug Ben when Pilgrim bust

out of the bathroom. He looked so startlingly different with his shaved head and no beard that Erin and I both screamed.

"Nononononononono... it's too weird." I said, covering my eyes.

"Who ARE you?" Erin said, laughing.

"Cool... thanks, you two," Pilgrim said, looking just a little annoyed. "Just what you want to hear, that your face is too weird to look at."

"I don't like it," I said.

"Jesus, Sally," Ben shot me a look.

"No, I agree. It's no good," Erin said, backing me up. "Your face is fine, it's just you look like a totally different person."

* * *

After we got over our shock, we all sat down again and decided to hash out a mileage plan for our finish. We settled on a summit date—July 15th. We planned our stops for the remainder of the mileage, making sure to include as many town stays as possible, knowing we would need them to keep morale up and make it to the end. We all vowed once again, to stick together. Everyone who had someone coming to hike the summit with them—Erin, Pilgrim, Ben—called their family and let them know our plans.

The boys really wanted to stay at Gull Pond over July 4th, to go watch the fireworks around the lake. Erin and I decided that we would hike ahead, so that we could do two easy days over what looked like pretty big climbs, while the boys could take a zero day and do one 30-mile day to catch up. Now that we knew we wouldn't lose them, it felt okay to split up temporarily.

That was how Erin and I found ourselves in the middle of the woods, alone, on July 4th. It felt good to talk and laugh, just the two of us. We marveled at the beauty of the mountains we had climbed over that day. The three summits of Saddleback Mountain—the main peak, the Horn, and Saddleback Junior—had been thrilling to hike over. The clear skies had allowed us to see the whole ridge laid out in front of us as we walked. We talked about what it was going to be like to enter the real world again, how we were a crazy mix of excitement to be done and never wanting this to end. We talked like we were back in my childhood bedroom, laying side by side on twin beds, both tired, but neither of us wanting to be the first to fall asleep.

"Isn't it weird... this might be our last night camping, just the two of us," I said sleepily. "I love you, Ernie."

"I love you too, Sal." She may have said more, but I fell asleep first. Just like always.

CHAPTER FIFTY-SIX

DAY 132, MAINE, 202 MILES TO KATAHDIN

Erin and I hiked together again the next day, starting early so we could set a leisurely pace to the road where we would hitchhike into Stratton, Maine and wait for the boys at the White Wolf Inn. When we got there, the owner told us that four packs had been dropped off earlier that day. We figured that meant the boys got a slack pack from Bob and wondered who the fourth person was. Erin and I got a room, had showered and were down in the adjoining pub drinking Guinness when the mystery hiker walked in.

"Awww, Turbo! I was hoping it was you!" I stood up to hug him. "Where is Peaches? Is she with you?"

Ben, Sug, and Pilgrim had walked in behind Turbo and were quickly bellying up to the bar.

"So, whatsit, I'm going to like, finish with you guys and then go back and finish with her and Cream."

"He's going to do a yo-yo for love!" Pilgrim laughed.

"Fuck yeah, Turbo! Yo-yo for Love!" Erin called up, pumping her fist in the air. A yo-yo hike is the term for a thru-hiker who finishes the whole trail and then turns around and hikes the other way. A true yo-yo would be Georgia to Maine and then back to Georgia.

I was happy to have Turbo back. With the way the group had been feeling lately, it was going to be nice to have his special dose of ridiculousness to keep our spirits up.

We all ate dinner at the pub and as we settled our checks Erin turned to me, "Hey. I'm going to go in on a room with the boys, why don't you and Ben share the room we got?"

"You're the best," I said, hugging her.

* * *

The next morning, Ben and I lay in bed.

"Okay," I said, rolling on my side to face him.

"Okay.... what?"

"Okay, I want you to move to Cincinnati."

"Okay!"

"But. I think we should get separate apartments. I mean, we just met each other. What if we get there and you find out that you don't like me in the real world or you hate Ohio? I just... I need you to have other things going on besides me." The words spilled out.

I'd been thinking about it for the last few days and I realized that a big part of my hesitancy was that I was scared to be Ben's whole world. I was going to have law school, which I knew was going to be hard and one of my best friends, Hadley, lived there, so I already had a social circle (not to mention most of my family lived only 45 minutes away in Dayton, Ohio). When Ben said he wanted to move with me, on top of the excitement, I also instantly felt worried about the pressure of being responsible for another person.

But when I'd said that to Erin the night before, she'd looked at me like I was stupid. She'd said, "I don't think Ben is a needy kind of guy. I mean, he's the one who's always taking care of all of us, right? And he likes you so much he wants to move to fucking Ohio with you? I don't want to tell you what to do but I think you'd regret not taking this chance. Just tell him how you feel... he'll get it."

"Sally, first, I'm not going to stop liking you in the real world," Ben said. "And okay, separate apartments is probably a good idea. Look, I'm not asking you to marry me, but don't you want to see where this goes?"

"Yes, I do," I leaned in to kiss him and just as our lips touched, there was a loud knock at the door. We pulled apart and then heard someone yelling, "Ben, are you in there? Ben?"

"Oh shit," Ben laughed, "it's my dad."

* * *

Ben slipped out of the room and then came back a few minutes later and said, "Well. Yeah, so, my dad is here. I sent him to the diner, but we should go out there soon."

His dad, Tim, had already been headed to Maine when Ben had called about postponing our summit date. An avid backpacker and constant traveler, he figured that he would do some hiking on his own before meeting up with us. He'd grown up in New England and had lived in Maine before Ben was born and relished any chance to hike up there. Ben had called home and talked with his mom the night before and she in turn had told his dad where we were staying. He happened to be nearby so he headed over in hopes of catching Ben.

"Dude. I feel like such a hussy. Does he know you're in a room with a girl?" I said, only half joking, burying my head in Ben's chest.

He hugged me tight. "It's okay, he's really very nice. I told him all about you. Don't worry. But please... put on some pants."

We rounded up the other hikers and met Tim in the diner. He was, as advertised, amazingly nice. There was no doubt from looking at him, that he was Ben's father. They had the exact same build, the same curls, although Tim's were white rather than Ben's brown.

I was nervous to talk to him, because I felt like I had already made a bad impression, but he asked me questions about what I was going to do after the trail and seemed genuinely interested in my answers. He kept telling us how amazing he thought we all were for thru-hiking. And then to top it off, he bought all our breakfasts, the surest way to a thru-hiker's heart.

By the time he dropped us off at the trailhead, I was a fan.

"So... is your dad just going to... hang out in his van for the next 9 days?" Turbo asked as Tim drove off in his VW camper van.

No, Ben assured him, his dad was planning to go up to Katahdin and in a day or two he would start hiking South in the 100 mile wilderness, hopefully meeting up with us a few days before the summit.

"Dang," Erin said, "your dad really is nice."

* * *

It's both a blessing and a shame that Maine is the last state for Northbound hikers. For my money, it's the singularly most scenic and interesting state for hiking on the whole trail. Its beauty is both necessary to keep tired hikers engaged and mostly wasted on people who have been in the woods for over four months. It took true splendor at this point to make me slow down and really appreciate the view as more than something that I was just hiking past.

That day, hiking over the Bigelow range, did that for all of us. The hiking itself was hard, you gain close to 10,000 feet of elevation over the range and the trail is mostly rocky boulder fields. The range consists of four peaks—South Horn, West Peak, Avery Peak, and the ridge of Little Bigelow. The day was perfect, not a single cloud in the sky. We really did have luck in having good weather when it counted. When we got to the West Peak, we could see all the way South to Mt. Washington and to the North up the ridge and beyond to what seemed like endless green mountains, dotted all over with bright blue lakes. Avery Peak, with its narrow, rocky summit, made me feel like I was precariously balancing on the tippy top of the tallest mountain. At that moment, with all of us standing, looking out over the wild North, it felt like we were the only people on earth.

It was one of the few days where everything else slid away —Ben, law school, life after the trail, moving, the chaos in the world, wondering how I was going handle talking to Kevin again, when I was going to get my next hot meal—and the only thing that mattered was the hike. These were our last big views before we reached Katahdin and I wanted to savor the feeling of standing on top of the world.

CHAPTER FIFTY-SEVEN

DAY 134, MAINE, 172.5 MILES TO KATAHDIN

If that day was awe-inspiring, the next day was truly perfunctory. In my memory that day was just a series of trees and ponds. We hiked 20 miles and arrived at Pierce Pond Lean-To just as the skies opened up. At the back of the structure someone had set up a huge tent. I rounded the corner to find the inside of the shelter completely full of 9-10 year old boys. A scout leader greeted us, and Erin asked if they were going to be staying in the shelter that night.

The leader looked at her dismissively and said, "Uh huh. It's pretty full in here."

"But you guys have tents, right?" I asked, trying to keep my voice reasonable.

"Yeah, but I don't want to have to put them up in the rain." The scout leader said, not looking me in the eye.

"What about the giant tent in the back?" I asked.

"That's my tent," he answered, plainly.

"Are you serious, dude?" Erin pushed, "It's pouring and these guys have no tents. These shelters are kinda meant for thru-hikers."

"Sorry," he said, not sounding sorry, "We were here first. Guess you should have tents."

He gave a shrug.

I looked at the faces of the boys under the shelter and then back at the scout leader. Having taken campers on overnights when I was a summer camp counselor, I had a tiny bit of sympathy for the guy. He'd probably had a long day. "Okay, can we at least just make our dinners under the shelter? And then we'll..."

"There's not really room," he answered before I could finish. My sympathy vanished and all I felt was white hot anger.

"Good example you're setting for your scouts, dude," I yelled at his back as he walked back to the dry shelter.

"Fuck this, I'm leaving," Pilgrim announced. He told us he was going to walk the last mile down to the Kennebec River and that he'd wait for us there in the morning. "If I'm going to get soaked, at least I won't have to be around this shithead."

Erin and I set up our tarp, trying to make it as big as possible to shield the two of us plus Ben and Sug. Turbo squeezed in, too, to cook a quick dinner and then got in his hiking hammock to get out of the rain. No matter how we configured it, none of us was staying dry and as we lay there we got angrier and angrier. At one point, Erin got up to go pee. When she came back, she was giggling to herself. I turned over and gave her a questioning look. She whispered, "I just peed on that dude's tent."

* * *

After a night of almost no sleep, we were all completely soaked and eager to leave the next morning. We knew there was no point in hurrying because we couldn't catch the ferry until 9am at the earliest. The Kennebec River is the one water crossing on the AT that is deemed too dangerous to ford by yourself. A hiker died once trying to cross it and ever since there has been a ferry that carries hikers across. In the early months of the hiking season, the ferry only runs between 9am and 11am, which is why we'd wanted to sleep close by the night before. If you got there past 11am, you had to wait until the next day to cross.

We took off before the scouts, making our way down to the river's edge. About 10 minutes into the walk, Erin told me to go ahead, she was going to poop. I figured it was only a few more tenths of a mile, so she'd probably be okay without me behind her.

I made it down to the river and caught the tail end of Pilgrim and a hiker who I hadn't seen since early in our hike, Indiana, talking about how they'd run into each other the night before. Indiana and his dog had graciously shared his two-man tent with Pilgrim.

"Who spooned who?" Sug wondered and then, noticing me, "Where's Sweets?"

"Pooping. She should be here soon."

After five more minutes passed, and Erin didn't appear, I started to get a little anxious. I could tell Sug and Pilgrim were, too. We all remembered all too clearly the scary afternoon in Virginia when Erin hadn't shown up because she'd passed out on the trail.

"I'm going to go back."

"I'll come with you," Sug said. We'd walked maybe 50 yards up the trail when Erin came hurrying towards us.

"DUUUUDE...." she said, eyes wide, "You guys are not going to believe what just happened."

Erin told us that she had been pooping off to the side of the trail, and that she'd been trying to hurry because she didn't want to miss the ferry and she knew the scouts, those "little fuckers," were behind her. She'd pulled up her pants and at the same time realized she was basically at the edge of a huge drop-off. She somehow lost her balance, slipped on some moss and fell off the cliff. She was barely able to grab onto a root before she fell the full 20 feet down.

"I was fucking dangling! Off of a cliff! Like in a fucking movie! And then who comes along but the GOD DAMN BOY SCOUTS!"

She said the boy scouts had quickly pulled her back up to safety, barely saying a word to her. I asked where the boy scouts were.

"I don't know, I fucking RAN, dude," she said. "Man, now I kinda feel bad about peeing on that guy's tent, ya know?"

My cheeks hurt from laughing, despite knowing how serious the incident could have been. By the time the ferry showed up, a few minutes later, Erin had earned the new nickname, "The Dangler."

CHAPTER FIFTY-EIGHT

DAY 135, MAINE, 151.2 MILES TO KATAHDIN

O n the other side of the Kennebec, three miles up the trail was the small town of Caratunk. We were all soaked and exhausted from the night before, so we decided to go into town and see if we could get breakfast at the Caratunk House Hiker's B&B. We shed our wet gear outside, hanging up our rain gear and sleeping bags in hopes of drying them out. The B&B was a large old Victorian. The owner, Paul, greeted us and immediately took pity on us. He sat us down at the large farm table and started cooking us breakfast, charging us each only $4 for the feast.

I wistfully mentioned that it would be nice to not hike the rest of the day. Everyone agreed, but we all knew that our end date was set, making deviations from the plan hard. We continued to chat while we ate, mostly about our horrible night, and Erin's ridiculous brush with death.

"I've got a plan," Ben said, looking up from the guidebook, in what had become a common refrain. "I think we should stay here tonight. It'll be our last quasi-zero day before we hit the 100-mile wilderness."

He looked at Erin, "But listen, the hiking is supposed to be pretty easy in this last stretch, but it's going to mean a couple of 30 mile days."

"Okay," she said. "I want to do it."

Ben re-configured our mileage and we talked to Paul about rooms. Ben and I got our own room at the top of the stairs and the others shared a bunk room over the barn space. Paul offered to do a slack pack if we wanted, so Turbo, Erin, and Sug decided to do a quick 10 mile hike that afternoon to shave some mileage off of the almost 30 miles Ben had planned for the following day. Pilgrim, Ben, and I decided naps were more appealing.

As Ben and I climbed the stairs to our room, I said, "Look, I find you *very* attractive, but when we get in that room, the only thing I want touching me is the pillow."

"Agreed."

I caught a whiff of myself and revised my statement, "Okay, maybe shower first, but then I'm sleeping until dinner."

* * *

The following day, Ben, Pilgrim, and I took off early while everyone else stayed for breakfast. I was excited to hike a long day, and Erin had told me that the 10 miles they'd hiked the day before had been easy. Soon, we reached Bald Mt. Brook Lean-to, about 14 miles into our day. Ben went to find the privy while Pilgrim and I had a snack at the shelter. There, we found Erin, Sug, and Turbo's packs.

"What the hell?" Pilgrim wondered out loud, confused because those guys were nowhere to be found.

"Oh!" I said, "Paul dropped these off so they could hike a few miles this morning without packs. I guess they haven't made it here yet."

Pilgrim got a glint in his eye. "We should fuck with Turbo. He's always fucking with me."

Since we'd met him, Turbo had acted as the annoying little brother to Pilgrim. The dynamic amused me to no end.

"What, like put a rock in his pack?" I joked.

"YES!!!"

"Oh my god, that is so fucked up. He's just going to be like, 'So, whatsit, why does my pack feel so heavy?'" I laughed, doing my best Turbo impression.

Pilgrim found a giant rock and put it in the top pocket of Turbo's pack. We figured he would notice right away. After wearing your pack for long enough, little imbalances of weight would start driving you crazy. If I put my stuff in a different order, I would be adjusting my pack cords all day long.

We started back up the trail, immediately climbing 1400 feet up to Moxie Bald Mountain. We hung out at the top, enjoying the view, when Turbo appeared. I looked at him, wondering if he was going to say something about the rock, but he just launched into telling us about his breakfast.

Pilgrim, Ben, and I exchanged looks and shrugged. We all started hiking again. A few miles later, we arrived at Moxie Bald Lean-to and sat down to take a break. Turbo unstrapped his pack, saying, "I think it's because we slacked yesterday, but my pack feels so heavy today."

We all started giggling, and Pilgrim said, "Did you check your pack?"

Turbo looked at us with big, sincere eyes, "Yeah, so whatsit, I thought it was heavy when I put it on and I went through it but there was nothing?"

"You checked the *whole* pack?" Pilgrim asked, grin on his face.

Turbo was already unzipping the front zipper, and the one

compartment he'd apparently missed earlier. He held the giant rock in his hand as we laughed.

"You fuckers," he said and turned and threw the rock in Pilgrim's direction.

"DUDE. WHAT THE FUCK? You almost hit me in the head with that rock." Pilgrim yelled.

"You put a fucking rock in my pack!" Turbo yelled back.

"Okay, okay. Calm down, both of you," Ben intervened. "Turbo, it was just a joke, we thought you'd find it right away."

Turbo shot Pilgrim an angry look, but I could see the edge was gone.

"And this is why I never do pranks," I said.

* * *

At the shelter that night, Turbo retold the rock story to Sug and Erin, who had been just a few minutes behind us all day. Already, he was telling it as a funny anecdote, including the part where he almost took Pilgrim's head off. We looked again at our mileage for the last stretch. Tomorrow we would go through Monson, our last trail town, to pick up supplies, and enter into the 100-Mile Wilderness.

The 100-Mile Wilderness is the last stretch of trail before you get to Baxter state park, the home of Mt. Katahdin. It's considered the wildest part of the AT because there are no official roads in or out, meaning no chance for resupply and no easy escape route. The terrain wasn't exceptionally hard, although there is still plenty of elevation gain and loss, but the black flies were legendary.

We arrived in Monson the following morning after a 9-mile hike. We had 15 miles to go, so while we couldn't linger all day, we had time to check out the town, grab a meal, and get groceries. Erin and I were hiking together when we arrived in town. We stopped by Shaw's Hiker Hostel to see if we could drop our packs while we wandered around.

Sitting on the front porch, we found a familiar face.

"Oh wow! Sweet n' Low and Not Yet!" It was Vic, a hiker we'd met back in North Carolina. Vic was thru-hiking with her husband, Irish. We'd known they were ahead of us from the trail registers, but didn't anticipate ever seeing them again. Even though we'd only hiked together a few nights, months ago, Vic was one of the few other women we'd met on the trail and because of that we felt a special bond. The three of us sat together and caught up, sharing stories of our adventures, reveling in the fact that we were probably within several miles of one another at so many points during our hikes.

"Are you guys staying here tonight? Let's have dinner!" Vic said, calling over Irish to say hi.

We told her we couldn't stop, that we had to summit in five days.

"We've really been dragging this thing out," I told her. We all hugged goodbye and posed for a picture and promised we'd look each other up once we got back to the real world. It was a promise we'd made to many people we'd met along the way—both Erin and I had addresses and phone numbers lining the covers of our notebooks—and I wondered how many we'd keep.

Erin and I continued on to get groceries at the Monson General Store and then eat at the C&G Country Store. We sat in the window looking out at the town, full of hiker-types, eating our sandwiches.

"This place gives me the creeps," Erin said.

I agreed. Our interactions in the town had all been pleasant, but there was still something off-putting. "Right? I can't put my finger on it, but it's like a cult runs this place or something."

"Yeah, like we're in the Truman show."

As much as I had always looked forward to going into town, I thought I'd want to linger in our last true trail town. But possibly because we'd gorged ourselves on towns in the last few states, or maybe because I knew that soon all I was going to have was convenience and stores, I was happy to hike out of Monson and into the 100-Mile Wilderness.

CHAPTER FIFTY-NINE

DAY 137, MAINE, 117.8 MILES TO KATAHDIN

I f our hike was a movie script, editors would tell us that we had too many coincidental reappearances of characters. But that was how the trail worked, some characters made a huge impact never to be seen again, some minor characters showed up over and over. One major character would make a dramatic exit and another would randomly reappear the same day. Sometimes you lost people for weeks, only to find them again wading in a pond in the middle of Maine. That was how it happened with Lucky and Sparrow.

Only a tenth of a mile into the 100-Mile Wilderness we came upon the first of a series of gorgeous ponds. Ahead of me, I saw Pilgrim pause and then turn off the trail down towards the beach. I followed his eyeline and saw a tall woman in a black sports bra and underwear with braids down her back wading knee deep into what I imagined was freezing water. The scene was so surreal, with the idyllic mountain setting and clear waters of Spectacle Pond, the woman looking like a water nymph, that I almost missed the short, shaggy haired man standing off to the side. It clicked suddenly; I knew these people.

I watched as Pilgrim approached, throwing off his pack and embracing Lucky in a big bear hug. Lucky and Sparrow had been Pilgrim and Sug's first hiking partners, before they'd had to get off the trail to go to a wedding. Their exit was the start of Erin and I hiking with Pilgrim and Sug, back when they were just funny strangers we thought might be cool to hang out with.

"Why am I not surprised to see you two?" I asked when I'd made my way down to the water. This was now the third time we'd randomly crossed paths with them and it seemed fitting that we'd find them again at the end. Sparrow told us they were still skipping around hiking different sections. Lucky, who had hiked the whole trail four years earlier wanted to make sure Sparrow got to experience all the best parts of the trail. Like us, they had to be back in the real world soon. Sparrow was starting a master's program in psychology in August.

"We're actually on our way to Monson and then we're gonna do Katahdin." Lucky told us they'd hiked in on a logging road so they could do a day of the 100-Mile wilderness before heading north to Baxter State Park.

"I thought there wasn't supposed to be any roads in or out of here?" Erin said. "It kinda ruins the mystique." But of course, as we well knew, no matter how wild it seemed, you were never far from civilization on the AT. Even this place, supposedly the most remote of the trek, had escape routes.

Pilgrim announced that he was going to go for a swim. Sparrow had made the water look so tempting that we all took off our shoes and waded in.

"WHAT THE SHIT BALLS?!" I screeched the minute my ankles hit the water. It was freezing, like digging into the bottom of a cooler of ice for a soda. I quickly retreated. Sug,

Turbo, and Erin followed. Pilgrim pressed on, determined to make his way to the middle of the lake.

Ben stayed where he was, water up to his calves, gazing into the water. I watched him, my breath catching, taken in by this handsome figure, sunlight streaming through his curls, deep in thought. *I love him*, I thought and then banished the thought, embarrassed at my uncharacteristic emotional exuberance. But still, I wondered what he was thinking about—us, maybe, hopefully—when he suddenly looked up and yelled to Pilgrim, "Griz, there are leeches in this water!"

* * *

We left Lucky and Sparrow with promises to meet back up at Abol Bridge on July 14th to all summit together, and hiked on into the woods. Compared to the soaring views and granite tops of Southern Maine, this stretch of trail was densely forested--rocks, roots and pine needles making up the path; black flies buzzing around our heads, tree branches filtering the sun and blocking the sky. The hiking that day was easy, the elevation rolling a few hundred in either direction. It felt like a reprieve from the trudge of the previous month. We passed more ponds, forded streams, and chatted about inane topics, mostly about life in the "after."

"You know what we should do when we finish the trail?" Ben said while we navigated yet another stream. "We should all run a marathon. We wouldn't even have to train."

"We're basically doing a marathon today," Pilgrim agreed. "Imagine how easy this would be with no packs on flat ground."

I thought about it. In the shape I was now, I could definitely run a marathon. A year earlier, I'd actually been months into training to run the Chicago marathon when I'd pulled my IT band and sprained a muscle in my knee. I'd spent every Friday night of that spring and summer watching movies with my roommate, Bethany, instead of hanging with our friends at bars, so that we could get up super early on Saturday mornings to do long runs along the Chicago lakeshore path. I'd started getting up early before work to run in order to beat the heat. I'd fallen in love with Chicago in those early morning jogs along the lake. It was during a 20-mile run that my knee had given out, in front of Navy Pier and I'd had to take a cab I couldn't afford back to my apartment in Boys' Town. When it had come time for the marathon, I'd been on the sidelines, cheering for Bethany and my dad, watching them do the thing I'd tried for and failed. I'd had weeks of physical therapy but had fallen badly out of shape in the time between then and starting the trail.

"I'm in. We should do Chicago," I said.

We talked through all the logistics of this fantasy marathon, at the moment truly believing that it would happen (it didn't), vowing to each stay in hiking shape until October (we didn't), when we'd meet up in Chicago and run the marathon.

"I'll come from Kansas City; Sal and Ben will drive over from Cincinnati..." Erin was saying. I was struck by the "Sal and Ben" part of it. Of course, Ben and I had agreed that he would move with me, but it seemed almost unreal that this magical thing could exist outside of the trail.

* * *

The next day was one of those that Ben had warned us about when we'd taken the day off in Caratunk and he'd reconfigured our schedule. We'd need to do 33 miles in order to get to the base of Katahdin by the 14th. Instead of the mild, blue-skied day we'd had the day before, we woke up to cold and rain.

"I'm going to get started," Erin said, pack already on while I still sat in the shelter, shivering while I hurried through my Clif bar. She breathed in deeply, and stepped out onto the trail. I heard her grumble, "Why does this feel like Georgia?"

It did feel like a throwback to our early hiking days. We'd had sun and clear skies for a few weeks, and I had almost forgotten how utterly miserable being wet and cold was. How hiking up mountains when it was fogged in and raining was all the work without the payoff.

My strategy that morning was to keep my head down and hike as long and fast as I could without making stops. The weather actually helped. There was no lingering at ponds, or hanging at mountain tops when you had to move to keep your limbs warm. I was in such straight-ahead mode that I almost bumped right into Ben, who had stopped in the trail in front of me.

"What are you doing?" I asked impatiently. The rain was now a fine mist that permeated everything, and I wanted to keep walking.

He put his finger to his lips and pointed to a clearing in the trees about 50 feet off to our left. At first, I saw nothing, but then as the trees began to rustle, I realized that what he was pointing to was a giant moose. It was the first time I'd seen one. In fact, it was the largest animal I'd ever seen in the wild. I was momentarily dumbstruck.

"Oh my god," I whispered, surprised to feel tears springing up. "That's amazing."

"Are you crying?" Ben whispered back, sounding amused.

"I'm... just, like... whatever."

The moose moved on and we did too, catching up to everyone else at shelter about 20 miles into our day. It was our first real stop of the day but none of us wanted to stay long. We were all thoroughly soaked and as we sat, our sweat cooled and body temperature dropped to where we shivered despite putting on fleeces and hats. Ben ate a Pop-Tart, not wanting to waste time making lunch.

"This is miserable!" I said.

"Yeah," Ben agreed, "But think about it. This is probably the last time we'll sit freezing in a shelter."

His words shifted my mood. Instead of being just miserable, I was now miserable and nostalgic. I watched him take off down the trail, thinking about all the days in Georgia, Tennessee, and North Carolina when I'd sat in a lean-to just like this one fighting between wanting to rest my body and wanting to get warm again. It felt the same, I thought, except now I wasn't dreading the miles ahead like I had in those days, worried that I wouldn't be able to hack some unknown climb, that I wouldn't be able to finish the last miles of the day. Now I knew that I could hike whatever was in front of me. This kind of physical confidence was completely new for me. As I sat in my self-reflection, I looked down and saw I wasn't alone. Beside me was a tiny field mouse, no bigger than a golf ball, holding a crumb from my sandwich in her impossibly small paws.

"Hey there, little guy," I said to the mouse, breaking off another crumb. I knew I was getting sentimental about the end of this journey. Mice in a shelter is never a welcome addition.

* * *

I powered through the rest of the 33 miles, walking mostly by myself, listening to a mixtape my brother, Damien, had sent me. I rewound and relistened to Jill Scott's "A Long Walk" over and over; the dreamy quality of her voice matching this misty, chilly day. At the very end of the hike, probably a half mile before the shelter, I caught up with Erin and Sug, who'd been hiking together a lot more in the last weeks. We walked together until, just as the lean-to came into sight, Sug power stepped around Erin and I.

Pilgrim called the race from where he sat at the edge of the wooden structure. "Here comes Sug, making a move around the outside, is he going to come in at the number one spot? NO! Erin, sweeps by with a hip bump right at the end and wins the race. It's Erin in 1, Sug in 2, and Not Yet finishing it off in the number 3 spot. Better luck next time, Not Yet."

* * *

Our third day in the 100-Mile wilderness, we covered 21 miles. Erin's knee was hurting more than ever, but each morning she loaded up with ibuprofen, tightened her knee brace, gritted her teeth and walked. I think knowing that we were so close to the end, knowing that her constant pain would be over soon was driving her forward. She had started looking at the trail as her enemy that she was going to defeat.

At the shelter that night, black flies swarming around, we met two kids who were just starting their southbound thru-hike. They were four days in, fresh and excited and nervous and full of questions. They were us, in Georgia. In comparison, we were old timers, grizzled from our months out in the woods, laughing internally at their rose-colored glasses.

As we sat and chatted and doled out our hard-won trail advice, I was excited for them, for the life-changing adventure they were just starting. But, I realized, not jealous. Even though I was in reach of the end and I was already missing this life and these people, I wasn't sad. I looked at Ben, and could only see all that was ahead of us.

"Oh hey," said one of the South-bounders, "Is one of you Ben?"

The two had met Ben's dad the night before. Although he'd planned to meet up with us somewhere in this stretch, apparently, he'd gotten a few days in and realized that he'd never be able to keep up with us if he did catch us, so decided to double back and wait for us just outside of Baxter State park.

* * *

The fourth day, our last full day in the 100-mile wilderness, was slated to be another 30-mile day. I looked at the trail book in the morning, mentally picturing the mileage markers (1.4 miles to Pemadumcook Lake, lunch at Rainbow Stream Lean-to, etc.) and noticed a notation for a logging road a little over 2 miles away. I flipped to the back found an entry: *Right .9m to White House Landing Wilderness Camp... pizza, burgers, ice cream, snacks...Use air horn to summon pickup by boat.*

"Guys. Do we or don't we want to make this a true 30 mile trail day?" I asked the group.

Sug eyed me warily, "What do you mean?"

I told them about the store and the boat, and made my pitch to Pilgrim, Sug and Erin, "Remember our first 30 in Shenandoah when we hitched into town to eat and then got snacks at the snack machines and then ended up hiking in the dark? Remember how epic and fun that was?"

"Yeah...."

"Well, shouldn't we go on this one last detour just for old times' sake? This is our last trail store! Plus, someone's going to pick us up in a boat!"

To my surprise, no one objected, not even to the fact that we were going to be adding nearly 2 miles to our already long day.

The prospect of ice cream in the morning was enough to motivate any of us, so we started the day on a collective high. But since we were thinking ahead to the detour, we weren't prepared for what we saw just 20 minutes into the day. There, as we arrived at the edge of Pemadumcook lake, we had our first clear view of Mt. Katahdin. We were still over 47 trail miles away from its peak and yet there it was.

"Well that just got real," Erin said. She looked at me, "Dude, are you crying?"

"I think I'm PMSing. I cried at a moose the other day."

"It's true," Ben said to Erin. "It was weird."

* * *

We followed the directions to the White House Landing, and took a blue-blazed path through the woods. Sure enough, at the edge of a small lake was a dock and an airhorn. We blew the horn and waited. Minutes later a man and a child arrived in a fishing boat and loaded us in. In the five minute ride across the water we learned that the boy was 5, his name was also Ben, he loved Snickers bars, ninja turtles, and he lived at the White House with his parents. His dad just smiled, probably happy that his kid had someone else to talk to for a few minutes.

"You're the first thru-hikers I've met!" Little Ben told us excitedly.

We all took our time picking out food and candy, savoring our last junk food raid, acting like we didn't have 28 miles still to hike. It was July 13th, the last day with just us. The next day at Abol bridge, we were meeting Ben's dad, Pilgrim's brother-in-law, Cara and Chris, and Lucky and Sparrow; all coming to hike the final miles up to Katahdin with us on July 15th. Abol bridge was the entrance to Baxter State park where the final miles of the trail and Mt. Katahdin stood.

I don't remember what we talked about during those last big miles, probably about American Gladiators or things we were going to do "all day long" when we got home (sleep, read comic books, eat, watch TV, be inside), but we stuck together the whole day, wanting so badly to be finished but also to hold on to this moment for as long as we could.

CHAPTER SIXTY

DAY 141, MAINE, 18.6 MILES TO KATAHDIN

"This is it," Erin said to me the next morning. We were still in our sleeping bags, but were itching to get going. We were only 3.5 miles from Abol bridge and it's like we could feel the pull of family and friends.

"Dude, this is it," I said. "It's going to be weird, not seeing you every second of every day."

"I know. I got used to you," Erin said. In two days, we'd be waving goodbye to each other and going separate ways for the first time in five months. Erin was going to go back with Cara to New Hampshire before flying to Ohio, and I was going to go with Ben and his dad to Delaware.

"I mean, we'll see each other in like a week in Ohio, right?" I said, trying not to get emotional.

"Right," Erin nodded, also looking a little misty, "and then, like, all the time, for the rest of our lives until we move into houses with connected porches."

"Promise?" I asked.

"Of course."

Somehow while we'd hiked through Maine, Ben and I had

formed a plan for our new life together. We'd go to Delaware for a few days, and then drive Ben's car to Ohio to my dad's house. From there, we'd go up to Cincinnati to look for apartments and then Ben would go back to Wisconsin to get his stuff and I would figure out a way down to Florida to get mine. That last detail, where I'd have to face Kevin and Ben would be seeing his ex-girlfriend, made me anxious, but I was trying not to focus too hard on anything past Katahdin.

I unzipped my sleeping bag with a flourish. "Let's finish this thing."

That day was a reunion party from the minute we started on the trail. The first person we saw, as we started our day, was a complete surprise. Coming towards us, with a huge smile on his face was Mike.

"I told you I'd wait and summit with you guys, too," he said, a bit sheepishly. He told us that he had, in fact, summited on his 21st birthday, by himself and that it had, "kinda sucked."

"I'm glad you're here, man," Ben told him.

Only a few tenths of a mile later, Cara and Chris came up the trail. The joy and relief on Erin's face was instant.

Then, in another mile, Ben's dad found us.

By the time we got to Abol Bridge parking lot, we were in full-on party mode. Pilgrim's brother-in-law, Steve, Mike's mom, and Lucky and Sparrow were there, along with Chris's parents, Bill and Sue. We'd bonded with Bill and Sue when Erin, Cara, and I had hiked the Long Trail two years earlier and again at the wedding. We were delighted they'd made the trip up from New Hampshire.

Cara pulled Erin and I aside, "I know it's a lot, but Bill and Sue rented a cabin and they want everyone to come stay after you guys summit tomorrow. They did the same for us when we finished the trail."

"And we're making you surf and turf!" Sue called over, "Everyone is welcome! Parents, hikers, everyone!"

Bill and Sue had both worked in mid-level jobs most of their lives before they started a business of their own building specialized computer cabinets. They'd recently sold the business for a lot of money and were enjoying being generous with their newfound wealth.

"I can't believe this. Thank you," I told Sue, the seemingly ever-present tears back in my eyes, "I would hug you, but, you know... I stink."

She pulled me in, anyway. "We're so proud of you girls."

Cara pulled out a cooler of beers and there were rounds of cheers and picture taking. It felt like the celebration had already begun.

"I don't want to be a bummer," Ben said eventually, after the gathering had quieted down a bit, "but we still have over 10 miles left to hike today."

There was a collective groan, but he was right. Even though we felt done there were 10 miles between Abol bridge and Katahdin Stream campground where we'd sign-in at the ranger station to hike Katahdin the next day. Ben wanted to hike with his dad, so they took off down the trail first. Pilgrim, Steve, and Mike went next. Erin, Sug and I looked around. Everyone else there was going to either meet us at Katahdin springs in the morning or at the cabin after we finished.

"I guess we should go, too." I said.

"You know..." Erin started, "There's another trail that is only 8 miles long..."

"Sold."

* * *

When we had all made it to the campground and it was just the hikers again, we went to the ranger station. There we signed in as official thru-hikers, Erin, Pilgrim, Sug, Turbo, Ben, and I were numbers 10-15 to make it from Georgia to Katahdin that season.

CHAPTER SIXTY-ONE

DAY 142, MAINE, 5.2 MILES TO KATAHDIN

That night, I slept like shit; too much anticipation, nervousness, excitement. I had weird, fragmented dreams, and woke up every hour.

By 6:30am, we were all packed up and ready to go. We were meeting everyone who was hiking Katahdin with us—Lucky and Sparrow, Ben's dad, Steve, Cara and Chris—at the ranger station at 7am to head up the mountain.

"I'm nervous," I told Erin.

"Dude, I know," she said, "but it's just a fucking mountain, right? I mean, we can hike another fucking mountain."

Katahdin isn't just another mountain, though. It's the most technical mountain on the trail. It rises out of the relatively low elevations of the 100-Mile Wilderness and climbs up 4,000 feet to the 5,268 foot summit, making it the tallest mountain in Maine. There are large boulders to climb over, and places where you have to scramble hand over foot. Even though I was in the best shape of my life, I was worried about Katahdin.

We gathered our crew and started up the trail. Erin hiked with Cara and Chris while I stuck with Ben and his dad. The first mile of the trail lulls you into a false sense of security. We followed a stream, and gained only slight elevation until we got to Katahdin stream falls.

"Wow, you're really fast," Tim, Ben's dad, remarked during that first mile.

I laughed and told him to just wait for the climbs.

After the falls, the elevation climbed and soon we were above tree-line, giving us amazing views of all of Baxter State Park. The reward of the views was bought with boulder fields, and I found myself climbing the boulders, only to have to drop down the other side. On some portions were handholds to help with the climb. For roughly three miles we scrambled up the edge of the mountain, stopping for breaks, or to give each other a hand up.

It took over two hours to reach Thoreau Springs, a mile from the summit. We rested for a minute.

"You ready to head up?" Ben asked, holding out his hand to me. I let him pull me up and hugged him tightly.

"You guys go ahead," I told them.

I sat back down on the rock and waited for Erin. I needed to finish this with her.

I looked out on the endless trees and lakes and felt an immense wave of gratitude. I thought about the phone call when Erin had told me she was going to hike the trail. I'd only joined in out of a sense of not wanting to be left out, of wanting to go on a trip with my best friend, of wanting to do something new and different with my life. I'd had no idea what I was signing up for, but yet here I was, alone on a mountain in Maine, almost finished with the hardest thing I'd ever done and I still felt strong. I felt strong and happy and fucking grateful to these mountains and the community that it brought me.

When Erin emerged from the boulder fields, she looked anguished, but triumphant. We sat together, not saying anything for a long time. She leaned her head on my shoulder. I leaned my head on hers. Grateful, together.

Eventually, Cara and Chris caught up and the four of us hiked the last mile to the top. It was 10:00am on July 15th, and we'd completed our thru-hike of the Appalachian Trail.

CHAPTER SIXTY-TWO

DAY 142, 0 MILES TO KATAHDIN

At the summit, everyone was excited. We popped little bottles of champagne and took endless pictures at the iconic sign at the top that says "Katahdin, northern terminus of the Appalachian Trail." We took pictures as a group, pictures with our Justin Timberlake poster, pictures of Erin and I re-enacting her becoming "the Dangler." Pilgrim stripped down to the pair of bikini bottoms I'd given him at Cara's wedding, threw on his aviator flair and took pictures posing on top of the sign. Ben and I took a picture, his arm around me, me leaning into him. We took pictures with Cara and Chris, with Ben's dad, with a random section hiker who also happened to hike up that day. When we couldn't think of anything else to take a picture of, we decided it was time to head down.

Later that evening, after the steak and lobster, after a game of wiffle ball, after trips to the souvenir store to buy Baxter state park t-shirts, after endless cheers and pictures, we all sat around one last campfire.

I felt strange being showered and wearing my real-life

clothes, a long skirt and coral colored tank top, everything hanging off me in a way my clothes had never done. I remembered packing these clothes in Florida before I left and mailing them to Cara.

I was a different person then, I thought.

But that wasn't quite right. I wasn't a different person. I was the same person who'd packed those clothes, but then I'd been so bogged down by who I thought I should be, by all the things I wasn't, by what other people were doing, that I couldn't see myself. The last five months had stripped me down and built me up. I'd always been strong and adventurous, but somewhere along the way I'd lost my confidence and perspective. The reason I'd said yes to this trip was because something inside of me needed to escape the narrow life I'd felt fated to live. I'd been too tired from trudging up and down mountains every day to put up facades, to worry about "everyone else," to be anything but 100% me.

I looked at the faces of these people, most of whom I hadn't known less than five months ago; Erin and Sug in deep conversation, Mike and Ben laughing, Pilgrim play-fighting with Turbo, Lucky and Sparrow cuddled together. If it was the mountains that had worn away my bullshit, I knew it was the people that had built me back up.

* * *

The next morning, after saying goodbye to everyone else, I hugged Erin for what felt like an hour.

"You've got to go," she said, looking at Ben and his dad standing by his dad's camper van.

"No, *you've* got to go," I said, watching Cara and Chris pack up their car.

"I love you," we both said and pulled apart.

I reached the van and Ben opened the door for me.

"You ready for this?" he asked, green eyes sparkling. With no hesitation, I stepped into the van.

"I'm ready for anything."

EPILOGUE

MARCH 2018, ESTES PARK, COLORADO

"Oh dude, some little fucking parking lot attendant was trying to get me out of the car while I still had my boob out feeding Oren," Erin said dramatically, scooting Ben and I over so that she and her husband, Jeff, could sit in the row with us.

Erin and Jeff had gotten married in 2005, before she started her internal medicine residency in Chicago, but they'd met before the trail. He'd been the 100% perfect guy she'd emailed me about. Erin held a car seat with their 9-month old baby, while Jeff carried their sleeping 3-year-old.

She looked down the row at me and Karleen, Pilgrim's wife and our dear friend.

"You guys still happy you didn't bring your kids?" Erin asked Karleen and I sarcastically, looking gorgeous in a green dress that set off her long red hair, and only just a little bit harried.

Karleen just laughed at Erin, and I knew, like us, she wasn't regretting leaving their 2-and 6-year-olds with Pilgrim's parents for the weekend. Erin and Jeff had driven up from their home in Durango, Colorado while the rest of us had flown to Denver and then carpooled up in a rental car to Estes Park.

Karleen and Pilgrim now lived outside Rochester, NY, where they were both college professors. Karleen is a rock star in Political Science, and Pilgrim is a brilliant writer and English professor. For several years, before they'd moved to Rochester and we'd moved to New York City, Ben and I, and Pilgrim and Karleen had lived within blocks of each other in Morgantown, West Virginia. The three of them had taught at West Virginia University (Ben is now also a college professor), and I'd travelled the country as a touring stand-up comedian.

I started to say that I hadn't even thought about our 2-year-old son, Max, in the past two days, but a hush had come over the crowd. Ben squeezed my hand as we watched Pilgrim and the other groomsmen walk into view. Then Sug was at the front, looking happier than I'd ever seen him, looking perfectly at home against the backdrop of Rocky Mountain National Park.

Music started up and we saw Jen emerge, looking like a snow queen in her long white dress and blush pink fuzzy wrap.

"I hope it's okay, we brought someone with us," I said later, at the reception. We were now all gathered outside, waiting for the photographer to come take a group picture. We'd finished dinner and had all cried at Pilgrim's best man speech. I pulled out the Justin Timberlake poster I'd found on eBay. "It's not the original, but that one is 15 years old and also I have no idea where it is."

"Dang, when did Timbo get so old?" said Erin.

We taped up the poster on the wall and squeezed in around it, recreating a picture we'd taken at the summit of Katahdin. I wished that Mike, Turbo, and See Blue were there, but the last time all of us had gathered around a Justin Timberlake poster was at Ben and my wedding in 2006 (which Pilgrim had officiated).

"I'm so happy you guys all made it," Sug gushed, looking handsome in his suit and cabbie hat.

"Where else would we be?"

EPILOGUE, PART II: THIS TIME WE GO THE RIGHT WAY

APRIL 2022, SPRINGER MOUNTAIN

Erin and I stood in the parking lot at the base of Springer Mountain, the Southern terminus of the Appalachian Trail. Ben dutifully took pictures of the two of us with our packs on, recreating photos we'd taken the first time we'd stood here.

Ben and I now lived in Atlanta with our son Max, less than two hours' drive from the AT. Erin had flown in the night before from Durango so that she and I could spend three days hiking together from Springer to Neel's Gap.

Ben pulled me aside. "I love you. I hope you guys have the most fun."

"I love you, too. You're my favorite."

"Dude! Let's go," Erin said, giving Ben a final hug before he drove off, back down the mountain, back to our home and our son.

I turned and looked at the trail up ahead. The canopy of trees formed a tunnel, looking like a secret passageway.

"Not falling for it this time, trail," I said out loud and turned to face the other way, following Erin across the dirt road and into the woods. Erin and I talked giddily as we walked. Although we talked or texted most days, any time we could spend together in person was magic. In less than an hour we came to a clearing. On a rock that looked out to the valley below was a plaque that read "Appalachian National Scenic Trail, Springer Mountain, Elevation 3782', Southern Terminus."

"Whoa," Erin said.

"I know," I replied.

Only nineteen years after we'd started our thru-hike, we'd finally made it to Springer.

LEARN MORE

Can't get enough of this story? Visit sallychaffinbrooks.com to see pictures from the hike, listen to the music mentioned, get updates on the people involved, and read more stories from the trail.

ACKNOWLEDGMENTS

This book, the hike, everything, would not have happened without Erin, my best friend. You inspire and amaze me and make me laugh harder than anyone. I'm so glad both of us were friendless weirdos at that 7th grade sleepover.

And Ben. You are the best thing that ever happened to me. Thank you for being the best partner, friend, person, and parent. I am truly so lucky. You really are a chill, cool, hottie. Max, my sweet kitty, I hope this story of your parents falling in love doesn't scar you too much. I love you infinity times infinity plus infinity.

To the hiker crew—Steve, John, Turner, Mike, and Kevin W. (and so many more I met along the way). The thru-hike changed my life because of you all. Thank you for letting me write about our lives. To Cara, thank you for letting us follow in your footsteps.

To my family, who loves me despite my intense fear of the phone—my dad (David), Damien, Keith, Tosha, Owen, and Theresa. I am privileged to be related to such excellent people. Thank you for your unwavering belief in me; you may have created a monster. Thank you to the Brookses—Martha, Tim, Ross, Jason, Melissa, Natalie, Charlie, and Brian—I seriously hit the jackpot when it came to in-laws.

Thank you to my brilliant friends who read drafts of this book and gave me invaluable feedback—Emily Galati (I'm honestly not sure I would have finished this book without your encouragement), Jen O'Neill, Alex Stone, Katrina Helz, Joe Smith, and Jonas Schrodt. Thank you to everyone who read parts of the book way back when it was a blog called Trail Tuesdays and encouraged me to keep writing. Thank you to Grace—I'm so lucky to have you in my corner. Thank you Bobcat, for inspiring me to pursue a creative life on my own terms. Thank you Karleen, the Best Buds, and the Sophisticated Ladies; I am blessed with the best, most supportive friends around.

Thank you, "Kevin," for being a great human. Sorry I was kinda a shit girlfriend.

Thank you to my editor, Rebecca Dimyan, who was encouraging and thoughtful and truly made this a better book.

And finally, thank you to my mom, Risa Grimes, who never let me believe I was anything but amazing and always made sure I knew I was loved. I see you in the rainbows and miss you every day.

ABOUT RUNNING WILD PRESS

Running Wild Press publishes stories that cross genres with great stories and writing. Learn more about us and our stories at www.runningwildpress.com